South by Southwest

South
by
Southwest

The American South Series • Edward L. Ayers, Editor

Planter Emigration and Identity in the Slave South

JAMES DAVID MILLER

Published in cooperation with the William P. Clements Center for Southwest Studies, Southern Methodist University

University of Virginia Press • *Charlottesville and London*

UNIVERSITY OF VIRGINIA PRESS
© 2002 by the Rector and Visitors of the University of Virginia
All rights reserved
Printed in the United States of America on acid-free paper

First published 2002

1 3 5 7 9 8 6 4 2

Library of Congress Cataloging-in-Publication Data
Miller, James David, date.
   South by southwest : planter emigration and identity in the slave South /
James David Miller.
      p. cm. — (The American South series)
   Includes bibliographical references (p.   ) and index.
   ISBN 0-8139-2117-1 (cloth : alk. paper)
      1. Slaveholders—Southern States—Social conditions—19th century. 2. Farmers—
Southern States—Social conditions—19th century. 3. Slaves—Southern States—
Social conditions—19th century. 4. Southern States—Race relations. 5. Southern
States—Social conditions—19th century. 6. Migration, Internal—Southern States—
History—19th century. 7. Group identity—Southern States—History—19th century.
8. Plantation life—Southern States—History—19th century. 9. Agriculture—Social
aspects—Southern States—History—19th century. I. William P. Clements Center
for Southwest Studies. II. Title. III. Series.
   E443 .M55 2002
   305.5′67′097509034—dc21   2002005251

To my parents,
Kate and Bill Miller

Contents

But schoolmen write on while man works. They
build theories and systems while ordinary men
build empires.
—*Magnolia Magazine*

Nature and Freedom! These are glorious words
That make the world mad. Take a glimpse at both,
Such as you readily find, when, at your ease,
You plough the ancient military trace,
From Georgia to the "Burnt Corn" settlements.
—William Gilmore Simms

Acknowledgments

I have so many people to thank. It is perhaps ironic, given the argument at the heart of what follows, that I must do so as much by reference to place as to particular people.

Archivists from Columbia to Chapel Hill, Montgomery to Montreat, Athens to Auburn, Durham to Tuscaloosa, have given me the benefit of their enthusiasm and expertise. I enjoyed all of these archival destinations, but I have to say that Montgomery was my favorite if only because it allowed me to enjoy, on several visits there, the hospitality of Howard and Gloria Goodson. I thank them for their understanding of the great truth that historians too march on their stomachs.

Many teachers, friends, and colleagues from East Anglia to Atlanta, Winnipeg to Dallas, and Davidson to Ottawa have contributed either directly or indirectly to this work. Among the many great teachers at the University of East Anglia, special thanks are due to John Ashworth and Howard Temperley who, through their classes on the nineteenth-century United States and comparative slavery, led me toward the part that really matters. During an exchange year at Georgetown University, Emmet Curran did so much to help me. At Emory University, I was fortunate to have as members of my dissertation committee two historians, Dan T. Carter and Elizabeth Fox-Genovese, whose extraordinary grasp of southern history is matched only by how much they care about that history and its continuing significance for our own times.

A year spent as a Summerlee Fellow at Southern Methodist University's Clements Center for Southwest Studies allowed me to make great progress on this work. The Center provided me with a generous fellowship that included both a subvention for the publication of this manuscript and the organizing of a seminar in which eminent historians gathered together to tell me what was wrong with it. In truth, the participants defined the ideal of engaged scholarly criticism, and that day remains for me a wonderful experience of what it means to be part of a community of scholars. Special thanks are due to David Weber, Terry Jordan, Edward Countryman, Sam Truett, and Chris Morris. Chris, then and later, was not only a conscientious, insightful, and generous critic of my work but also, along with Stephanie Cole, a provider of much social cheer during my year in Dallas. Jane Elder was never too busy running everything to be a great friend.

Many other people, in comments on parts of this work presented as papers or in conversations at conferences and archives, have provided me with suggestions and encouragement. I would especially like to thank Joan E. Cashin, David Moltke-Hansen, and Johanna Shields (who also participated in the SMU seminar) for taking an interest in this project and giving me the benefit of their own research and thinking on southern history and culture. Were it not for Richard Holway at the University of Virginia Press, I might still be working on the eighty-ninth revision of the eighth paragraph of chapter 2. Dick also took an interest in this project early on, and his encouragement, enthusiasm, and advice have made the publishing process go more smoothly than I could have hoped.

As an emigrant myself I have been fortunate always to find myself among people who made me feel at home. In various places in the United States, my social circumstances never came close to reflecting my official status as a "non-resident alien." Steve Goodson, Martha Goodson, Mark Schantz, Nancy Barr, John Rodrigue, Chris Snyder, Renee Snyder, Ruth Dickens, Andy Dickens, Renee Dye, and Jennifer West all helped to make Atlanta home for five great years. During the year I spent at Davidson College, even the paradoxical pleasure of having an office in a converted inn once owned by Hinton Rowan Helper's brother could not compare with the happiness derived from spending time in the company of many Davidsonians, especially Alan Parker, Felicia Van Bork, Michael Strysick, Earl Edmondson, Judith Jackson, and, most of all, Brother Bill Jackson. In Winnipeg the Senior Common Room at the University of Manitoba's University College and the Beverage Room at the Cambridge Hotel were unassuming places made wonderful by the many unforgettable friends who gathered there. In Ottawa all the members of Carleton University's history department have made me feel welcome from the beginning and contributed to an environment in which I could continue work on this book while adjusting to the demands of a new job. Special thanks to Rod Phillips, Ruth Pritchard, Carter Elwood, Jill St. Germain, and Trotsky for all the advice on fine wine and carrots.

James L. Roark has been extremely generous in the time, energy, and wisdom he has devoted to my work and career. He has gone far and beyond what could reasonably be expected of even the most conscientious of dissertation supervisors. His usually sound judgment deserts him, however, when it comes to his underestimation of the great contribution he has made to this book. It remains a great academic and personal pleasure to count him as both a mentor and a friend.

My parents-in-law, Roy and Betty Johnston, and my grandmother-in-law, the late Margaret Marr, made me feel part of their family from the beginning and encouraged my studies in numerous ways with their kindness and generosity. I am extremely grateful to them for all they have done over the years. My sister Elizabeth and my brother Calum have provided love and friendship and conversation over the years and over the distances that more often than not separate us. Thoughts of them are both frequent and sustaining. They have contributed to this work more than they know.

Some might question the wisdom of swearing eternal love and loyalty within sight of Fort Sumter, but that is what Mary Margaret Johnston-Miller and I did one fine June day in 1991 at the Battery in Charleston, South Carolina. William Gilmore Simms bore silent and statuesque witness to the proceedings. We have driven the South in pre-malaise Chevrolets, eaten too many biscuits and too much BBQ, and together tried to understand a little better the people and the times that fascinate us both. Her contribution to this book is immense, and my appreciation for her help in writing it can be expressed only in love.

My parents, Kate and Bill Miller, have been a constant part of my thoughts in all the years I have worked on this book. Without their love, patience, and unselfishness over the years, I would never have reached this point. If they take from this book a fraction of what they put into it, I will be happy.

South by Southwest

1 When Planters Roamed the Earth

Towards evening, we passed six waggons, conveying ninety slaves, belonging to General ——, removing from his plantation in Georgia, to his settlement on the Cahawba, in Alabama. I mention these little occurrences, to put you more familiarly in possession of the habits of the country.
—Adam Hodgson, *Letters from North America*

IN 1846 SIR CHARLES LYELL TOOK A TRIP FROM THE Georgia coast to the interior of Alabama. Along the way Lyell could not help but be impressed by the great numbers of travelers he encountered heading in the same direction. On a January morning in Claiborne, Alabama, Lyell and his wife shared their inn's veranda with "a family of 'movers'" on their way to Texas, "enjoying the warm sunshine after a shower of rain." At the tavern in Claiborne, Lyell was mistaken for the Methodist minister the locals had been "expecting to come from the north, to preach a trial sermon." As he shared accommodations with these and other movers and as he met them on the road, Lyell was often asked, "Are you moving?" Both the inquiries and the assumption spoke to the fluidity and mobility of a time and place where much was not as it seemed, and did not stay the same for long even when it was.[1]

Lyell came as a scientist rather than as a settler. One of the era's leading geologists, the Scotsman had come to Alabama for a spot of fossil hunting. He was particularly anxious "to examine the geology of the region" near Clarksville, Alabama, where "the fossil skeletons of the gigantic zeuglodon," a whalelike dinosaur, had been unearthed by new settlers clearing ancient lands. Lyell understood that it was modern-day movement and settlement that had done so much, so rapidly, to enrich his own journey into the prehistoric past. As slaves rowed his handcar through Georgia's new-cut railroad gorges and as he spent "many pleasant hours" hunting for dinosaur bones or "gathering hundreds of beautifully preserved shells" on the riverside cliffs of Claiborne, Lyell read the layers of passing time newly uncovered by the quickening human movement of his own modern age.[2]

By the time Lyell made this, his second, visit to Alabama, many of the movers he encountered were leaving that state for lands farther to the west. It had not been long since Alabama itself had been the emigrants' principal destination. One of Irish actor Tyrone Power's lasting *Impressions of America* in the previous decade was of a December evening spent journeying westward on a stagecoach from Augusta along with "nine other victims" of Georgia's notorious roads. During the night Power and his fellow travelers passed "several camps of emigrants, on the move from the Carolinas and Georgia." For light and warmth these travelers had set fires in huge toppled pines that they kept blazing in spite of the rain. From Augusta "to the banks of the Alabama," Power found the road "covered" by emigrants.[3]

Power recorded scenes of westward voyaging that would have been familiar to even earlier visitors. In March 1820 Adam Hodgson, an English businessman and trader from Liverpool, broke his own westward journey at the Indian Agency on Georgia's Flint River. Observing cultural characteristics that would persist with great tenacity, Hodgson found Americans to be "enterprising and migratory" while nevertheless possessed of "a great aversion to walking." Among all the "waggons of emigrants from Georgia and Carolina" heading to Alabama and beyond, Hodgson found the most striking evidence for the scale of westward movement in the "solitary party" he was "astonished" to encounter returning "against the stream" from New Orleans to Georgia.[4]

People on journeys observing other people on journeys: from the 1840s, to the 1830s, to the 1820s. Indeed, even before 1820 a new and telling name for the phenomenon was on the lips of the region's residents. Samuel McDonald, for one, described a "disease prevalent" in his area of Georgia. First "the patient" discovered "a great love" of talking with his neighbors about "the new country, Jackson's Purchase." Next he tried "to make sale of his stock," and "lastly he makes an attempt to sell his plantation." According to McDonald's diagnosis, "scarce any of those who were attacked by it ever recover; it sooner or later carries them off to the westward." Such was the condition called "Alabama Fever."[5]

This fever hardly made the southern United States a distinctive portion of the transatlantic world of the nineteenth century. European observers who also traveled the highways of their own continent knew how human mobility was changing the face of the "old" world as well as the "new." In the opinion of another traveler in America, Alexis de Tocqueville, "nothing in history" could compare with "this continuous movement of mankind, except perhaps that which followed the fall of the Roman Empire." Yet as Tocqueville also went to some lengths to point out, there was little in history's existing repertoire to compare with the rise of the American empire. So although mobility in the United States was not a discrete phenomenon, Tocqueville did accord Americans' transcontinental trek an exceptional role in the society-convulsing movements of the wider world. The United States was the focus of an unending "double movement of immigration" to and across the continent, in which "millions of men are all marching together toward the same point on the horizon."[6]

Domestic commentators added their voices to the claims of European visitors that some serious history was afoot. Writing of the "Old Northwest" of the 1830s, author Caroline Kirkland described a time that would "long be remembered . . . as the period when the madness of speculation in lands had reached a point to which no historian of the time will ever be able to do justice." "The 'man of one idea' was every where," wrote Kirkland (herself involved in land speculation); "no man had two." Her description of speculative frenzy was just as apt for the influx of settlers and squatters into the Alabama Territory in the wake of the War of 1812. In the summer of 1817, the *Charleston Reporter* remarked that the population movement out of the Southeast had reached "unprecedented proportions." To the *Alabama Republican* emigration into the Southwest was "unparalleled in the History of the world."[7] Hyperbolic to be sure, but perhaps not by much. Offering a retrospective endorsement of contemporary accounts, historian Malcolm Rohrbough describes "the migration that engulfed the eastern half of the continent" as "one of the greatest in the history of the world."[8]

Emigrants caught up in the flood also struggled to estimate its force and impact. "The emigration will exceed all calculations," wrote William W. Bibb in 1818. Bibb, who had emigrated from Georgia to Alabama the previous year, doubted that his Georgia friend Charles Tait would be able to "imagine the number of persons who are engaged in exploring the Territory." Perhaps not, but Tait could imagine himself as one of the explorers. He was in the process of moving himself, along with his son James and his daughter-in-law Caroline, to the lands of the Alabama Territory.

Moving was a central theme of Tait family history. Earlier generations of Taits and Goodes (Caroline's family) had moved south from the Chesapeake region where they had first settled after arriving from Great Britain. The Goodes had already moved on to Alabama. James and Caroline Tait planned to follow.[9]

Now, the thoughts of the patriarch himself had turned to the West. The father admitted to his son, who had gone on ahead to scout the land, to having "indulged my imagination somewhat" on the subject of the "Home, where we all shall meet soon & sit down for the rest of our lives and spend our days hereafter in peace & prosperity." Charles Tait fancied he saw a place blessed with various qualities, both practical and pleasant, a place which "unites fertility, salubrity & navigation" as well as other "advantages" such as a stream for a mill, an extensive range for cattle and hogs, and a "never-failing spring at the foot of a hillock on the summit of which a Mansion-house can be built in due time." In "the catalogue of human comfort" he compiled in his mind's eye, Tait included a post office as well as good land on either side "where will settle a number of good neighbours & from whom the pleasures & benefits of society will soon be realized."[10]

Yet neither past familiarity with moving nor daydreaming about his ideal new home could assuage Charles Tait's anxiety regarding the move. He fretted, in particular, over how James Tait would fare at the January land sales and worried that he should have gone himself. Throughout the winter of 1818–19, father deluged son with advice and exhortation. Charles Tait worried about cost and quality, his fear of paying too much vying with his desire to acquire the best land available. He instructed James to "buy good land & none but good at the sale," specifying that he "need not fear any engagement to the amount of thirty or five & thirty thousand dollars." He told him to get "a choice settlement and don't higgle about the price." At other times he worried that James was not "higgling" enough, expressing his doubts that any land was worth the forty or fifty dollars an acre his son seemed prepared to pay. On the other hand, Tait acknowledged, "we can hardly give too much for good bottom land; and poor is a hard bargain at almost any price." Charles Tait hoped that the eventual purchase would "be a fortunate one for us both not only as to soil but as to price," and that his son might ultimately acquire the land "for less than you imagine."[11] Tait also encouraged his son to seek advice from friends and family such as the Goodes and William Bibb, from whose "extensive acquaintance & influence" James Tait would no doubt "derive much benefit."[12] Charles

Tait trusted in his son's judgment yet beseeched him to take advice. He worried he would spend too much but insisted that he not penny-pinch. He was content to "go where you go & stay where you stay" as long as he could continue to take the lead in family affairs. As to what constituted good land, at least on that score the message was unequivocal. "Have in mind at all times the unity of Fertility, Salubrity, & Navigation," chimed the land seeker's mantra.[13]

Eventually, Charles Tait followed his son and daughter-in-law to the banks of the Alabama River. The spring of 1819 would find three generations of Taits settled together there. Charles Tait's avalanche of advice notwithstanding, James had not yet purchased land, and so the Taits remained squatters for the time being. As it turned out, the family patriarch would be there after all when a place was eventually purchased.

In their anxious pursuit of western lands, the Taits appeared a lot like their fellow Americans elsewhere on the continent. Yet the Taits were not the same as emigrants to Michigan or, indeed, many of those with whom they shared the muddy roads to Alabama. If Kirkland was right that those moving to the Northwest had only one idea, then many of those heading for the Southwest had at least two: land and slaves.

Slaveholding emigrant families like the Taits proved incapable of thinking about western land without reference to the human property they knew would transform it for them. Charles Tait, still in Georgia and writing to Caroline Tait in Alabama, expressed his pleasure with how "cheerfully" "our black people" were so far responding to the prospect of leaving for the West. This attitude had earned them "much consideration," in the master's view. "They deserve to be treated well; not only with justice but with tenderness. . . . I have strong hopes that every one will go without a murmur." Tait's words of praise imply his awareness that slave attitudes toward departure might well be otherwise. Nevertheless, they would simply have to bear it as their lot, make the most of it, and know that it would not go unappreciated. After the slaves had been sent to Alabama, Tait asked his daughter-in-law to "present me kindly to all our people" and to tell them that he would see them in the spring. He remained confident "that they will give cheerfully all their exertions to our establishment in the Alabama. I hope there will be no discontents, no murmurings." Those prepared to "do their part willingly," Tait went on, would "be gainers by it." Caroline Tait was soon able to report that the family's slaves had apparently reached Alabama in the same frame of mind as they had left Georgia. "The negroes all arriv'd here on the fifth of January safe and in high spirits as they were heard some time before they were seen." [14]

We must surely be skeptical of the master's use of words like *willing* and *cheerful* when it comes to understanding how enslaved people felt about their forced removal to the West. But Charles Tait's words leave no doubt that although they could do so with varying degrees of cheerfulness and murmuring, the slaves had little choice but to go where their masters took or sent them. Cheerful or murmuring, they still had to go. Cheerful or murmuring, their masters' power over them and dependence upon them would remain as strong in Alabama as in Georgia. And so in that spring of 1819, the Taits shared their new home on the banks of the Alabama with about sixty enslaved men, women, and children. They were pioneers who owned other pioneers.

There were many emigrant families like the Taits. Few travelers failed to recognize the black and white character of southern mobility. Charles Lyell encountered a family of movers "carrying away no less than forty negroes." Tyrone Power remembered the groups of field slaves surrounding their owners' carts and carriages and numbering "from half a dozen to fifty or sixty." Adam Hodgson "saw many gangs of slaves whom their masters were transporting to Alabama and Mississippi." These groups were among the more than three-quarters of a million enslaved men, women, and children transported to the Southwest in the years between 1820 and 1860. Throughout the period the planters traveled west as the freest of Americans, moving in lockstep with the casualties of one of modern history's great forced migrations. [15]

Their ownership of human property gave families like the Taits an elite status shared by few other emigrants, either in America or Europe. Charles Tait, for example, shared Charles Lyell's fondness for fossils and dinosaurs. Tait was also a pioneer when it came to the study of Alabama's geology, and his work in the Claiborne area would win him election as a corresponding member to the Philadelphia Academy of Natural Sciences. [16] Before quitting Georgia, Tait had been a judge and later one of the state's senators in Washington, D.C. When he moved to Alabama, he joined other public figures who had left Georgia for greener pastures, both private and public. Friend and colleague John Williams Walker had moved to northern Alabama before the War of 1812 and was now keen for his friend to settle in that portion of the territory. William Wyatt Bibb, who was born in Virginia in 1781 but had lived his adult life in Georgia, had sat in the Senate with

Tait. Losing his seat, in part due to the Georgia electorate's intemperate response to the pay raise Bibb and his colleagues voted themselves, Bibb had moved west at the same time as the Goodes, acquired a great deal of land, and became Alabama's governor during the territorial period and the early months of statehood. Men like these remained correspondents of powerful Georgia friends such as Tait and Secretary of the Treasury William H. Crawford. Now they labored to bring southern culture, and southern colleagues, to a new country to join what, thanks to their numbers and influence in Alabama, had become known as the Georgia Machine.[17]

If their elite status distinguished the slaveholders as emigrants, their emigrant status distinguished them from other elites. The Taits' peers among the northern upper classes exhibited no such restlessness. For the rising bourgeoisie of the northern states a disinclination to roam increased as their power and property grew. In the incessantly mobile America of Tocqueville and Kirkland, only the poorest residents of northern cities moved as much as the leading citizens of the slaveholding states.[18] The mobility of families like the Taits was even more striking because they belonged to an agricultural elite. Such families must have startled European eyes accustomed to roads clogged with the landless, in the habit of measuring social esteem by geographic immobility. The ownership of land and slaves gave the planters the kind of wealth and status that elsewhere would have rooted them to the scenes of their success. The mobile ways of the southern elite thus distinguished them from both the new urban elites of the North and the old landed elites of Europe.

As the region's leading citizens and their human property continued to head for their society's borderlands with a fervor unmatched by any comparable class, so too talk and thought of what it all meant spread and intensified. Discussion of movement and its meanings encompassed a remarkably large number of slaveholders: old and young, male and female, those who moved, those who stayed, and those who could not make up their minds what to do. They recorded what they thought and felt about mobility in various ways: in personal diaries and family letters, in agricultural reform literature and political pamphlets, in fictional works of verse and prose, even in advertisements selling land and on tombstones recording death. Many wondered what emigration could do for them as individuals or households. Others, far fewer in number, contributed to a varied public discourse conducted around the central question of what emigration said about the planters, both as individuals and as a class. In the years between the War of 1812 and the Civil War, debate over the meaning of emigration occupied a significant place in the elite discourse and culture of the plantation states. One way or another, most planters were thinking about moving. Why and how they did so is the subject of this inquiry into the cultural and spiritual meanings that slaveholders gave to the mobility in their midst.[19]

This study focuses on emigration from Georgia and South Carolina to the states to the west from Alabama to Texas. This emphasis derives from the study's broader concerns with the thought and culture of the slaveholders in the region where slavery's hold was firmest. Without drawing too hard a line between upper and lower Souths, it is reasonable to acknowledge differences between the two areas, differences reflected in such things as the relative importance of slavery to their economies and their contrasting approaches to the possibility of disunion. Having said that, the arguments made here do not depend upon any strong claims for qualitative differences between upper and lower southern states when it comes to emigration. Planter emigration was important to every slave state. As existing studies make clear, there were broad similarities across the region regarding motivations for moving as well as some similarities when it came to the ways in which planter emigration was debated publicly. Yet given what historical geographer D. W. Meinig describes as the "broadly latitudinal" character of westward emigration in America, it is also clear that Georgians and South Carolinians took the lead in settling southwestern society and shaping its culture.[20]

The study observes and interprets how the planters of Georgia and South Carolina responded to emigration both in private discussion and in public debate. From pillow talk to public oration, careless barroom chatter to carefully crafted broadside, discussion of emigration ranged back and forth between public and private. This study does the same, in the conviction that historical understanding of emigration's meanings is enhanced by exploring the private discussions of people like James and Caroline Tait alongside the public debate that developed around planter mobility throughout the period.

In the private realm motivations behind emigration remained largely unchanging over time. When James Tait's son Charles W. and his wife Louisa moved to Texas in the 1840s, they did so with the same kinds of hopes and motivations, expectations and anxieties, that infused James and Caroline Tait's move to Alabama in 1817. Whatever the period, motivations were shaped by the planters' extensive involvement in the commerce and culture of the transatlantic world. The Taits' anxious pursuit of western lands cannot be understood apart from their desire to prosper in the cotton marts of the nation and the world. Indeed planters like the Taits were more likely to talk of "cotton and slaves" than "land and slaves." The anxieties and ambitions of men like the Taits must also be understood in terms of the relations existing within the plantation household. This study views the plantation household not so much as a place but primarily as the complex relations of kinship and commerce that formed among all the residents of the plantation: slave and free, male and female. These relations encompassed all aspects of family life, black and white, as well as the productive labors that sustained the household and connected it to the wider society and beyond. These relations in turn formed the human mold in which the planters' worldview took shape, including their view of emigration.

To Taits of every generation and gender, new homes to the west held out different hopes and expectations. For Charles Tait, who wanted to remain active in political life, his new home was where he hoped that his private standing and his work in the Senate on behalf of Alabama statehood would encourage his new neighbors to reward him with a Senate seat. But it was also where he could work to preserve ties to, and authority over, his family and to strengthen its place in the ranks of the region's ruling elite. James Tait shared none of his father's public ambition, which was a further source of tension between the two men. Instead, the younger man intended to do as well as possible in the private sphere of planting. There, success would certainly be measured by profits, but also by his ability to pursue authority, independence, and happiness in his own name and in his own household. Resistance to following in paternal footsteps in one sphere of life only fueled James Tait's desire to outdistance his father in the other. Independence, for James Tait, would take the form of selective emulation within the opportunities and constraints established by the plantation household and plantation society.[21]

Women like Caroline and Louisa Tait were raised to their own particular family pressures and obligations. Their task was to maintain comfort and order in the private sphere, a demanding role in a household that was both a family and a business. In new places planter women would strive in support of the familiar goals of household success, progress, and independence. Emigration often made those challenges more difficult to meet for planter women. Charles Tait, explaining to Caroline Tait what she surely already knew, described the great inconveniences involved in settling in a new country and declared his confidence that she would "bear them with resignation & firmness." "You will cherish hope & look forward to your situation being better every year till you get a comfortable establishment," he went on, expressing the hope that this could be achieved "in a few years." After arriving in Alabama, Caroline Tait wrote to thank her father-in-law for the cabbage seeds and to assure him that she would "endeavor to make our home as agreeable as I can and hope you will be satisfyed to make yours and our home the same as heretofore." She did so even though her new location was as "completely in the wild woods as any body ever need to be," with not even a fence around her house. If rudimentary household circumstance made planter women's lives more difficult, so too the undeveloped nature of the infant communities in which they often found themselves stoked their desire to nurture and strengthen the wider relations of community. Thus for planter women like the Taits, new homes to the west would offer a new, but not too new, life pursuing the bounded ambitions of the plantation mistress.[22]

As the land-purchase correspondence between James and Charles Tait illustrates, strong intergenerational tensions often existed within plantation households populated by white men born to rule yet raised to obey. Also, planter men and women often brought very different perspectives and priorities to the emigrant venture. These different perspectives and priorities grounded in generation or gender nevertheless fueled a shared commitment to the success of the move and to the remaking of new places in the image of those left behind. Taken together, the Taits' varied but related aims and expectations suggest the impetus toward both change and consolidation inherent in the emigration experience.

Ties of gender and generation and the tensions they often created surely were on display in any emigrant venture, whether in the South or the rest of the nation. In this regard the planters were hardly unique. But the particular forms they took were very much shaped by the unique circumstances of plantation households that also included enslaved men and women. Male and female planters of all ages were profoundly shaped by their ties to the enslaved members of their households. This was true of all slaveholding households, of course, but perhaps especially so for emigrating households. The ways in which enslaved men, women, and children themselves understood emigration are not addressed to any great extent in this study. The profound impact their presence had on the thought and habit of planter men and women is, however, very much central to its approach and conclusions. The ownership of slaves was itself a major factor in encouraging planters to leave the East and settle in the more fertile lands of the Southwest. Yet, as the private discussion of movement, settlement, and separation illuminates, as capital and labor those same slaves bound planter families together over great distances, even as their own families and communities disintegrated.

Spiritual bonds also proved crucial to maintaining ties that transcended space. In particular, the evangelical Christianity that increasingly shaped the slaveholders' understanding of life in general also proved crucial in ameliorating and explaining the physical separations demanded by emigration. A faith that demanded that its adherents disdain the dangers of earthly journeys and give priority to ultimate, eternal destinations was ideally suited for emigrant women and men living and moving in anxious times. Thus the human relations of slavery and the spiritual assumptions of Christianity formed the bricks and mortar that bound together the plantation households of the slave states. Indeed, in many cases these bonds remained so strong as to call into question the very utility of viewing these households as separate entities.

Countless letters back and forth preserved and embodied these ties. Their content also reveals the relatively unchanging nature of private motivations over time. This was far from being the case with the public circumstances in which household ambitions were pursued. Westward movement itself helped to make sure of that. For one thing, the pursuit of private ambition itself changed the collective character of the southern landscape. Moving to Alabama in 1837 was a different proposition from doing so in 1817. Travel became easier; movement was less likely to be into "the wilderness" but rather toward a landscape that in its broad features resembled "home." New places were increasingly likely to be populated by people one actually knew or at least by people whose habits and values one appreciated and shared. Old ties remained strong while new alliances were formed. This did not make for complete consistency in such things as religious affiliations or political loyalties. Significant differences certainly existed between the subregions of the South. Nevertheless, from the persistent dispersion of interlocking slaveholding households and communities emerged an increasingly cohesive planter class.[23]

The continuing movement of slaveholders also played a critical part in the changing political circumstances that themselves formed part of the context for that movement. When James and Caroline Tait moved west, they did so in a period of intense national optimism. Few seemed to doubt the compatibility of individual, local, and national interests. Yet westward movement fueled the sectional divisions that eventually split a Union that had once counted southern planters among its most loyal and nationalistic of adherents. Following the panic of 1819 and the compromise over Missouri the following year, a rising chorus of concern increasingly intruded on discussions of emigration's political meanings.

Sometimes discussion of emigration could illuminate internal differences. As nullification divided friends and families within South Carolina, for example, nullifiers saw the emigration of others as one more negative consequence of federal tariff policy. Some Unionists came to see departure as a means to escape the state's seemingly irreconcilable internal differences. More insistently, discussion of emigration reflected the growing concern in both South Carolina and Georgia that to lose people was to lose power. That so many elite families were gripped by Alabama Fever only intensified the public scrutiny of emigration's implications for the slave states' place within the nation. It was one thing to see the poorer or even the "middling" classes lighting out for the territories. It was quite another to see the "best people" leaving and taking "their people" with them. Loss of wealth threatened weakness in relation to other regions of the nation. For some, this included the new region being created in the West where southeastern slaves and southwestern soils would give emigrants unbeatable advantages in the production and sale of cotton. Politically, loss of people, whether they counted as one or as three-fifths of one, threatened to diminish the slaveholders' representation in Washington just as such representation had never seemed more essential.

By the 1840s, when Charles W. and Louisa Tait moved from Alabama to Texas, American nationalism had taken on a forthrightly imperialistic tone which, if anything, enhanced its appeal to many Americans. Yet many in both the South and the North blended their love of nation with an intensifying sense of sectional identity. As sectional priorities came to dominate debate, emigration looked less like a problem in itself and more like a solution to other problems. As North-South differences grew, so Southeast-Southwest differences shrank. Westward movement strengthened the slaveholders' sense of themselves as a class with common interests even as debate over the territories' development deepened their fears that they might no longer have a place in the Union they had done so much to create. As the emigration of slaveholders became the expansion of slavery, so anxiety that emigration was weakening the Atlantic states diminished. The public debate over emigration reflected these changing circumstances and the slaveholders' changing perceptions of their place in the Union.

The emigration debate offers more than just one more way to trace the planters' journey from nationalism to sectionalism. It also reveals the planters' engagement with the internal development of their society. How slaveholders debated what they were becoming cannot be separated from how they perceived their growing differences from other Americans. Nevertheless it was the kind of debate that would have been going on anyway. To draw a loose contemporary parallel, one suspects that Americans would have found ways to talk about themselves in the second half of the twentieth century even had there been no Cold War. Too often, the nature of this "internal" debate is obscured by the assumption that antislavery thought and action was the primary, even the only, catalyst for the proslavery worldview that developed in this period.

In this internal debate anxieties of a different kind emerged regarding the social and cultural consequences of planter emigration. Much of the criticism of emigration was grounded in a worldview that has been called agrarian republicanism. In this view the ideal society was one in which land was exalted as a cultural resource and the "agriculturist" was duty-bound to nurture a spiritual relationship between himself and the soil. Only if the relationship between people and place was both secure and sacred could community health and social stability flourish. Critics of emigration feared that the planters' departure from particular places was symptomatic of a wider rejection of agrarian values and a dereliction of the agriculturist's most sacred duty to nature and community. Leaving was treason; the embrace of mobility the mark of the savage. From such a perspective the mass movement of elite agriculturists could scarcely appear as anything other than source and symbol of social disorder and decay.[24]

This view of emigration declined over time, as the ideas and language that shaped it lost their force. Agrarian republicanism grounded in the classics gave way to a proslavery argument infused with the beliefs and assumptions of Christianity. A commitment to order was also at the heart of the proslavery ideal. But it was an order that derived from stable, reciprocal relations between people (slave and free, male and female, parent and child), not between people and place. From the proslavery perspective land was not the essential cultural or spiritual foundation of the good society.

Mobility was not perceived as an insuperable barrier to continued community. Ties within and between plantation households were what mattered. How, not where, was what mattered. The period between the wars saw a shift from agrarian republicanism toward Christian proslavery as the primary ideological prism through which the planters viewed emigration (and, of course, much else). How the planters' responses to westward movement reveal this ideological shift, with its attendant changes in the very vocabulary of planter self-definition, are set out in the chapters that address and interpret the public debate over planter emigration.

The changing nature of the public debate reflects, in one important sense, a society's elevated public ideas catching up with its everyday private realities. Slaveholders seldom confused themselves with shepherds. They knew that the real agriculturists were the slaves who remained all but invisible in the idyllic images of the agrarian ideal. Furthermore, when it came to emigration, mover and stayer alike had long known that physical separation did not mean an end to the ties of slavery and spirituality that bound together households and communities. The ideal and the reality of plantation household and society did not, of course, merge in the seamless fashion envisioned by proslavery ideologues. Tensions between private practice and public prescription remained inescapable and important. Nevertheless what was central to much of slaveholding society—slavery and religion—did become central to plantation society's public discourse on the nature and destiny of that society. The debate over emigration richly reveals both the extent and the limits of this developing convergence between the private and public worlds of a southern elite increasingly inclined to view themselves, not as landowners who happened to own slaves, but as slaveholders who happened to own land.

The debate over emigration reflected and shaped the planters' understanding of their development as a class, both in relation to each other and to other Americans. Yet these interlocking discourses of internal examination and external defense themselves fit within a wider realm of anxious analysis that slaveholders shared with other Atlantic world elites of their age. Slaveholders acknowledged that they were increasingly at odds with their peers in the North, Great Britain, and elsewhere. Unlike those peers, slaveholders did not assume that arriving at different answers to the insistent questions of modernity somehow placed them at odds with the modern world itself. Rather the planters' view of themselves and their world was profoundly shaped by the questions they shared with other elites of their time (including their northern critics) regarding the pressing tensions of modern life: between individual and society, rootedness and deracination, tradition and progress, people and place. No less than their peers across the Potomac or the Atlantic, elite southerners searched for coherence and stability in a world that often appeared fragile and volatile. All that was solid may very well have melted into the nineteenth-century air, but Karl Marx and Friedrich Engels were hardly alone in their ceaseless desire to distill new personal and historical meaning from the modern world's persistent assault on all that was familiar. It is the fate of humans to strive to reconstitute meaningful substance from the inchoate vapor of constant change; to apply the cooling agents of thought and necessity to the affairs of life, however darkly arbitrary those affairs might seem. The Sisyphean labor of humankind was no less the labor of humans of the slaveholding kind. For many planters the ceaseless mobility in their midst made the task of securely locating themselves in new times as well as new places seem especially urgent. For the historian interested in how the planters answered the questions posed by the modern world they inhabited, their responses to mobility take on particular significance precisely because mobility was, and is, seen as a defining characteristic of that world.

Thus this study fully shares the view of previous interpretations of planter emigration that slaveholders' attitudes toward mobility offer a fruitful guide to their broader understanding of their place in the modern world. It departs, however, from certain of the assumptions underpinning those interpretations. One such assumption is that attitudes for or against westward movement offer a reliable guide to differences between slaveholders who espoused "modern" or "liberal" forms of thought and behavior on the one hand and those who maintained a commitment to "traditional" or "conservative" values and practices on the other. To embrace mobility was to embrace the future. To reject mobility was to cling to the past. Furthermore, while these studies differ in appraising the relative strength of these groups in slaveholding society, they do tend to share a narrow definition of conservatism as reactionary opposition to change. They also agree that conservatism and modernity are to be understood as polar opposites. Thus they combine a misleading definition of conservatism with misunderstanding of its relation to modernity.

The limitations of these assumptions are suggested by the interpretation of mobility's meaning offered by William Freehling in his study of the *Road to Disunion*. Freehling argues for deep and significant differences between the "colliding gentries" of the Southeast and the Southwest, contrasting the shrinking reaction of "post-seventeenth-century South Carolinians" and the "expansive imperialism" of "pre-twentieth-century Louisianians." He describes South Carolina as a state that not only "wanted out of everything modern, not least the Union," but also wanted to "secede from the century" itself. Freehling thus locates these differences not only in the planters' relationship to time but also in their location in space, drawing a sharp line between the stagnant, reactionary culture of the Atlantic seaboard states (especially South Carolina) and the go-ahead, risk-taking regions of the wild southwestern frontier. Whether one opposed or embraced mobility was, furthermore, a reliable indicator of these respective broader sets of attitudes and characteristics.[25]

Yet, as Freehling himself describes, it was the very "entrepreneurial army" that had "lately roamed away from" the Palmetto State that led the way in settling the Southwest. We are left with the less than satisfactory conclusion that people left the Southeast driven by attitudes and habits that characterized the places where they had not yet been, having somehow developed those attitudes and habits in a society that considered them anathema. In Freehling's formulation the emigrants can tell us little about the places they left but a great deal about the places they had not yet arrived at. He neglects, in other words, precisely what needs to be explained: how and why such an enthusiastic army of emigrants could be recruited in such supposedly inhospitable territory. Freehling's ultimately unconvincing effort to ground ideological differences in place suggests the deeper definitional problems that arise when conservatism is understood as reaction and modernity and conservatism are viewed in opposing rather than symbiotic terms.[26]

This study seeks to explore the planters' understanding of mobility in a way that avoids such definitional dichotomies in favor of a more flexible understanding of conservatism and its relation to the modern world. Conservatism was, and is, itself an effort to come to terms with the modern world. Indeed just as the rise of southern slavery itself has to be understood in relation to the development of the modern capitalist world, so too the planters' developing and distinctive worldview cannot be understood apart from that world's cultural as well as economic life. This was not a relationship of clear dichotomies and straightforward opposition. Rather the planters' developing worldview in this period "faithfully captured," as Elizabeth Fox-Genovese has suggested, "the complexities of a southern slave society torn between its commitment to the most advanced developments of its time and its determination to protect and justify slavery as the foundation of a just social order." In this sense the planters were modern because they were immersed in the task of meeting the demands made upon them by the wider world in which they lived. The slaveholders' struggle to shape, rather than simply accept or reject, a modern future for themselves is reflected in their responses to planter emigration.[27]

How responses to mobility reveal deeper shifts in planter culture and identity in these years is set out more fully in the coming chapters. The story told here will, I hope, contribute to a fuller sense of the planters' ideology (understood as the coming together of habit and thought), and so to a fuller sense of the planters' understanding of themselves as a class and as a culture. It shows that to track the slaveholders' private and public perceptions of their society's geographical transformation is also to follow the complex, often crooked, intellectual and spiritual paths that paralleled that transformation and eventually converged with it to create the mature plantation society of the American South.

2 The Spirit of Emigration

The spirit of emigration is still rife in our community. From
this cause we have lost many, and we are destined, we fear,
to lose more of our worthiest citizens. Of this we complain
in private. Let it now be the subject of discussion in public.
—William Gilmore Simms

IN 1820 JAMES E. CALHOUN RETURNED FROM NAVAL
duty in Canton, China, to Norfolk, Virginia. There he heard the latest
news from his uncle at the War Department in Washington. While he had
been gone, John C. Calhoun told his nephew, "many of our friends in
Carolina" had made shorter but more permanent journeys to Alabama.
Their relatives Colonel Andrew Pickens, his brother Joseph Pickens, and
Ezekiel Pickens with Mr. Simpson and his family, as well as Dr. Hunter
and his family, were "among the emigrants from Pendleton." From Abbeville the movers were "no less numerous." Similar lists of the notable and
the restless peppered the correspondence of elite Georgians and South
Carolinians throughout the 1820s and 1830s.[1]

Mrs. S. A. Robson of Charleston remarked that "there is nothing talked
of but Alabama." Her brother had recently returned from there, "much delighted" and "speak[ing] of removing there before long." He was thinking
about Mobile, where his friend Wheeler was "doing well." For her part
Mrs. Robson had "no opinion of these new countries. I would rather have
comfort than wealth." To the north, in Camden, William Blanding reported to his wife Rachel, in the northern city of Philadelphia, on the
"great party at Mr. Deas this evening; the whole family start for Mobile on
Saturday next, Mrs D. and all." They were going "on a visit of observation,"
but Blanding had "no doubt they will settle there—young Deas is prac-
ticing up and down the streets, four in hand." In the up-country Robert

Gage kept a skeptical eye on the neighborhood's comings and goings for his brother James, who had left Union, South Carolina, to study medicine in Paris. "T. J. Hughes left here last Wednesday evening for New Orleans—making quite a show in his sulkey," reported Robert. "Mitchell of York a sort of lawyer went with him." Hughes had "a goodly portion of money & I wish him well," but Gage feared that he would "never do much for himself." Later he reported that the Merrills had all left for Mississippi. "God grant they may do well—they have ever been kind to ours—but Jack still drinks & I dread the consequences." Such gossipy intelligence of departures made or imminent proved a common feature of elite correspondence throughout this period.[2]

People losing friends might be expected to exaggerate from their inevitably narrow observations to broader generalizations regarding the scale of westward emigration. Yet statistics from the time support their accounts. This was no ordinary emigration. Census taking before 1850 did not record a person's native state, thus making accurate counts difficult.[3] It has been estimated, nevertheless, that almost half the white people born in South Carolina after 1800 left the state, nearly all of them for the Southwest. Overall, free South Carolinians were almost 80 percent more likely than other Americans to have left their state in the first half of the century.[4]

South Carolina's larger neighbor to the west presented a more mixed picture. From 1820 to 1840 Georgia's population doubled. And although the population grew to 906,185 during the 1840s, that decade saw the lowest increase in the white population recorded for the state, while the black population was only marginally higher than it had been in 1840. That there was an increase in population was due in significant part to Georgia itself still being a destination for emigrants (often from South Carolina) and to the high number of those who left Georgia's older eastern counties to settle in the rich cotton-growing lands opening up in the state's southwestern corner. Even so, 25 percent of white, native-born Georgians lived outside their own state by 1850. This figure nevertheless disguises the full extent of emigration from many of the state's older eastern counties because it excludes those who moved to southwest Georgia rather than to Alabama and beyond. As one correspondent to the *Southern Agriculturist* insisted, with customary resort to aquatic imagery, people were leaving "in shoals."[5]

Images of shoals and tides, streams and waves, suggest the amorphous as well as the mass nature of westward movement and the consequent difficulty in differentiating among the various kinds of movers. It is difficult to know how many emigrants were members of elite households. Just as census practices before 1850 complicate calculations of emigration itself, they also create problems in estimating how much property emigrants had when they left, including how many enslaved emigrants they took with them. The numbers were certainly large, especially in the context of the relatively small numbers of white southerners who belonged to plantation households (defined as a household containing twenty or more slaves). The numbers are greater too when one includes, as I do, emigrants who may not have begun life in the West with more than twenty slaves but who remained part of the southern elite, either as members of extended plantation households or as the lawyers, doctors, and ministers of religion who culturally and socially belonged to the region's leading class.[6] Whether anecdotal or quantitative, then, reports told the same story: emigration was a central fact of life in the southern states.

Many residents believed that the scale of departure was so great that it was transforming the social landscape of the places left behind. Returning from a visit to Pennsylvania in 1833, James Hemphill found "scarcely a single family" in the Chester District of South Carolina who had been there when he left. "Whole families are emigrating to the western wilds," he recorded with amazement; "almost the whole face of Society appears changed." Like the person standing on the riverbank or by the railroad track, those who stood still often seemed most impressed by the speed with which others were moving. Not themselves consumed with the expectancy and anxiety of departure for places new, those who remained were more likely to contemplate the impact of emigration on neighborhoods and communities they already knew. Emigration was as much about those who stayed as it was about those who left.[7]

Many of James Hemphill's peers shared his vision of a social landscape rapidly transformed by emigration. Many, again like Hemphill, confined their musings on movement to private correspondence. But a growing number of elite southerners did their pondering in public. The meaning of private journeys changed as they were drawn into wider discussions concerning the development of plantation society. At different times emigration's observers adopted different forms, different tones, and different emphases, ranging from celebration to jeremiad. Whatever their view of the matter, those who stayed behind sought the meaning of movement as keenly as they appreciated the speed with which it was taking place.

The debate surrounding elite emigration often fixed on its immediate causes and consequences. Yet discussion of a particular social issue frequently offers insights into the deeper thoughts and habits animating a class or a culture. This is the case with emigration and the slaveholding elites of South Carolina and Georgia. Debate about movement through space reveals much about the questions planters asked about their society's development in time. What kind of people are we? What kind of people should we be? How should we live and work? How should we organize our families, our households, our communities, our society? These particular questions fell into three broad categories. What kind of relations should exist between people? What kind of relations should exist between people and place? What is the relation of the past to the present to the future? Whether asked and answered with descriptive or prescriptive intent, all these questions had to do with the efforts of people, as individuals and as groups, to locate themselves in time as well as space.

Certainly the planters of the American South were far from alone in asking such questions. Perhaps these fundamental inquiries are heard in most, if not all, societies, regardless of time or place. Yet such questions were asked with unusual urgency in the societies of the nineteenth-century Atlantic world where change was most rapid and where long-standing ways of understanding the relations of people and place seemed increasingly inappropriate or endangered. New kinds of social mobility and new ideas about freedom's meaning made for new ways of understanding the individual's relation to family, community, and society. Unprecedented levels of geographic mobility challenged the notion that a "place" should be something more than a mere geographical location. Did people owe patriotic loyalty or political allegiance to places of birth, nurture, and residence? Should people look to such places as sources of psychological strength and spiritual sustenance? Should, in other words, place continue to shape people? Or, in a world of seemingly greater individual autonomy and social atomization, should people be free to redefine their connections to place just as they felt increasingly free to redefine their ties to one another? However differently these questions were answered, the intensity with which they were asked spoke to a shared sense of participation in what many understood to be a modern world qualitatively different from what had existed only a short time before.

Questions of gender, generation, and geography—of people and place—and their relations to one another frequently proved to be inseparable from questions of the present's relation to both past and future. Discussion of present change was infused with concern for what that change meant for relations to the past and to the future. Did, for example, the birth of the modern world mean a radical break with a past increasingly seen as the enemy rather than the foundation of progress? Or, however radical its nature, did the modern world still have to be understood as emerging from, and still shaped by, the past? It was no accident that the places that saw the most rapid change in everyday life also embraced most enthusiastically the developing discipline of historical study.

The slaveholding states and territories of the United States were among those places. In some respects the slave states were changing less than other societies to the north and in Europe. But in other ways they changed more than most, especially when it came to the geographic mobility that for many seemed the most striking source and sign of changing times. Thus the slaveholders occupied a particular place in a broader, shared modern landscape. Their approach to broader concerns can deliver up answers that illuminate shared ideological ground while also identifying important points of divergence when it came to seeking an understanding of the modern world and their place in it. For these reasons it is essential to establish just where the planters stood, as it were, as mass emigration of slaveholders and slaves began, and how the planters understood their "place" in the Atlantic world and in history at that time.

Our story of the planters' westward progress begins in 1815, the first year of what many historians, with a tellingly teleological tip of the historiographical hat, like to call "the antebellum era." Whatever the benefits to be gained from naming an entire era after an event that did not happen during it, there are certain decided drawbacks. More than a shorthand convenience, the adjective inevitably privileges some—or even just one—of the era's meanings over others. Whatever the eventual importance of the Civil War, no American alive in 1815 thought of himself or herself as living in an antebellum world. Indeed Americans inhabited a postbellum world.

That "antebellum" so often modifies "South" simply compounds the problem. An event that had not yet happened defines the principal significance of a place that did not yet exist in 1815, or in 1835, in the way that it did in 1861. In 1815 there were few if any "Southerners" of the kind that there were in 1861. Nor did they, any more than their compatriots to the north, look out on their nation through the spectacles of unforeseen secession and fraternal bloodletting. This is not to deny that sectional interests and tensions were not already in evidence. Indeed they were to some extent cemented into the Constitution, while the debates over the recent war with Great Britain had hardly been devoid of sectional differences. It is to say that like most Americans of the time, the residents of the southern states had not yet learned to look to the North as the principal reference point by which to define what they were and what they were not. Poised between the colonial and the imperial, southern writers and observers began to probe for the causes and consequences of emigration. They sought to answer the questions of identity raised by their novel and dynamic circumstances. As they did so, they looked east and west as well as north, back as well as forward in time. As they sought to orient their westward movement to the maps of civilization they carried in memory and imagination, they looked east and back to a continent filled with cultural reference points, west and forward to another continent of great imperial expectations.

The meanings that slaveholding men and women gave to emigration reveal how they understood the tangled, shifting connections of time and place that shaped their identity: from the household to the nation, and most points in between. At times public discussion of emigration was imbued with nationalistic pride and optimism. At others, priorities grounded in local loyalties to community and state framed understanding of planter departure. As the period progressed a sectional tinge did spread from the edges to the center of debate, and a developing sense of regional identity proved increasingly important in coloring public perceptions of emigration. As questions of identity and destiny came to the forefront of the slave states' cultural and intellectual life in these years, so the planters' responses to emigration offer one avenue of retrospective inquiry into the varied and changing ways in which slaveholders answered those questions.

In the confident wake of the Battle of New Orleans and the ensuing Treaty of Ghent, it was the voices of the nationalists that echoed most loudly and insistently in the southeastern states of Georgia and South Carolina. The War of 1812 had eradicated many of the barriers—west and east, native and foreign—to the spread of Thomas Jefferson's "Empire for Liberty." As a speaker on the "Permanency of the American Union" assured an audience of Charlestonians in 1815, "Our union is not to dissolve, but to augment in vigor, and bear new blessings and new glories." Many leading Georgians and South Carolinians shared this enthusiasm for the nation's future prospects.[8]

The nationalists' absorption in their own country's development did not preclude, indeed it encouraged, a great deal of attention to peoples and affairs beyond America's liquid boundaries. Nationalists understood that the task of national self-definition required attention to relations with the continent that Americans had so recently broken with (politically if not culturally). It also required attention to relations with the other peoples of their own continent. Furthermore, these contemporary relations had to be understood as part of a progressive historical process. William Gilmore Simms, man of American letters and leading analyst of the slaveholding condition, exhorted his fellow Americans to make a priority of understanding the young nation's past and present connections to East and West. The acquisition of such knowledge was an essential element in forging a distinct sense of national identity shaped by both European heritage and American circumstances. Those who would seek to shape the nation's future must first "learn to dwell," Simms explained, "upon the narratives of the brave fathers who first broke ground in the wilderness, who fought or treated with the red men, and who, finally girded themselves up for the greater conflict with the imperious mother who had sent them forth." Americans had to study their struggle with (and continued connections to) one empire even as they searched for the historical significance of their many and continuing conflicts with the native populations who stood in the way of their own imperial destiny. Americans, in other words, had to be both postcolonial and imperialistic in outlook.[9]

This outlook profoundly shaped the nationalists' understanding of westward movement and its consequences. South Carolinian John C. Calhoun was among those whose support for a strong, united, and expanding nation was motivated in part by his view of America's place in the world. Looking east, influenced by his experiences as secretary of war and with his suspicions of Great Britain largely undimmed, Calhoun insisted that "the *liberty* and the *union*" of the United States "were inseparably united."[10] National strength, in this view, was a prerequisite of American liberties; national expansion would be a guarantor of the nation's ability to defend both its ideals and its interests.

In the happy days before nullification and Peggy Eaton, the "Hero of New Orleans" himself seemed to be singing from the same nationalist song-book as Calhoun. "Nothing," insisted Andrew Jackson, looking to the West, "can promote the welfare of the United States, and particularly the south-western frontier so much as bringing into market at an early day, the whole of this fertile country" for sale to settlers.[11] The expansion of the 1820s only fueled Jackson's enthusiasm for the universal benefits of westward advance. In 1830, now president and offering his view on the State of the Union, Jackson asked a question to which he already knew the answer: "What good man would prefer a country covered with forests and ranged by a few thousand savages to our extensive Republic, studded with cities, towns, and prosperous farms, embellished with all the improvements which art can devise or industry execute, occupied by more than 12,000,000 happy people, and filled with all the blessings of liberty, civilization, and religion?"[12] The many South Carolinians and Georgians who rallied to the national hero's vision of American development knew that Jackson's words were informed by more than a sense of the nation's economic and security interests. They also responded to the views and visions of Simms, Calhoun, and Jackson as statements of the nation's historical intent. Expansionists appealed to visions of history and progress that cast westward settlers not only as the agents of American empire but also as the vanguard of advancing civilization.

Political and intellectual leaders of the slaveholding states such as Simms, Jackson, and Calhoun viewed westward movement in the dual light of national destiny and universal progress. They defined America as a successor nation in relation both to the children of the forest whose savage civilization it was replacing and to the imperial parent it had outgrown. The images they drew upon and the visions they created profoundly shaped their understanding of emigration as the physical and geographical manifestation in space of a triumphal advance through time. In manifold private decisions they saw a manifest national destiny. Whether they knew or even cared, westward emigrants were making history as integral links in the expansionist logic of Greater America.

In focusing attention on the new nation's relations to those beyond the nation, this imperial vision inevitably encouraged another powerful tendency in nationalistic assessments of emigration's impact: if it was good for "the nation," it was good for every person and every place within the nation. Expansionists like Jackson confidently assumed that "civilization"'s extension to the new places of the West could be accomplished without significant cost to the eastern cradles of that civilization. Indeed, as Jackson insisted, the older-established areas would themselves benefit from the "great" revenues derived from land sales and from the security that "a permanent population" on the frontier would provide.[13] Visions of mutual gain often found grander expression. A *Savannah Daily Republican* editorial in May 1821 rejoiced that "the 'tide of emigration'" continued "to set strongly Westward." Looking "through the vista of futurity," the writer envisioned the "sublime spectacle" of "wildernesses, once the chosen residence of solitude or savageness," converted into "populous cities, smiling villages, beautiful farms and plantations!" This new West would be home to "a happy multitude, busy in their daily occupations," living in "manifest contentment and peace, [and] breathing their gratitude and their prayers only to the King of Kings!"[14] Many elite southerners of the time shared the *Republican*'s confidence that the emigration of Americans would play a crucial and unproblematic part in the young republic's triumphant development. From the perspective of swelling nationalism, all boats—private and public, local and national, regional and sectional—would rise together on the emigrant tide.

Calhoun captured best the temper of the nationalistic times. Arguing before the House of Representatives in 1817 in favor of improvements to internal transportation as one means to "bind the Republic together," the South Carolinian gave the era as apt and untroubled a watchword as any: "Let us conquer space."[15]

Acceptance of the national unity argument and its assumptions was, of course, far from total. Opposition to it, rooted in matters both of intellect and interest, grew as time passed. Skepticism regarding the possibility, much less the desirability, of creating a continental republic long predated the Republic's birth. James Madison had assuaged the fears of some by his efforts to overturn the conventional "small is better" wisdom of traditional republicanism. Subsequent events such as the Louisiana Purchase did much to help southerners as well as other Americans set aside their reservations about the nation's geographic spread. But not all southerners possessed the ingenuity of a Madison or the sanguinity of a Calhoun when it came to accepting that the best kind of politics need not be local. Those who found the Federalist vision of a vast republic oxymoronic rather than inspirational lost the argument over ratification. But many continued to live uneasily under the Constitution and to share classic republicanism's doubts that social cohesion and political representation could be reconciled with geographical expansion on an immense scale.

Thus for those accustomed to measuring the good life on smaller scales, the nationalists' confident belief that geographic mobility would actually contribute to increased social stability remained far from self-evident. These doubts were intensified for some whose daily observations of departing planters and decaying plantations seemed to mock grand claims for expansion's universal benefits. Even eager nationalists were not oblivious to the local impact and personal costs of expansion. Secretary of the Treasury William H. Crawford of Georgia admitted to his friend Charles Tait that he looked forward, "with some degree of despondency," to finding himself "a stranger in my own neighborhood," either "compelled to form new political associations, or to abstain entirely from mingling in the political discussions of the state." Yet Crawford saw the loss of friends and influence as "individual evils, which will not for a moment disturb the general repose, or obstruct the progress of the nation to the fulfillment of its high destinies." For Crawford, personal sorrow counted for little when set against public pride.[16]

Other elite southerners arrived at a more depressing bottom line after calculating emigration's costs and benefits for local communities and national greatness. Thomas Spalding of Sapelo Island, one of Crawford's fellow Georgians, was among the first to question whether national expansion, and the leading role of his class in fueling it, really served both nation and locality as well as the nationalists claimed. Addressing the Union Agricultural Society of nearby Darien in the early summer of 1824, Spalding set a tone of anxious ambivalence on the subject of planter emigration that others would soon take up. He spoke approvingly of the "independence that belongs to our government" and the "liberty which belongs to the individuals who compose it." But Spalding feared that along with their "mighty blessings," national independence and personal liberty also brought "some moral feelings, which had better far been left behind." Spalding had in mind "the restless energy, which liberty stamps upon the character of Free Men" and which "makes them look to their Common Country as their Common Home, and breaks down those local feelings, which, under, other Forms, take deep hold upon the Human Heart."[17] Spalding recognized the developing connection between American freedom and American nationalism. But he saw less of the glory in that revolutionary mix and more of its corrosive effect on local loyalties.

The fear that individual liberty was the enemy of local survival only increased. In 1835 Hugh Swinton Legaré of Charleston found it to be "truly afflicting, for one so much under the influence of *local* attachment as I am, to think of the old families of the State leaving their homes in it forever. Legaré also felt that the "moving off *en masse* to the West" showed "what I have always *felt,* how terribly *uncertain* our whole existence in the South is." "And is it wonderful," he demanded, "that we, the haughtiest of the free,—the most enthusiastic lovers of the blessed order of things under which we were born and educated,—that we should feel our hearts breaking as we survey the appalling prospect around us." For those, like Spalding and Legaré, who loved localism as well as liberty, the fear was that emigration threatened both.[18]

The words of Spalding and Legaré suggest the tension between imperial progress and social stability, between the national and the local, that would increasingly find expression in the developing debate over emigration's meaning for plantation society. Viewed from Washington, D.C., emigration looked like a creative force, establishing the new nation's independence from Europe while breathing the civilizing spirit of the age into a waste, howling wilderness. Viewed from Sapelo Island the twin pursuits of individual liberty and national expansion seemed to undermine rather than extend the order and culture of longer-settled regions. From the shores of Sapelo Island, it seemed far from clear which "spaces" were truly being conquered.

Events as well as ideas played their part in fueling elite southerners' increasingly ambiguous attitude toward the ceaseless westward journeying of their slaveholding peers. Doubts about movement were intensified by doubts about an American nationality supposedly able to harmonize all lesser interests within it. Throughout the 1820s growing concern about planter emigration emerged in broader debates over a series of political issues ranging from territorial organization to tariff policies. Increasing emigration disabused even the most optimistic of nationalists of the belief that an easy harmony of national, local, and regional interests was to be the hallmark of the new republic.

The year 1819 marked a turning point in the slave states' relation to the wider Union. The question of whether or not Missouri should enter the Union as a slave state was increasingly answered along sectional lines. Despite the eventual "Compromise" the Missouri controversy revealed a regional divisiveness that would greatly influence national politics over the next decade or so.[19] The year 1819 also brought financial panic, as economic boom turned first to slump and then to depression. Planters read the signs of the times in the declining prices offered for their cotton. Sold for twenty-seven cents in 1816, a pound of cotton brought only fourteen cents by 1819.[20]

Falling cotton weighed heavier on slaveholders whose enthusiasm for national unity and expansion had been dulled by dismay at scenes of stagnation close to home. In 1829 Eldred Simkins, a member of one of Edgefield District's leading families, found himself "humbled" by the sight of "young" states like South Carolina and Georgia already disfigured by "bald hills, and extensive wastes, as desolate as if the besom of destruction had passed over them."[21] Many joined in Simkins's lament for landscapes lost. William Elliot of Charleston conjured up a past visitor to "our shores in the day of our prosperity," returning in the present only to see "the stamp of depression and decay every where imprinted on us" and "the whole country wearing the aspect of hopeless despondency."[22] Contrasting images of past glory and present disorder proved popular rhetorical devices for those intent on bringing the escalating ills of the old seaboard states to the forefront of the public mind. This was especially so in South Carolina, where present distress was hard to take for a class so conscious of their state's recent history of agricultural wealth and Revolutionary glory.

Nor did Elliot have any doubts as to the "besom"'s identity. His visitor would learn that this "dreadful calamity" had been caused, not by war, pestilence, or famine, but, shockingly, by "the paternal care of Government!" "Yes Fellow Citizens," Elliot insisted, "we must look to our own government as the fountain head of our distresses!"[23] Many elite southerners joined Elliot in blaming the federal government's policies for their communities' economic misfortunes and anxieties. In particular they blamed the series of trade tariffs passed during the 1820s, intended to encourage the growth of American manufacturing and culminating in the Tariff Act of 1828.

Outraged slaveholders lambasted this "Tariff of Abominations" as the most egregious example yet of federal indifference to slaveholding interests and as a further blow to social and economic health in the southern states. Thomas Fuller Hazzard of West Point, St. Simon's Island, Georgia, also blamed the tariff for the problems of Sea Island cotton, while William J. Alston, addressing the Anti-Tariff Agricultural Society of Broad River, deplored the "direful effects" of the federal government's "execrable laws." To many slaveholders it seemed that a highly selective understanding of "national progress" was being implemented at their expense. In response they proposed, under the intellectual and political leadership of onetime nationalist and tariff supporter John C. Calhoun, a theory that asserted a state's right, in certain circumstances, to nullify federal laws considered to be against its interests. Most slaveholders, however much they despised the tariffs, did not support nullification. Yet the extended controversy over tariffs and nullification worked permanent changes in the slaveholders' perception of their relation not only to the policies of the federal government but also to the idea of the American nation itself.[24]

Signs of the shifting times could be seen and heard in many places. In August 1832 John Berkeley Grimball witnessed an event where both words and their absence spoke to the great shift in sentiment that had taken place over the preceding years. Attending a states' rights sing-a-long at the Circus in Charleston one Saturday, Grimball recorded how an otherwise "convivial Evening" spent drinking "sour Claret and Punch" and singing French songs—"particularly The Marseilles hymn"—was itself soured when "Old West—(of the Theater)" sang Yankee Doodle. It quickly became obvious that his selection was not to the taste of the meeting, when "no one applauded or joined in the chorus of a song—which may be called our National song—and which a few years ago every man in the house would have strained his throat to swell." Grimball interpreted the audience's response as evidence for how "the sentiments of the people" had been "so completely changed" by the actions of the federal government. Many slaveholders feared that national and sectional interests were turning out to be less harmonious than postwar pride and profits had once led them to hope. Antagonism toward government policies prompted reconsideration of an idea of American nationhood that many elite southerners increasingly viewed as threatening rather than enhancing local and regional interests and identities.[25]

This atmosphere of political uncertainty and threat inevitably shaped attitudes toward the elite emigration that was itself becoming a major public issue. The year 1819 also had brought the beginnings of heavy elite enlistment in the army of emigration, especially in South Carolina.[26] Previously the movers had been mostly nonslaveholders who took little with them and left behind land and fields that their planting neighbors could add to their existing holdings. As more of the leading citizens of the seaboard states joined the exodus, westward expansion began to look more complicated to their own kind than it had in the days of war-fueled enthusiasm for conquest and country. Many still viewed emigration as a prerequisite of future national strength and success. But a growing number of slaveholders found it difficult to share the disengaged wonder of the tourist or the involved optimism of the American nationalist for westward movement. Growing attention to planter emigration as an important matter of public concern in its own right was, then, frequently bound up with growing anxiety regarding the slave states' economic and political relations with the rest of the nation.

Compromise notwithstanding, the Missouri question accentuated the slaveholders' awareness that some Americans questioned the compatibility of slaveholding advance with national progress. In some respects northern opposition to the expansion of slavery strengthened slaveholders' belief in the political necessity of westward movement, but as a prerequisite of preserving slaveholding power rather than advancing national unity and glory. Yet as the drive west now coincided with economic decline at home, fears grew that westward movement was at best a two-edged sword. Even as one side carved a wider place for slaveholders in the West, the other undercut economic and social stability at home. Judge John Belton O'Neall of South Carolina estimated in 1842 that a third of his state's "wealth and population" was to be found in the Southwest, carried there by the "disastrous spirit of migration."[27]

To make matters worse, what had once been the capital and labor of the Southeast was now being employed in the fabulously fertile lands of the Southwest. The Southeast was not just losing its people, it was gaining a new competitor. Were southwestern settlers not "destined at no distant day," as James Henry Hammond later argued, "to supply the foreign markets of the world" with cotton? Hammond felt sure that the planters of the Southwest, having "just overcome all the incipient difficulties of the enterprise," were "now prepared to put forth, on the finest soil and in the most favorable climate of the earth, an energy which must inevitably crush all serious competition." A correspondent to the *Southern Agriculturalist* urged caution on those who believed that westward movement would increase the older slave states' political influence. Rather, Y. Z. feared, "in the attempt to control the East" they might "establish a power in the West, which will, in the sequel, overwhelm both the East and the South." For Y. Z. the answer was to "stunt their growth by *low diet*—that is by withholding from them our money and our labor—for which we get no equivalent in any form." These writers were far from alone in questioning the assumption that settlers in the Southwest would continue to share the political and economic interests of those who remained in the Southeast.[28]

Almost as worrying as the departure of so many leading citizens was that the loss of "our people" also meant the loss of "our people's people." And it was not just the loss of slaves who traveled west with emigrating owners. Critics of emigration worried that the Southwest offered too tempting a market for southeastern slaveholders eager to rid themselves of underproductive slaves. Whitemarsh Seabrook, an agricultural reformer and later governor of South Carolina, complained that "the amount of property, particularly slave property, sold" during the past year had been "so great as to excite the liveliest apprehensions of every friend to our domestic institutions." Seabrook was concerned that emigration not only threatened to cause economic and social instability at home but also to diminish the planters' voice in national politics. "In proportion to the withdrawal of capital and the necessary reduction of income," he calculated, "will be the diminution of the political influence of the state, in the national councils." Whether emigrants counted as one person or three-fifths of a person, the departure of so many residents, with little or no balancing migration to the Southeast, raised fears of a reduction in congressional representation "and hence," as Seabrook continued, "of the decrease of our moral power, and ultimately, perhaps, of our numerical strength, in successfully maintaining the strength of our local policy."[29]

Seabrook expressed the growing fear that the westward flow of the best people and their property represented the draining away of class and community capacity to defend the slaveholding way of life. Seabrook's fears were borne out as South Carolina's congressional delegation was reduced by two members in the following years. Seabrook and others spoke for those for whom emigration meant more than the personal loss of a neighbor or a family member. It also meant the loss of collaborators in the public battle to assert and maintain slaveholding interests. For those who agreed with Seabrook, the society that slavery made possible had more to fear than gain from the continuing westward movement of slaves and slaveholders.

Thus events from the Missouri controversy to the tariff crisis encouraged a more ambiguous understanding of westward movement in the older-established slave states, especially South Carolina. For some the westward movement of slaveholders meant the welcome spread of the right kind of people and practices. For others it threatened the established slave states with a diminution of their economic and political power at precisely the time that many Americans in the rest of the nation—prodded in large part by westward expansion itself—were questioning the compatibility of slaveholding interests and the national interest.

Growing differences between the nation's regions provided part of the context for growing concerns about emigration. Planter emigration also raised questions about possible divisions among the slaveholders themselves. The view that departure meant disloyalty and competition, hinted at in the words of Seabrook, Hammond, and others, found increasingly widespread expression. This elite discussion of emigration could reflect differences over issues—such as nullification—other than westward movement itself.

The Nullification Crisis generated profound divisions among the slaveholders of the southern states. Some slaveholders, Louisiana sugar planters for example, supported tariffs. Others, like President Andrew Jackson, supported tariffs for some purposes but not others. The great majority, however, opposed the Tariff of Abominations. Yet a majority of the tariffs' opponents rejected nullification as an appropriate form of resistance to federal policies. Many planters retained a powerful faith in the Union that transcended opposition to particular, and hopefully passing, policies. They saw the doctrine of nullification as a threat to the Union itself, not just a response to particular federal policies. In the only state where a majority of the slaveholding elite supported nullification, South Carolina's radical nullifiers were quick to chastise their fellow slaveholders in other states for their lack of support.

Yet there were also South Carolinians who opposed nullification, and tensions between nullifiers and Unionists ran highest within the Palmetto State itself. In countless speeches and the occasional street fight, both sides proved themselves as implacably opposed to each other as the nullifiers were to the federal government. Charge and countercharge of treason and unreason filled the air. Nullifiers took steps to enforce "loyalty" to their state through legally prescribed oaths. Unionists lamented the virus of fanaticism sweeping their state. Fevered conflict within the state was linked to the Alabama Fever that continued to carry off planters to the West. Writing at the end of 1833, seeking an explanation for his neighborhood's changing face, James Hemphill looked to "the vestiges of the late political conflict" that remained "perceptible in the conduct and conversation of the people." "This Spirit of Emigration arises," he concluded, "in a great measure from the prevalence of nullification."[30] Other residents of the state—Unionists and nullifiers—agreed with Hemphill that emigration was linked to the current political conflict. But they disagreed about why emigration was both source and symbol of the deeper crisis.

For the nullifiers tariffs helped to create the depressed economic conditions in the Southeast that drove so many slaveholders west. Their laments often twinned decay with desertion, agricultural decline with the absence of agriculturists. Wealthy South Carolina rice planter and politician James Hamilton encouraged his Walterboro audience to "look abroad through this once happy, this once prosperous land" and observe "the wilderness regaining her empire." Exhorting them to "look at those waste and desolate spots which once teemed with fertility and life," Hamilton asked what had happened to "those beautiful homesteads and venerable chateaus which once thronged this land of our fathers." "Gone," Hamilton lamented, "fallen into irreversible decay." If decay was written in the landscape, it was also evident in the absence of people from that landscape.[31]

Staunch Unionists, for their part, did not necessarily dispute the connection the nullifiers traced from tariffs to depression to departure. But they also saw emigration as a potential response to the policies of the nullifiers. Some Unionists began to think of leaving themselves should the nullifiers' extreme policies of loyalty oaths and state defiance prove triumphant. James L. Petigru, among the firmest of South Carolina's Unionists, lamented how "fanaticism of every kind" was on the rise while acknowledging his own "complete state of uncertainty" as to what the nullifiers, the Congress, or the states would do next. Petigru remained "doubtful" as to his own course of action should "a revolution [be] effected" but felt that "should it come to an affair of force in the State I must take my share, and if proscription and penal laws are enforced I must emigrate." If the Union was to be "severed," Petigru had determined "to quit the negro country" altogether. "But where to go?" he added. "There's the rub."[32] For Petigru emigration offered an escape route of last resort from conflicts that threatened to overwhelm ties of interest and affection at home.

Other South Carolinians shared Petigru's understanding of emigration as the only alternative should the nullifiers win. Not all who contemplated leaving South Carolina considered leaving slave country. William Haynsworth of Sumter thought about fleeing to Alabama to escape the conflicts over nullification that raged within his own family. "Who can say that he will not remove to Alabama," pondered his niece Sarah Gayle in

September 1832, "when he and his brothers are warmly opposed to each other?" Gayle consoled herself with the thought that her uncle's removal close to her family in Alabama "would truly be good out of evil." Gayle also noted the spread of conflicts over nullification to Alabama. She recorded in her diary her husband's attendance at an antinullification dinner in Clinton on the same evening as a similar event in Marion to which Gayle herself had been invited. On the last day of the year, Sarah Gayle felt "emotions of mingled pain and pleasure" regarding her uncle's chosen course. She felt "pleasure" that he had "a settled intention of remooving to Alabama" but also "bitter regret that a cause so calamitous" had led him to it. Gayle was "grieved" by the depth of family division she inferred from letters too "thoroughly imbued with a spirit of melancholy" to reflect concern for "publick affairs" alone. "Can it be that unkind feelings have grown up amongst you of one household?" Gayle asked. Nevertheless she hoped "that the period is not remote when friends & brothers will meet again in confidence and affection." Political tensions, mingled with who knows what other private rivalries, could thus divide families.[33]

Others shared the concerns of Petigru and Haynsworth, as well as their consideration of emigration as a last, regrettable resolution to conflicts seemingly beyond compromise. An angry William Gilmore Simms agreed with Petigru's sense of the "state of excitement little short of phrensy" that had engulfed his state, an atmosphere only fueled by the Nullification Convention's passing of a "villainous ordinance" which embodied loyalty tests that Simms considered "most dishonorable to honest men, and the most degrading to free men." Anticipating violence in the streets, Simms had purchased a new pair of pistols.[34]

Alienated by his political foes, Simms claimed to consider himself a "visitor" rather than a "citizen" in his own state. He agreed that departure would be the only acceptable response to a complete nullifier triumph and "had already determined on expatriation" from South Carolina. Should the nullifiers prove victorious, Simms did not look, with Petigru, to the North but, like Haynsworth, "to the stabling place of the Sun." Simms had already corresponded with his uncle in Mississippi about the possibility of settling there. Simms's thoughts of westward flight went beyond the personal. He feared that the population was so divided that exile and exodus would be the only resort for all Unionists. Simms felt sure the nullifiers would pass legislation demanding of South Carolina's residents "an oath of paramount allegiance to the State." Simms insisted that such a move—"if our party have any soul left"—would drive the state's Unionists "to arms or emigration *en masse.*" Simms further insisted that these political refugees would have to move to a territory set aside for them by the federal government, carrying with them "such of our gods, goods, and spirit of Independence, as in these troublous times may have been left." They would leave behind the "damnably defiled scene of brutal prostitution and tyranny" to be divided up among its "more loyal" neighboring states. Simms, then, saw emigration as a consequence not only of personal alienation but of ineradicable public divisions.[35]

Inverting familiar contrasts between frontier and civilization, Simms prophesied cultural disaster. He pictured "a mournful, but a proud spectacle" of one-third of South Carolina's white people "in sad and solemn procession" departing "the homes of their birth and growth" for "the unhewn woods and the desert wilderness of rocks & trees." He portrayed an apocalyptic landscape of civilization crushed and history in retreat. In the East "commerce, trade and peace are all in exile," while "even agriculture, dreadfully reluctant, is preparing to take up her implements of culture, and in the more fertile quiet regions of the west and southwest . . . seek for the repose she has here been denied." No empire for liberty this, rather a reservation for freedom.[36]

We may doubt the seriousness of Simms's belief in a Unionist trail of tears leading to a federally established western enclave. Yet he was not alone in seeing emigration as a drastic and final means of escape from the nullifiers' treasonous tyranny. For the nullifiers emigration was one more symptom of a federally imposed sickness that had ravished familiar social landscapes almost beyond recognition. For both sides emigration, whether as cause or effect, represented one more sign of the crisis facing their society.

Leading figures on either side of the Nullification Crisis may have hoped that emigration would ease as economic depression abated or political tensions eased. They were to be disappointed. As Joseph Jenkins, a planter of Colleton District, South Carolina, pointed out in 1835, the Nullification Crisis, "with its raw-head and bloody-bones, has passed by, and the tariff, with its concomitant evils, is gradually reclining its iron sides." Yet, as Jenkins unhappily observed, "the tide of emigration is sweeping from us with increasing rapidity." The slaveholders' westward movement from Georgia and South Carolina did indeed reach unprecedented levels in the 1830s.[37]

As more and more people left, South Carolina experienced little of the immigration evident in other regions of the nation that might have gone some way to balancing the demographic books. The state's population grew by 15.5 percent in the 1820s but by only 2 percent in the 1830s. Backcountry areas, recently a destination for movers, now saw the heaviest departures. Between 1800 and 1830 the population of Fairfield and Chester Districts, for example, had grown by 114 and 110 percent respectively. Between 1830 and 1850 the respective increases were only 3 and 5 percent.[38] Planter emigration continued to fuel slave emigration. John Gage of Camden was among the many who recorded his estimates of this black exodus. He thought that two thousand or so slaves had recently passed through his town as part of "the immense quantity of negros going on" to what he tellingly described as "the Cotton growing States." Small wonder that Joseph Jenkins seemed preoccupied by a "tide" that emptied places of people while leaving "the memorials of desertion [that] crowd thick around us." Jenkins's lament reflected a growing inclination on the part of elite southerners to view emigration as an intrinsic, and troubling, feature of their society rather than a phenomenon rooted in a particular event or controversy.[39]

Jenkins still saw the problem of emigration in the wider context of national expansion and division. The tariffs and the Nullification Crisis might not have "caused" emigration, but Jenkins, as Whitemarsh Seabrook had done, located emigration's most negative consequences in its weakening of the slaveholders' ability to repulse future threats. The iron sides of abolitionism were rising even as those of the tariff were reclining, strengthening the slaveholders' sense of external threat and intensifying appeals to slaveholders to fortify their defenses. "If the flower of her chivalry" was to be "drained from" South Carolina, Joseph Jenkins feared that "of her territory a conquest must be made, not by victory, but by desertion."[40]

It followed that strength would come from the "chivalry"'s staying put. "South-Carolina has very properly been called the Frontier State," Jenkins explained, the state "in which the battles for Southern Institutions are to be fought." Jenkins thus followed Simms in inverting the prevailing imagery of the West and the frontier. But he did so in a different way. During the Nullification Crisis the West had seemed to Simms a calm refuge from a wild and chaotic East. Jenkins's "frontier" would always be in the East, an ideological line of defense facing north rather than moving west. From this perspective emigration was the prelude to, rather than the consequence of, defeat. Faced with the "evil" of "desertion," Jenkins declared it "the high and bounden duty of every patriot to lend his efforts to stay the growing calamity." Jenkins called on his fellow slaveholders to resist the temptations of one frontier and to stay and play their part in defending far more important frontiers against political and cultural attack.[41]

Jenkins was one of a growing number of slaveholders who increasingly viewed emigration from a sectional rather than (or as well as) a national perspective. They saw emigration primarily in terms of its relation to a threat that came from beyond the boundaries of the slave states. Yet a significant number of elite southerners who sought the meaning of this movement chose to view emigration as largely an internal problem and to look within the slave states for its causes. Those causes, they felt sure, lay deeper than federal policy or passing political conflict. Indeed, some believed that the recent focus on tariffs and nullification had distracted elite southerners from a serious search for the real causes of their society's problems. South Carolinian William Ellison, for one, considered it wrong to identify tariffs "as the cause of our decline." Ellison expressed his frustration that his peers' absorption in "much argument and angry discussion" over federal policy had led them to neglect the internal self-examination necessary to expose the homegrown causes of problems such as emigration.[42]

In their own ways both Jenkins and Ellison reflected the growing view that planter emigration represented a crisis in itself. Both, in their own way, were participants in the widening effort to direct the public gaze inward in search of mobility's causes and meanings. To many it was a good thing that more people were talking about emigration. "The spirit of emigration is still rife in our community," declared William Gilmore Simms. "From this cause we have lost many, and we are destined, we fear, to lose more of our worthiest citizens. Of this we complain in private. Let it now be the subject of discussion in public." Simms must have been encouraged to see a growing number of his peers agree that a public coming-to-terms with "the spirit of emigration" was essential to understanding the nature and character of the planter class and to plotting the future direction of plantation society.[43] It is to that continuing coming-to-terms that we now turn.

3 Public Thoughts

> Now if it be true that fixed land property is of the essence
> of civil society, properly so called, what shall we think
> of our prospects as a nation,—a people,—South of the
> Potomac!
> —Hugh Swinton Legaré

WILLIAM GILMORE SIMMS'S DEMAND THAT MORE PUB-
lic attention be paid to elite emigration reflected his concern that too few
of his peers shared his view of planter mobility as an ambiguous force in
slaveholding society. Not for the first time Simms overestimated both
his isolation and his prescience. By 1836 many other elite southerners had
joined Simms in exploring the connections between private movement
and its public consequences. Even more would join them. In 1838, to take
one example, South Carolinian Joseph Johnson reminded the Agricultural
Society of South Carolina that "most of us have children, relatives and
friends, who have left the State and gone Westwardly, to seek for new lands."
"Many more" would follow, Johnson believed, including those "distinguished for talents and enterprise and public spirit," unless they were provided with "profitable occupation" at home. Johnson, in his choice of words,
reflected the concern about emigration's consequences shared by Simms
and others. In his choice of venue, he reflected the increasing desire to discuss these concerns in public.[1]

Public discussion of elite emigration focused on both its causes and its
consequences. Observers wondered why so many privileged citizens would
choose to leave behind the places that had given them status. They asked
what the emigrants' departure would mean for those places. Inevitably,
particular questions about the meaning of planter emigration could not
be separated from wider questions about plantation society in general. As
it developed in this period, the debate over emigration reflected, and influenced, wider discussions of southern society's character and destiny. If

more were talking about emigration than Simms acknowledged, many more than he allowed shared his troubled perspective on the issue. By the 1820s and 1830s, the public debate was dominated by those who, like Simms, viewed emigration with a mixture of alarm and ambivalence.

Reasons for the observers' anxiety varied. Ideological frontiersmen like Joseph Jenkins emphasized external threats to southern institutions and lamented the "desertion" that undermined their defense. Even as Jenkins spoke out against planter desertion, the proslavery discourse that would come to dominate public debate in the southern states was well advanced toward maturity. Yet as men like Thomas Spalding indicate, other strands and streams of thought also ran through the region's public discourse in this period. Ideal notions of agrarian order and republican advance, ideals in which slavery was largely invisible, also provided much of the language and many of the categories that elite southerners brought to the analysis of elite emigration. Especially important in shaping perceptions of emigration was what might be called agrarian republicanism. An outlook shaped by classical and republican assumptions about the appropriate relations between people and between people and place, agrarian republicanism placed great stress on good husbandry and good citizenship as the foundation for a healthy, orderly, and progressive society.[2]

Emigration was discussed, then, in the more traditional language of agrarian republicanism as well as in the developing discourse of what came to be called the positive good theory of slavery. The debate, as it developed, also reflected an ideological shift in slaveholding thought from agrarian republicanism to the proslavery argument, a shift that emigration as a social phenomenon itself did so much to encourage. The more that the fact of slavery's centrality to southern society became central to public discussion of that society, the more perceptions of planter emigration changed. By the 1850s elite emigration had become such an accepted part of the southern order that it no longer aroused much public debate at all.[3] Yet in the period when Simms was calling for more debate, many who discussed emigration's meaning did so in terms of a social ideal that placed attachment to place— as land, as community, and as spiritual resource—above all else. From such a perspective, emigration could scarcely look like anything other than a sign of social crisis. It is necessary, then, to look at emigration through the eyes of the agrarian-minded commentators before later returning to the question of why emigration eventually became no more than peripheral to

the vision of southern society that the region's thinkers and writers had created by midcentury.[4]

Most critics of planter emigration agreed with Thomas Spalding that it
loosened, even severed, the ties of kin and culture that bound local communities together. Just as political ties could be strained, even broken,
other centers of community activity also suffered. Chief among them were
the churches of the eastern states. John Witherspoon, a Presbyterian pastor
in Camden, South Carolina, noted how even Mr. Douglas, "the father of
this church almost," was expected to "remove before long." "We live in a
changing world," Witherspoon concluded.[5] Emigration thinned out entire
churches; whole congregations disappeared or dwindled below the point
at which a church could support a pastor. Four churches in Hopewell
Presbytery, Georgia—Clarkesville, Gainesville, Eatonton, and Hickory
Grove—were, by 1837, "almost extinct in consequence of emigration." The
departure of some disheartened those who remained. "The impression
which [emigration] makes and deepens on the community," wrote "Rusticus" in the *Southern Religious Telegraph* in 1835, "is that the country *must
ultimately be abandoned and entirely depopulated.*" In this atmosphere of
uncertainty, "efforts for building houses of worship, settling pastors, establishing schools and the improvement of society in other ways are *paralized*
if made, and frequently so paralized as to prevent them from being made."
Thus emigration was seen as undermining those congregations that it did
not entirely uproot.[6] Some consolation could be found in the hope that the
East's loss would be the West's gain. With mingled sadness and pride, a
member of the Bethel Presbyterian Church in South Carolina remarked
how his own church, "now in its decline and greatly weakened," nevertheless had been "the fruitful mother of many other Christian Societies" to the
west.[7] As time passed such consolation seemed increasingly meager, and
the churches of the South Atlantic states increasingly opposed emigration
as a threat to church organization and religious community.[8]

Emigration's impact on religious communities appeared to many observers to be part of a wider unraveling of community ties. John Witherspoon worried that the entire town was "going down fast," as "many of
her best citizens are removing to the South and West."[9] Emigration's de-
bilitating impact on entire communities was addressed by a "Pine Land

Planter"'s meditation on the meaning of "Emigration," published in the *Southern Agriculturist* in the summer of 1839. There were "few" people, the writer believed, who had not been made "uneasy, not to say unhappy," on hearing "flattering accounts" of the West from "relatives or friends" already there. Many had visited the West, where they had seen their friends' and relatives' "deep rich soil, their luxuriant fields," and listened to "their boundless discourse of hundreds of thousands and of millions." Such sights and sounds "seldom failed to make us look back with absolute contempt upon our own barren and spiritless land." Many were moved to buy their own land on the spot, returning home only long enough "to pull up stakes and abandon all the endearing associations of infancy, youth, and manhood, for the glorious prospect of unbounded wealth in more favored climes." [10]

Not everyone pursued this path, of course. There were those who returned to the East with every intention of emigrating but on whom "the lapse of time" and renewed acquaintance with "the comforts of home and friends" combined to "wear away his first vivid impression, and deprive him of the resolution to go." Yet these people made their own unwelcome contribution to community instability. In most cases, the "Pine Land Planter" insisted, "the thorn rankles in his bosom," and he "feels that he has made an immense sacrifice" in surrendering "to his unfortunate attachment to the spot where an unkind destiny has cast his lot." The desire "to break away" lingers, and he "looks upon the soil and institutions of his father scarcely as his own—certainly as not his children's." [11] Discontented where they were and still dreaming of departure, such men added to the sum of social anxiety. The words of the "Pine Land Planter" describe a class alienated from the communities of their birth and dangerously adrift from its proper moorings in the connected course of generations.

While some lamented emigration's consequences for ties between people, others focused on its destructive assault on the ties that, in a healthy society, ought to have bound the conscientious agriculturist to the land. Many critics portrayed the departure of people and the decay of place in shades of elegiac gray. A correspondent to the *Southern Agriculturist* found it "humiliating to look over large sections of this and the neighbouring States, in the lower districts especially, and witness the frequent recurrence of dilapidation that every where presents itself." [12] A South Carolinian once "a sojourner in a smiling portion" of his state now saw "a wilderness" in which "the beautiful homesteads of the hospitable planters" were "fast disappearing" while "fields which once teemed with golden harvests" had become "mere water-wastes!" Such scenes of decay and dislocation inspired something close to desperation in those who saw only the signs of social regression written on a once-fat landscape. "How should this be?" asked the South Carolinian. "I repeat the question—how should this be?"[13]

In addressing this very question, many elite southerners became convinced that a decay so clearly written on the land must have its strongest and deepest roots in the planters' relation to that land. The South, after all, was an agricultural society, "emphatically" so as their orators were fond of expressing the point.[14] "The Patriot," as one "well-wisher to agriculture" insisted, "in contemplating the progress of our extended country, must look with anxious attention upon the Agricultural interests, for in them, in a great degree, depend the wealth and strength of the country and the happiness of its people." To many concerned observers it was in their primary role as agriculturists that planters should seek to understand both themselves and the challenges they faced.[15]

A growing number of observers turned their "anxious attention" to agriculture and to the agriculturists. In doing so they sought not only the sources of present decay but the solutions to future regeneration. If this was an age of anxiety, it was also one of optimism. If it was a time of frequent resort to the overwrought romantic image, it was also a time of great faith in the power of human reason to put together again whatever human unreason had once put asunder. At times, opponents of emigration could sound like authentic reactionaries: curmudgeonly Canutes seeking to reverse the westward flow of humanity and capital that symbolized to them the wider tides of progress and modernity. Thomas Spalding, for example, considered it the "duty" of "lovers of our country," even "if we are unable to recall those that may have gone, to do every thing in our power, to fortify those that remain, against this love of change."[16] Yet Spalding, although more resigned than most, was no reactionary. Indeed he insisted that to resist change in some areas required the encouragement of radical transformation in others. Spalding and his fellow reformers rejected the love of change for its own sake that modernity at times seemed to breed. But they enthusiastically embraced the assumptions and methods of modern science and experimentation as the means to foster agricultural improvement and, therefore, social progress. William Ellison noted that "the time is fast approaching when science must be called in to the aid of labour, and old habits be exchanged for new." "The times are changing, and we must change with them," he insisted.[17]

Thus while Ellison decried the focus on tariffs and politics as the sources of current ills, he was optimistic that good was emerging from evil as planters' anxieties about politics and prices were "beginning to awaken a spirit of inquiry among all classes, which may be productive of great good." Furthermore, "planters of enterprize, capital and information, will lead the way," Ellison hopefully proclaimed, "and point out the best methods of general improvement." If planters harnessed the power of modern knowledge and science to their agricultural ambitions, they could meet their stewardship responsibilities to soil and society alike. Thus pessimism regarding current circumstances combined with a heartfelt faith that people could reform themselves and in so doing rejuvenate the places they inhabited. However strong the reformers' romantic laments for Alabama Fever's undermining of the agrarian ideal, their proposed cures for the condition revealed their faith in reason as the means to republican restoration. For most reformers it was an article of faith that new knowledge would provide the power needed to achieve traditional ends.[18]

Many reformers insisted that making the pursuit of knowledge a collective endeavor would bring even greater potency to reforming efforts. John D. Legaré, editor of the *Southern Agriculturist*, explained that even "with the greatest industry and perseverance," a single planter could "make but comparatively few experiments in the course of his life, whilst in every department, so much remains yet to be ascertained and settled."[19] Reformers advocated the founding of agricultural societies as a means to deepen and develop the ties between the individual planter and his class. William Harper praised gatherings like those of the Monticello Planters' Society of South Carolina, of which he was president, for such associations improved the people's "character and intelligence" and "promotes mutual benevolence."[20] The local agricultural society, this "creature of our exigencies" in Simms's description, was seen as an essential venue for conducting experiments and sharing ideas. Such organizations also would promote among planters a sense of their collective mission as agriculturists.

Agricultural journals also were welcomed as evangelizing organs of modern agricultural methods. Thomas Fuller Hazzard, for one, proved laudably ecumenical in his enthusiasm for the *Southern Agriculturist*. Hazzard likened his fellow planters to the children of Israel, pursuing their own way and failing to learn from the successes and failures of others. He rejoiced that they now had an "agricultural Alkoran" in which to "communicate all their sins and errors in farming." Its editor, Hazzard believed, would be "a centinel in the agricultural temple." Other reformers shared the hope that journals like the *Agriculturist* and the *Southern Cultivator* would serve as two-way conduits, irrigating minds and nurturing communities as they carried back and forth across the region the general principles and practical knowledge that together made for wisdom.[21]

State governments also were called upon to overcome their indifference to agriculture. Arguing that agricultural improvements were worthy of its "attention and protection," William Harper urged the South Carolina legislature to sponsor annual or semiannual fairs and offer small premiums for successful agricultural practices. Thomas Spalding recommended that state governments should dispense prizes for agricultural experimentation and support the judicious importation of "rare, and useful, and valuable animals from distant countries."[22] Many reformers argued that the scientific study of agriculture should be established in the colleges of the various states. "Why should the scholar, who has accompanied the Mantuan bard through smoking Troy and hard fought fields, not follow when he teaches to till the earth, points to waving harvests, or would recline in pastoral scenes," asked Robert Roper, not unreasonably. Reformers like Roper believed that its establishment as a serious subject of academic study would raise agriculture to the level of public esteem enjoyed by other professions.[23]

This blending of the classical ideal with the modern means for its realization proved to be a staple of articles and orations promoting agricultural reform. General agreement on the need for experimentation and innovation in no way precluded earnest, sometimes heated, debate as to what kinds of experimentation and innovation would work in practice. Suggested reforms ranged across a broad spectrum. Some believed that careful attention to architecture and horticulture would make plantations more efficient, attractive, and homelike (and so less likely to be deserted). Many called for new methods of plowing, manuring, and crop rotation; others for greater crop diversification and reduced reliance on cotton. Favored alternatives to cotton included fruit orchards, silk farming, and vine growing. One article in the *Southern Agriculturist* began with the bold declaration that "the Sugar Cane is henceforward to be a staple crop of South Carolina." Others explored the outer limits of optimistic inventiveness by lobbying for opium production in Georgia and the transformation of the barren regions of the Southeast into the world's next great tea-growing country. Despite their utopian moments, most reformers recognized the need to take account of the strength of cotton's grip on the planter, even as they sought to loosen that grip.[24]

Yet in their own way the most outlandish of the reformers' visions of the possible told most eloquently of their unbounded faith in the power of land. If only its cultivators would treat it with due care and reverence, anything could be built upon its sustaining soils. The reformers believed, with Nicholas Herbemont, that soil exhaustion was "not an unavoidable evil," and that "even the exhausted fields are susceptible of being restored to their primitive fertility." Praising "the capabilities of our three Southern Atlantic States," Thomas Spalding "wished to impress others with the belief, that in *soil* and *climate* and in *local situation,* no portion of the American continent, from Labrador to Cape Horn, could promise to man a better, and a happier home." If planters could be convinced of such claims, they would begin to see their land from a less detached perspective, Spalding believed, and would come to appreciate how people and place might blend in progressive rather than destructive ways.[25]

The reformers' vision of the good society was infused with the belief that at the heart of a healthy society existed an almost mystical connection between people and place. A correspondent from Orangeburg described the bond that emigrants were breaking. "We are the children of the soil," he wrote; "a relationship exists between us. It is the nurse which has supported us in our infancy, which has added bountifully to the means which fostered our manhood." Reformers argued further that good relations between people and place were the indispensable foundation for good relations between people.[26] Rather than a society characterized by anarchic relations between humans and human mistreatment of the environment, reformers posited a society in which humans and nature would be partners in the production of a progressive, civilized order. It would be a society in which crops and trees—the olive tree and the grapevine were favorite symbols—would be chosen for their ability to maintain or restore soil and soul alike. The case for such products was certainly made on economic grounds (particularly self-sufficiency). But their greatest worth would lie in their capacity to reconcile the needs of the Good Society with those of Mother Nature. Such an environment, according to Thomas Spalding, "gives to man perhaps the sweetest hour he knows, when retiring from the oppressions he has met with abroad, he seats himself down under his own vine and his own Fig Tree, and then, and only then, feels that there is none to make him afraid."[27] Often expressed in intensely anthropomorphic language, the ideal envisioned a society in which firmly rooted humans would become more like nature and a cherished nature would become more like humanity. Together, nature and humanity could build a beautiful society where, in the evocative lyricism of the Book of Isaiah, "the mountains and hills shall break forth before you into singing, and all the trees of the field shall clap their hands."[28]

From the reformers' perspective nature stood ready to meet its responsibilities to humanity. It remained an open question whether the southern agriculturist was either ready or prepared to meet his obligations. Reformers had a clear idea of the kind of man required for the job, an idea that found its embodiment in "The Good Farmer" "depicted" in the "mind's eye" of William Gilmore Simms and presented to the readers of the *Ladies' Companion* in the summer of 1841. But his broad character appeared countless times in the agricultural advice literature of the time.

The good farmer, as portrayed by Simms, stood "in the sight of God, in threefold aspect. As a subject of his power and his bounty . . . as the citizen of a community . . . and as an individual man." Unlike the roving archetype of the "Pine Land Planter," Simms's good farmer was trained by "early habit and education to subdue his duties to the narrow limits in which his lot has been cast." Subduing "the appetite which craves for change and various excitement," the good farmer understands that "no foreign attractions can beguile him" from "the few paternal acres" that, "through long cultivation," he "learns to regard with something of the same affection which he feels for the children of his loins." Resorting to the anthropomorphic imagery so common to the genre, Simms described a figure who finds all around him "the children of his thoughts, and hopes, and labors," in a place where "the old walks grow natural to his footsteps—the old trees wear the faces of familiar friends." As Simms's blend of the anthropomorphic and the paternal, the rooted and the generational, suggests, the agricultural life, properly lived, would bring the good farmer into an intense mutual intimacy, even communion (for "he must, indeed, be something of a religious man"), with nature.[29]

If such a paragon existed anywhere in the southern summer of 1841, then it was probably only in the mind's eye of William Gilmore Simms. No one knew that better than Simms himself. "The Good Farmer, in our country," as he admitted, "is not often to be found."[30] Agriculturists who refused to behave like agriculturists puzzled, frustrated, and ultimately angered reformers whose prescriptions for agricultural health went largely unfilled by people who gave every indication of being unaware that they were actually sick. So it was that their recommended regimens for agricultural health and social order were often laced with lamentations for the planters' failure to adopt them. Their scientific plans for agricultural and social health mixed with diagnoses of the individual and collective mental health of the planter class.

No figure proved more incomprehensible to the reformers than the planter emigrant: a man who not only abused his land but then deserted it. Whether viewed as source or symbol of deeper social disarray, the planters' unflagging westward mobility occupied a central place in a developing portrait of the antiagriculturist: a planter unable or unwilling to submit to the dictates of his true nature or to the greater good of social order and community stability. The critics' analyses of the departing planters proved as varied as the advice the emigrants seemed determined to ignore. Generally, however, the debate revolved around the planters' apparent failure to nurture the right kind of relations between people and place. The Bad Planter combined, just as his critics did, the traditional and the modern. In his case, however, the blend was all wrong. Far from a nurturing blend of the reverential and reformist, he produced a toxic cocktail of reaction and irresponsibility.

Almost all its critics agreed that a crucial cause of emigration, and of the poor agricultural practices believed to encourage it, was the planter's attachment to what Whitemarsh Seabrook called his "strong, and oft-times unconquerable prejudices." Seabrook did not know whether this condition should "be ascribed to his isolated situation, and its attendant peculiarities, or to the influence of education." But he did understand its consequences. He considered it beyond question that the slaveholder's "limited intercourse with society . . . betrays the ascendancy of a deceptive self-love" and "a settled conviction of mind, that his pursuit is independent of the aid of his fellow-man."[31]

A misplaced sense of independence that privileged personal experience over general principle and collective inquiry bred a stubborn and short-sighted aversion to the advances in science and agriculture that so impressed the reformers. "Practically denying the existence of elementary principles in agriculture, and rarely guided by any other monitor than the biddings of experience," complained Seabrook, the average planter apparently believed "that scientific inquiries are uncalled for by the legitimate wants of his profession." As the reformers saw it, the planters' reactionary disdain for anything that smacked of "book-farming" was among the most destructive consequences of their unhealthy blending of individualism, ignorance, and isolation.[32]

Too detached from his immediate world, the bad planter was too attached to past worlds. His sense of personal autonomy in the present was, in the reformers' view, reinforced by an equally misleading attachment to past ways of doing things. Addressing the Agricultural Society of Charleston, Francis D. Quash drew on what he considered a suitably reactionary analogy. He recalled Peter the Great's observation "that our ancestors were the worst enemies we have, for they transmit customs, which, however, inapplicable to the present times, can only be broken down by force."[33] Planters who thought they already knew it all were not best placed to profit from the knowledge of their neighbors or the scientific breakthroughs of their time. Knowledge is power, insisted the reformers. Power is knowledge, replied the planters with the eloquent silence of their indifference.

The planters' indifference to agricultural advance was symptomatic, some argued, of a deeper apathy toward cultural improvement generally. William Gilmore Simms, who managed to combine a life of letters with a life of planting, believed the South lacked the dense settlements and "commercial and populous marts" that in most countries provided the intellectual marketplaces where minds could go to be honed and expanded. Isolated as it was from "these fields of attrition and collision," Simms worried that "the mind of the Southern gentleman . . . is apt to sink into languor or indifference."[34] Furthermore, the problem lay not only in the insufficiency of mind-expanding marts of intellectual exchange. It was also rooted in the planters' unwillingness or inability to take advantage of the opportunities for intellectual and cultural improvement that did exist. "Absorbed by the cares and pursuits of a country life," one observer protested, planters "seldom allow their minds to reach farther than its drudgery, and become bound by the webs of prejudice and timidity, always attendant on contracted habits." Where "the cultivation of a few paternal acres" was the limit of the planter's "ambition," one could not expect "improvement," only continued toil "in the weary path of sameness and antiquity."[35]

Living in an isolation they mistook for independence, it was no surprise that the planters did not make of their "paternal acres" the place of agricultural abundance and spiritual sustenance evoked by Simms's use of that phrase. Rather they oversaw only a starved and shrunken retreat. These "paternal acres" offered no settled limits within which the planter could and should be content, only a barrier to his ability either to preserve or to progress. From this perspective the problem lay not in the planter's lack of attachment to the place where he lived. It was to be found in the nature of that attachment: reactionary, unproductive, and careless of the social consequences of prideful isolation. Life on a plantation more keep than castle reinforced the negative power of both past and personality, leading the planter into dead ends of habit and thought no longer appropriate to the modern world in which he should be making his way.

Reformers were convinced that the virus of emigration thrived in this reactionary atmosphere. Having lost "millions" as a consequence of their "ignorance of true principles of husbandry," the planters then, according to Robert W. Roper of South Carolina, "deserted their abodes, friends and comforts of civilized life, to seek in distant wilds those means of subsistence which art and education may have supplied at home."[36] Reformers disagreed, however, about the relation between bad agricultural habits and planter emigration.

For some, emigration was the unforeseen and unwanted consequence of the planters' poor husbandry. The planters left, in Roper's view, "with heavy hearts." Eldred Simkins, an advocate of horizontal plowing as the cure for emigration, agreed. Simkins acknowledged that there were "some wanderers, some restless people, who, with a roaming disposition and a fondness for frontier settlement," would always be in "pursuit of the Elysian fields, cheap lands, and golden prospects." But Simkins denied that this was true of "the great bulk of settlers who occupy any country." Only as bad habits, growing families, and declining land finally presented "the unpleasant alternative of living in poverty or seeking fresh lands in a newer country" did most planters decide to leave. For this great majority, Simkins believed, "it causes a painful struggle in families to be compelled to abandon their old homes, fire-sides, friends, and connexions, which from habit and many endeared associations had become identified with their happiness, to seek homes in a wilderness." Only as "field after field" deteriorated and the plantation finally "becomes useless and almost unsalable," agreed James Gregorie, did the "broken-hearted" planter forsake his home, "to seek relief in the western wilds."[37] From this perspective most planters saw emigration as a last response to the depressed circumstances their hidebound habits and beliefs had inadvertently helped to create. Hatred of change, it seemed, fueled the most disruptive change of all.

All this talk of the emigrants' "heavy," even "broken," hearts suggests many reformers' reluctance to accept the notion that agriculturists could take such an "unnatural" step willingly. Such a possibility was simply too much at odds with their assumptions about what constituted an agriculturist's "natural" behavior. Eldred Simkins spoke for many when he insisted that "the nature of most men as they settle down, make improvements, clear land, form acquaintances, make friends, and become identified with a country, its laws, manners, customs, and a thousand associations, is to wish to accumulate property and become permanent."[38] These assumptions, in turn, fueled the faith of Simkins and others that planters would respond warmly to the reformers' arguments that improvement at home would render removal unnecessary.

Other reformers found it more difficult to believe that emigration was quite such a reluctant last resort. Surely, some asked, if planters loved home and land, they would show greater enthusiasm for the agricultural improvements that offered the opportunity to remain in place. Furthermore, the ubiquitous usage of terms like *Alabama Fever* hardly spoke of regretful departure. Why did planters, supposedly too apathetic to ride out over their own fields, grow so giddy at the prospect of riding west to take up residence in the backwaters of Alabama and beyond? Disinclined to portray the emigrant agriculturist as the unwitting victim of his own bad habits, some reformers focused instead on a countercurrent they found coursing through the character of the planter. "A love," rather than a hatred, "of change," Thomas Spalding observed, "is stamped upon the heart of man." A universal trait, this restless desire seemed especially strong in the male planter, whose "roving disposition" led Spalding to liken him to "the Tartar of the Steppes" forever driving his flocks in search of greener pastures.[39]

Emphasis on the planters' restless receptivity to change also cast their relation to the lands of the Southwest in a very different light. No "wilds" or "wilderness" these, in the mind of the emigrant, but rather a "region of boundless extent and great fertility." For Spalding it was "not to be wondered at" that in the face of such temptation, the planter "yielded to this first impulse of his nature."[40] C. C. Pinckney of South Carolina believed that the planters' obsession with what they grew—cotton—had rendered them indifferent to where they grew it. Dreams of wealth through cotton made planters "content to abandon all the comforts of home and friends and civilization, in order to double our income." The "certainty of obtaining cheap and productive lands in the West" rendered them "careless concerning any benefit beyond the growing crop; satisfied, that when their present fields are exhausted, they can be sold for what will purchase fresh Western lands." Pinckney's damning verdict found an appropriate metaphor, as he concluded that the planters "pursue a system of husbandry, so reckless, that were the destruction of land and life equally felonious the Courts of Sessions would never adjourn." [41]

Others agreed that critics like Simkins had it the wrong way round when it came to the true nature of the connection between the planters' mobility and their attitude toward place. William Ellison insisted that the planters' "destructive system of culture" was an effect of their "disposition to emigrate." The cause was "the abundance and fancied cheapness of Western lands," in Ellison's view. The prospective emigrant "cares but little for the future condition of the country, where he considers himself but temporarily located." Far from bad habits forcing regretful recourse to the West, it was the emigrant's "dreams of the orange groves of Florida, his twelve hundred pounds of sugar to the acre in Louisiana, or two thousand pounds of cotton to the acre in Alabama, Mississippi, and Arkansas" that bred those very habits. For such a planter "the governing object is to 'skim the cream (as he expresses it,) of his lands . . . with a determination to abandon it when it is ruined or exhausted.'" [42] From this point of view, the planters' restless nature combined with their infatuation with western lands to fuel movement to the West and mistreatment of their land in the East. To pursue Pinckney's courtroom metaphor, departure took on a more malignant cast: closer to premeditated murder than to involuntary manslaughter.

To hold the planters responsible for agricultural decline was also to find them culpable for the social decay that, from the agrarian republican viewpoint, was its inevitable corollary. Many reformers linked disloyalty to place as land with treason toward place understood as community or state. Some critics saw departure as a dereliction of Christian duty, a failure of stewardship entwining with a failure of fellowship. One correspondent of the *Watchman of the South* chided emigrants who put their own worldly gain ahead of the welfare of the neighborhoods they left behind. "Those who forsake pastor and church and brethren and sermons and prayer meetings and Sabbath schools, and go into the woods for the sake of a fat piece of land, may get rich in money," the writer conceded, "but they will not increase in piety, nor exert a more holy influence upon their fellow men." [43]

The editor of the *Southern Religious Telegraph* was more understanding in his acceptance that there were reasons for and against emigration, but he warned people to remember that should they emigrate "for the purpose of acquiring wealth—let them not be surprised if they meet a frowning Providence." One contributor to the *Southern Cultivator* went so far as to conflate greed and mobility entirely. "It is this migratory spirit," he wrote, "this sordid love of money . . . that is tempting the people of this country to pass beyond its bounds." These correspondents joined Pinckney and many others in claiming that greed had replaced higher attachments in the hearts of the emigrants.[44]

Values, it seemed, had been turned upside down. Means had become ends. In an ideal world "every true Carolinian" would, in the interest of the state's welfare, "scorn the idea of abandoning her to the ravages of cupidity, and fleeing to the West because he can get richer lands," insisted William J. Alston of South Carolina. Drawing on ancient precedent, Alston insisted that just "as the title and privileges of a Roman citizen were his highest boast," so every South Carolinian should "ever feel that it is an honour to be a Carolinian."[45] But Alston and his home-loving peers did not live in an ideal world. Worse still, as the names of new towns like Marion, Alabama, named for the Revolutionary War hero Francis Marion, made clear, emigrants saw no discrepancy between leaving Carolina and retaining their honor as Carolinians.

That they were happy to leave the state and keep the name only fueled their critics' rage. A "Rustic" from Columbia, South Carolina, questioned the loyalty "of those who say, 'it cannot be helped,' when the smallest exertion to prevent it has never been made." "Where is their *amor patrie*," he demanded, "the love of the very soil that witnessed their birth, and the sports of their infancy; their love of their children and their posterity, when they suffer things to go on . . . to certain destruction, without taking one step to avert the impending calamity?" The editor of the *Southern Agriculturist* spoke for those who drew little distinction between environmental abuse and social irresponsibility. He described "this movement Westward" as both "unpatriotic" and "un-natural," a movement in which "we cast off our own mother; she who nursed our infancy, and bestow strength and energies upon another, an adopted one, who knows us not, and cares not for us, farther than we make her richer, or stronger." Numerous writers, by their choices of image and allusion, joined him in identifying love of mother earth with devotion to the land of one's fathers and in construing ingratitude to one as indistinguishable from disloyalty to the other.[46]

For some critics the unconscionable greed and inexplicable disloyalty that fueled this dynamic indifference to place could only have their roots in the irrational, darker places of the human heart. Critics like Spalding and Ellison acknowledged as much when they suggested the rage to roam lay beyond the reach of even the most rational and reasonable of reformers. William Gilmore Simms addressed the entwining of greed and mobility in verse. In "The Western Emigrants" he portrayed an "old patriarch" whose "discontent" and "vague yearning for a better clime, And richer fields than thine, old Carolina, Led him to roam." As Simms continued:

> Self-exiled, in his age he hath gone forth
> To the abodes of strangers,—seeking wealth—
> Not wealth, but money! Heavens! What wealth we
> give, Daily, for money! What affections sweet—
> What dear abodes—what blessings, happy joys—
> What hopes, what hearts, what affluence, what ties,
> In a mad barter where we lose our all,
> For that which an old trunk, a few feet square,
> May compass like our coffin!

Simms employed the language of lunacy that had been common currency almost from the beginning of the phenomenon colloquially known as Alabama Fever. Simms's telling choice of an "old patriarch" reinforces the sense of a fever that did not necessarily recede with age. That many never developed an immunity to this fever encouraged the growing despair of reformers reduced, at least in their darker moments, to locating the ultimate source of emigration in an incurable "madness" or a "mysterious love of change" capable of overpowering all love of land and homeland.[47]

Whether drawn in rage or regret, the sketch of the emigrant planter that emerged from his critics' articles and addresses was not pretty to contemplate. His fever, like its proposed cure, resulted from a coming together of traditional and modern strains. Tragically, however, the emigrant combined the worst of modern ends with the worst of traditional means. He was too content with his lot, or then again not content enough. Hopelessly resistant to modern trends in science and education, the emigrant planter, in his individual self-absorption and social irresponsibility, was devoted to the worst of modern-day excess. Wedded to the worst habits of his forebears, he yet lacked attachment to the hard-won land of his fathers. Unwilling to leave his plantation for purposes of culture and education, he somehow thought nothing of deserting it for money and forever. Whether portrayed as ambitious or apathetic, restless or reactionary, the emigrant planter combined the worst of modern times with the worst of days gone by. Together, his critics drew a composite mug shot of a most unsavory public enemy.

The critics who drew this portrait did so in what they sincerely considered the best interests of their society and those of the individual planters they addressed. They spoke to people who, when emigrants and prospective emigrants were added together, made up a significant portion of the class to which they themselves belonged. Although they divided the good and the bad, the stable and the mobile, for rhetorical purposes, emigration's critics knew it was not so clear-cut in practice. They knew that the public enemies who appeared in journal pages and society speeches were also the friends and neighbors with whom they shared so much of their daily lives.

Yet not the least of the critics' complaints was that so few people paid attention to what they had to say about proper planter conduct and the appropriate ordering of the good society. What explains this lack of resonance among members of the reformers' own class? Aside from the natural human reluctance to see one's own image in an unflattering portrait, there are several possible reasons. For one thing, agricultural reform could be expensive and time-consuming. Reformers often acknowledged this even as they insisted that it eventually would repay its practitioners in greater material and psychological security. In the short term or in hard times, however, reform could seem impractical given the pressing financial imperatives felt by most cotton planters. Furthermore, even the reformers recognized the potent lure of fertile western lands recently made safe for slaveholding civilization.[48]

Nevertheless, rejection of the proposed cures on practical or financial grounds need not have precluded an acceptance of the diagnosis or of the ideals and assumptions behind it. Yet it was not just emigrants who rejected the charge that they were soil-killing deserters. Such harsh judgments were largely absent from private discussions of emigration. Heartfelt regret for the loss of family and friends or the decline of communities seldom turned to accusations of treason or ignorance. William Gilmore Simms had called for the transformation of private concern into public debate. As that debate developed, something was clearly being lost in the translation.

Perhaps the source of this dissonance lay in a failure of communication rather than of content. Perhaps it was because, as Nicholas Herbemont lamented of himself, emigration's opponents lacked "the elegant pen of Virgil, Delisle, or of Florian, to portray . . . the simplicity of innocence, that rural felicity, which can only be obtained by cultivating, with the soil, all the mild, gentle, and peaceful virtues" of a "rural life." It was those virtues which, in turn, provided the groundwork for "cultivat[ing] in peace and plenty those relations which bind man to his fellow man."[49] Herbemont was wrong. The problem did not lie in a failure of presentation but in the inaptness to plantation society of the ideas that infused Herbemont's agrarian organicism. The problem lay not in the reformers' failure to match the literary skills of "the Mantuan bard" but in their attachment to the pastoral ideal of the good farmer and the good society. In actuality, there was too much Virgil.

All social commentators must, of course, operate within particular frameworks of belief and sentiment. These frameworks shape not only which subjects are discussed but how they are discussed. A language so powerfully anthropomorphic in its exaltation of the agriculturist's organic (even mystical) connection to mother earth ensured that rootedness in place was seen as the key to healthy social progress in time. It all but guaranteed that for those who spoke it, extensive geographic mobility could only spell trouble for an agricultural society. It made axiomatic the proposition that a class lacking in a sense of attachment to particular places must also be failing in its obligation to treasure and sustain essential ties (of citizenship and community) between people. For those who criticized emigration in the language of agrarian republicanism, neglect of one's land was part and parcel of a deeper alienation from all the important relations of life. These arguments were made time and again in speech and essay.

Yet just as striking a feature of the agrarian republican critique of emigration is its almost total neglect of the human relations that shaped the lives of planter men as slaveholders as well as "agriculturists." Slaves—the "real" agriculturists in many ways—rarely came between the agrarian and his ideal the way they habitually did between the slaveholder and his soil. Planter women, although at least implicit in many idyllic images of public peace and progress, rarely achieved on the reformers' page the central and complex roles they played within the plantation household. Planter men's relations with their own families and their own slaves were seldom discussed as either cause or casualty of emigration.

The silence was not total. The security of slavery as a system often formed the implicit standard by which emigration's impact was measured. When writers and orators like Joseph Jenkins spoke of defending their state's "domestic institutions," they were, of course, talking about slavery and expressing the fear that planter emigration eroded slavery's defenses. Yet even those who did raise the issue of slavery in relation to emigration did so to discuss movement's consequences for slavery. That slavery itself might be a cause of this socially destructive behavior was not considered.[50]

Unwillingness to indict slavery emerged in part from slaveholders' growing reluctance to make or accept criticisms of their society's most important institution. But it also resulted from the very nature of the language of agrarian republicanism employed by so many of emigration's critics. Agrarian republicanism's emphasis on attachments between people and place (between the agriculturist and his land) rendered invisible the connections between people (slaves and slaveholders, women and men) that were more important than ties to land and community in shaping male planters' behavior, including their ceaseless voyaging toward "the stabling place of the sun." That women were active participants in the affairs and, to some extent, the decisions of the household was seldom considered. That slaves were usually the ones doing the agricultural work (and not infrequently the plantation residents with the most knowledge of how to do it) could not be recognized. The agrarian ideal, so humane in its reverence for Mother Nature, could only retain its charm and simplicity through the inhumane reduction of women and slaves to invisibility or instrumentality.[51]

Perhaps, then, it is here, in the definitions of people and place that shaped the critique of planter emigration, that the reason for its lack of intellectual or spiritual resonance is to be found. The milder, gentler Mantuan model might have seemed like a good idea to those, like Herbemont, fixated on the citizen agriculturist's relation to nature and society. But it necessarily obscured the other relations that shaped the ordinary planter's understanding of life, work, and society. That is why, as we turn to questions of why so many emigrants would be so indifferent or antagonistic toward their own society, we should not be surprised if young men like James Asbury Tait (never mind older men like Charles Tait and women like Caroline Tait) failed to recognize themselves in the most-wanted flyers being circulated by those concerned citizens back home. Instead these inhabitants of elite emigrant households had a different view of themselves and their world.

Before we turn to the emigrants and the view from within the plantation household, a final word (for now) about their critics. In its pessimistic moments the critique of emigration told a tale of decline. It charted the demise of the ideal society at the hands of planter disdain and indifference.

The critics were never more pessimistic than when bemoaning their inability to convert the planters to their vision of the good life. Yet the planters' rejection of their critics' ancient ideal, and of the modern means to its realization, can itself be read as an unintended epitaph for the ideals and assumptions regarding human life and society that infused the reformers' vision. For most planters, emigrant or otherwise, their society was not dying; it was in the process of changing into something else. Whether they liked this change or not, whether they saw it as regressive or progressive, or even if they did not quite know what to make of it, most members of the southern elite were aware that they lived in a world moving at "railroad speed." What they needed was a new language and new assumptions better suited to understanding their place in that world.

The critics tried, but their blend of idyllic ideals and modern means left most slaveholders cold. As emigration itself increased in mocking step with their campaign to curtail it, the growing volume of its opponents' complaints proved less a barrier to movement and more a barometer of emigration's rising influence in slaveholding society. This is not to say that they had no impact on slaveholding society and culture at the time. Even if barometers record phenomena that cannot be stopped and so must just be accepted as natural, talking about the weather still seems to serve soothing social purposes. Similarly, the critics' impassioned ranting and reasoning may actually have served, albeit inadvertently, to reduce the public anxieties inevitably to be found in any place or time filled with minds racing in the midst of change. In important ways the critics conformed to a pattern of response quite common in the elite sections of societies undergoing rapid change. Such responses can welcome change even as they reflect a certain ambivalence and anxiety about some of its actual or predicted consequences. From Puritan divines lamenting the decline of order to late nineteenth-century conservatives deploring the dwindling of their own importance, from Scottish lawyer-novelists mourning the destruction of clan society to Wal-Mart shoppers bemoaning the demise of the corner store, people have found a certain relief in seasoning with a little sadness their pursuit of convenience, power, and progress. Thus the lamentations of reformers may have helped to ease, rather than prevent, the flow of a progress that in many respects most of their peers saw as not only inevitable but desirable. Their failed efforts to curtail emigration may have helped to increase public acceptance of it.

Yet that failure cannot be ascribed to the incompatibility between a yearning for the way it never was and a love of the new science that made all things possible. The reformers' forward-looking optimism and their backward-glancing nostalgia, far from contradicting one another, can be seen as two sides of the same modern coin.[52] The reformers' genuine sense of regret for the world they thought they were losing is itself evidence of their class's extensive participation in the creation of a new kind of world. Not the sour grapes of a reactionary fraction, the critics' nostalgia for the golden age of agriculture was the quintessential product of the modern, materialist mind seeking to reconcile a sense of the past with a yearning for progress.[53]

From this perspective the critics had more in common with the emigrants than they might have liked to admit. Like those they criticized, the reformers also offered a group portrait of people sliding back and forth between the modern and the familiar, in their case between the galvanizing advances of the century of science and the paradoxical dream that even in the slave society that mobility built, those advances could be harnessed to the task of holding people in place.

4 Moving Home

Glorious Young America with whom independence is
all and all, if it is also starvation: or rather if it is the most
ridiculous fallacy that ever entered the human brain. Who
ever was, who ever can be independent? Of all the bubbles
name another to compare with this.
—James Henry Hammond

SHE WORRIED ABOUT HER HUSBAND. HE HAD LEFT
Retreat for the Alabama Territory a few days before Christmas 1817. Now,
the January weather was bad, she had not heard from him in several weeks,
and she worried too "concerning the safety in traveling the road to the
Alabama." He had gone "entirely unarmed" from the family plantation in
Elbert County, Georgia, but she hoped, as she told her father-in-law, that
"the all protecting hand of God" would be with him, to "guard him from
every danger and return him in safety to his family." Nevertheless, she would
feel uneasy until she heard he had "arriv'd safely at his journeys end." James
Tait shared his wife Caroline's desire that he travel safely, by which they
both meant avoiding encounters with the Creek Indians. Given the continuing conflict between the United States and the Creek Nation in the wake
of the War of 1812, Tait intended to "shape my course on the upper roads.
I do not wish, at this time, to run any risk of losing my scalp." [1]

James Tait's present journey would not be the first time he had risked
violent encounter with the first nations of the South. He had volunteered
for service in the Georgia militia during the War of 1812, eventually becoming a captain in the 192d District Company. He had fought under
General John Floyd against the Creeks at Calabee Creek in January 1814. [2]
The Creek War ended with a treaty signed in August 1814 at Fort Jackson
on the banks of the Alabama River. The Creeks gave up more than half of
their lands, about twenty-three million acres, including almost all of their
land in what Americans called the Alabama Territory as well as in the south-

ern portion of Georgia. Many white Georgians were nevertheless disappointed by an agreement that left much of the land between the Ocmulgee and the Chattahoochee Rivers in Creek hands. To these Georgians the federal government had broken its 1802 promise to secure all Indian lands for the state of Georgia as soon as was peaceably possible.[3]

Georgians' annoyance was intensified by the increasingly frequent sight of their compatriots leaving the state for lands to the west now under American control. Far from bringing the expulsion of all the Creeks from their state, the war's end precipitated the removal of numerous white and black Georgians to the fertile and newly accessible lands of the Alabama Territory. James Tait, along with many other Georgians and veterans of the war, joined the frantic rush toward a new future in the country he had helped to win for the United States.[4]

Squatting on public domain along the Alabama River thirty miles or so north of Fort Claiborne, the twenty-year-old James Tait seemed more impressed by the isolation of his new situation. Tait was feeling lonely. "Oh! if you and my sons were here with me," he told Caroline Tait, "how agreeably I could spend my time, how happy indeed, I may say with truth, I should be." Yet Tait accepted the need to make "present and temporary sacrifices for an ultimate good." He encouraged Caroline to "bear cheerfully the inconveniences" brought on by their "necessary absence" from one another and reminded her that "absence heightens love."[5] His own "chief pleasure" lay in anticipating the arrival of his wife and children.

Tait may have felt the absence of his family, but he was hardly alone. If no other members of his family had made the journey with him, members of his household had. He had taken three slaves—Brunswick, Wily, and Gloster—with him and intended to buy more slaves in the West. Eventually the remaining enslaved members of his household would also journey west. Among them would be the slave families given to James and Caroline on their wedding day by their parents.[6] Tait's relative isolation was merely a preliminary step toward the permanent transplanting of his entire household to the banks of the Alabama.

James Tait's household was in many ways typical of the plantation household of the time, whether in the East or the West or both. The plantation houses of the South took a multitude of physical forms and settings, from mansions by the sea to cabins in the canebrake, from landscaped gardens to stump-strewn forest clearings. Yet the plantation household's principal defining features were not to be found in its appearance or location but in the human relations of kinship and ownership from which its true nature was constructed.

The nature of the plantation household's relations made it unique among the various kinds of elite household organization in the nineteenth-century United States. Unlike elite households in the North, from which market-related production was increasingly expelled as the century progressed, the southern plantation household continued to encompass the principal productive activities of the region's economic life. In the North the household became the "private" home, and work and business became activities conducted in other, "public," places.[7]

The plantation household encompassed bosses and workers, owners and owned, white and black. Although the household's enslaved inhabitants usually lived in families, ultimate decisions regarding food, shelter, and even marital and family relations remained the preserve of the master. Thus, the degree of family privacy and coherence afforded the slaves by the plantation household's organization did not diminish their ultimate dependence on the white master who stood at the apex of the household's structure.[8]

The master of the plantation was also head of his own family. Here again, the developing northern tendency to identify the private sphere with women and the public sphere with men proved of limited applicability to the plantation household. A great deal of the economic activity supervised by planter men remained within the household. Many planter women took an active role in plantation production for the market, through the supervision of domestic labor such as the making of slave clothes and, in some circumstances, the management of field labor. Thus planter women's lives were directly linked to the economic activities from which other elite women in America were increasingly divorced. Rather than viewing planter women and men as occupying separate spheres of public and private activity, it is more helpful to see them as filling distinct roles within a plantation household that encompassed the domestic and economic activity of men and women, free and slave.[9]

The center of productivity and domesticity, the household and its relations did much to shape its members' sense of themselves and of their place in society. This is not to say that they did not also see themselves as individuals or as members of their society. It is to say, however, that they understood self, society, and the relations between the two through the mediating prisms of elite family values and planter household necessity. The household came between the individual and the broader society, crucially shaping the slaveholders' understanding of the relation between them. That the public analysts of planter emigration largely ignored this crucible of planter character explains in part why their criticisms remained peripheral to the vision of men and women like James and Caroline Tait. By going inside those emigrating households, we can see something of what was central to the lives of the many planter men and women who took to the emigrant trail.

The critics of emigration were quick to argue that the lust for profit had overwhelmed all other attachments, especially those to the people and the places of the southeastern states. James Tait would not have denied the drive to make money. Like other emigrants he saw the abundant land to the west, and he heard the clamor for cotton from the east. But he also heard the call of powerful expectations generated by that same society, which, for Tait and many other young men, could best be met (perhaps only be met) by moving to the West.[10]

Chief among these expectations was that men like James Tait, when the right time came, would establish their own households. When James Tait wrote to his wife, he acknowledged that they would "live in a cabbin." But he also predicted that they "would feel ourselves more independent and more at home, than we have ever done yet." For James Tait independence in his "little cabbin" in the canebrake was preferable to dependence on his father back in Elbert County. Similarly, John Horry Dent left coastal South Carolina for Alabama with his wife and slaves in 1837. Born into a planter family of good name but moderate wealth in Colleton District, Dent successfully ran the family plantation "as a kind of Superintendent." Dent would remember how, despite the promising start he had made on his mother's plantation, he soon "tired of the dependent life I was living" and decided to strike out for the West when he was still in his early twenties. Many other young male emigrants shared Tait's and Dent's sense of purpose.[11]

Yet young men's desire for independence from existing households did not mean their rejection of the aims and values of those households. Young men like Tait and Dent understood departure as the pursuit rather than the rejection of what it meant to be a slaveholding planter. Both, for example, revealed attitudes toward agriculture that might have surprised those who saw emigration as the last resort of the "bad farmer." Tait, in part driven by the knowledge that his lack of political ambition was a disappointment to his father, was determined to prove himself a success in his "own sphere" of planting. Dent had learned the intricate and demanding craft of rice planting under the watchful eye of an experienced overseer. Indeed, he even believed that all planters should subscribe, as he did, to an agricultural journal. James Tait and John Horry Dent were far from exceptional among movers who viewed their chosen course as following, rather than fleeing, the priorities of their class and society. Emigration could be undertaken by men who had been notable for their successful attention to the welfare of the "paternal acres" of Georgia and South Carolina.[12]

Many members of the planter class agreed that emigration was not necessarily evidence of private or public irresponsibility but rather the means to meet the responsibilities of planting life. Independence did not mean the desire to establish the relations of life on a different basis from that of eastern households. This was nowhere clearer than in discussions of emigration that also dealt with the question of marriage. For many young men personal independence was linked to marriage and the establishment of one's own household. John Horry Dent remembered how, his decision for independence made, he "set to work in dead earnest to get a wife."[13] For Dent, as for others, independence and matrimony were related pursuits.

In a society in which the creation of a new household was viewed as the best time to get married, and in which the West often was seen as the best place to establish that household, questions of matrimony and movement frequently intertwined. Marriage, considered beneficial for young men generally, was considered by many to be essential for those who aspired to western success. And, as with any elite, much urgent advice was offered to young men on this most important of decisions. Reluctant to see his son leave his own plantation in Union District, South Carolina, David Johnson Sr. hoped at least "that you take unto yourself a helpmate as soon as you can."[14] Thomas Harrison of Columbia counseled his emigrant son James, who had evidently written about "an heiress" in an earlier letter. "It would be wrong to marry *for* money," wrote the father, "but it would be wrong to marry now *without* money." "Besides," as he further explained, "the best raised and most intelligent women" were generally to be found among the wealthy. Thus "a man should marry into a respectable family" and "by all means a woman of understanding," Harrison concluded in magnanimous vein. "Rise to eminence & you may marry whomsoever you please," he told his son.[15]

Some relatives worried that the dictates of Venus and venality might not blend as smoothly in practice as in theory. Distance often increased anxieties as to young men's matrimonial prospects. Abner Benson of South Carolina relayed the grim news to his brother Elias, in Alabama, that it had been "reported and believed" back in Spartanburg that their brother Nimrod, also in Alabama, was "married to a woman without beauty, respectable connections, fortune or even charactor." "I fear the report is too true," confessed the dismayed brother.[16] In their own ways Abner Benson and Thomas Harrison reflected the widespread belief that no responsible suitor should ignore matters of property and status.

No bride could bring more valued property to a match than property of the human kind. As Rebecca Latimer Felton remembered of life in Georgia, "If there was a prospect of plantation or slaves as a dowry there was a rush into matrimony." Slaves had been among James Tait's wedding gifts from both his own and his new bride's family. Mary Elizabeth Morrison brought hundreds of acres and forty-five slaves to her match with John Horry Dent, allurements that helped to make up for her less prestigious family name.[17] More slaves. What could be finer, in Mississippi or Alabama just as in Georgia or Carolina? Perhaps even finer in the states of the West, where, if there were fewer people around to admire one's "likely negroes," there were a great many trees to be felled, swamps to be drained, and prairie acres to be prepared for planting. Plantations had to be carved from the landscape before they could dominate and give new meaning to that landscape. With such tasks ahead, the more slaves at a household's disposal, the better.

The material mattered, then. But much more than the material mattered. Not all male emigrants were married to, or would marry, young women of substantial property. Yet not all relatives were as dejected about it as Abner Benson. Others understood that wives contributed to the success of men and their households in other ways. Joanna Townes's lack of wealth had led Samuel Townes's family initially to oppose their marriage, but most reservations seem to have been quickly dispelled. Henry Townes, the eldest son and chief adviser to his widowed mother, insisted that the family should avoid all impressions of dissatisfaction with Joanna. Henry Townes believed that his brother's wife had "pride, ambition & *excellent* sense" and would "stimulate Sam to 'deeds of noble daring.'" Henry thought it important that Samuel would "be thrown entirely upon his own resources." "As soon as a young man marries," Townes believed, "he ought to be made to feel that his own and his wife's salvation in this world depends on his own exertions alone."[18] Thus the presence of a new wife would be a further spur to suitable ambition, even if she did not necessarily bring with her the material means to fulfilling that ambition.

In Caroline Tait's case it appeared she brought steel as well as slaves to her union with James Tait. That was certainly Charles Tait's opinion. He told his son that he was "fortunate in having a companion who cannot be too highly estimated by you. She is sensible, discreet and devoted to your person & interest. May heaven preserve her long as the . . . principal support of your family." To Caroline Tait herself he wrote of the great inconveniences involved in settling in a new country but also insisted that "if I am not mistaken you will bear them with resignation & firmness. This it is our duty to do in all circumstances thro life." In words that were part prediction, part injunction, Tait told his daughter-in-law that "you will cherish hope & look forward to your situation being better every year till you get a comfortable establishment, which I hope . . . will take place in a few years."[19] Like Henry Townes, David Johnson, and others, Charles Tait felt sure that the right kind of woman was essential to the success of emigrant households. It could also seem that they held to such a belief all the more tenaciously the more they harbored doubts about the maturity, perseverance, and will to succeed of their male relatives. Henry Townes believed that a young man should be made to feel that his family's salvation rested on his shoulders alone, but he also made it clear how much the success of such an illusion rested on the ability and character of the man's spouse. In the case of his brother, Henry Townes had little doubt that it was Joanna who would be Samuel's "worldly savior."[20]

Male emigrants like James Tait and Samuel Townes were clearly less than happy about the doubts they knew their kinfolk felt about their prospects. But generally they agreed about the psychological and practical benefits that the right "helpmate" brought to western endeavors. In this respect, as in others, younger male emigrants showed themselves as imitative of rather than alienated from the prevailing patterns of planter life. Younger men looked to emulate their fathers by themselves becoming planter-patriarchs. The drive for independence involved the creation of one's own family or, more accurately, a new branch of existing families. It required the taking on rather than the shrugging off of traditional responsibilities. Establishing new independence meant the creation of new dependencies—wives, children, and slaves—through marriage. If planting and professional patterns were to be duplicated in the West, most planter men agreed that a plantation mistress was crucial to the design.

Planter women's understanding of emigration also was shaped by personal desires as well as social expectations and constraints. If marriage was deemed essential for men moving west, then emigration was a distinct possibility for women looking to marry. And most plantation women did look to get married. Just as few men understood their own independence except as part of their own newly created family, few women wished to forgo the status that came with being mistress of one's own household. In a class inclined to view spinsterhood as a genteel form of social death, few women feared leaving the East more than they feared remaining unmarried.[21]

Marriage certainly brought new anxieties and limitations, and these could just as certainly be intensified by emigration. Women's concerns about being separated from existing family by departure for another home could be compounded by the accompanying prospect of departure for another state. "Oh my dear Jim," Nancy Gage wrote to her absent brother as her wedding approached, "it almost distracts me to think of marrying." She could not do so "without shedding tears." Gage was to move from Georgia to Alabama after the wedding, which also weighed heavily on her thoughts. She worried that "I love my family too well for my own good," and that it "will kill me to be separated from you all." Henry Lea, about to take his new bride away from her Georgia family, also feared that "the thought of leaving Athens and an extensive circle of well tried friends—of going, and going too with strangers in some respects, to a strange, a distant country" would be "a source of great regret to Serena." Lea hoped that the prospect of an early return visit might mean "she will perhaps go without reluctance."[22] As Lea suggested, part of the pressure for newly married women whose new relatives were already in the West came from trying to conform to their unfamiliar desires while far from the comfort and assistance of their own family. Yet some women saw the separation of emigration as a desirable accompaniment to the new responsibilities of marriage. Martha Jackson of Athens, Serena Lea's mother, believed that a new bride's geographical distance from her own family was conducive to her better according with the wishes of her new family, something Martha Jackson considered essential if the new mistress was to make her household a success.[23]

For single women the West itself could be the place to make a good match or, perhaps, have one made for them. John Moore, who had moved his family to near Claiborne, Alabama, reported the good news to Richard Singleton in Manchester, South Carolina, that his daughters were all married now that Tabitha had wed a Mr. Hollinger, "brother-in-law to our member to Congress Col. Owen." Having transferred his daughter to a family that was "respectable and well off," Moore just had his "three little boys to take care of now."[24] For women who had been married for some time, emigration could hold out the promise of a new start that would ease family pressures and conflicts. Eliza Blassingame, sister-in-law to Joanna Townes, shared her family's hope that a new start might bring an end to her husband's abusive behavior.[25]

If marriage looks, in such discussions, like the contractual transfer of obedience and responsibility from one family to another or the mere shifting of fears and worries from one state to another, that is because, in part, it was. Yet the reality of replacing one focus of power and obedience with another or of continuing to endure the problems that many women faced in their marriages did not alter the fact that within the constraints of their society, marriage represented for many women a step toward greater responsibility and greater independence.

For wives who became emigrants, those steps could be lengthened as they became neither the first nor the last to discover that distance from loved ones' welcome affections could also be distance from their unwelcome control. True inequality did not necessarily mean chronic ineffectuality. A sense of surprise and excitement could be apparent in something as simple as Eliza Kennedy's discovery that camping was "more pleasant than I anticipated" (except when her husband burned his hands in the campfire) or as deep as Mary Maverick's appreciation of the vastness of the horizons that framed her family's endeavors in 1830s Texas. "We find ourselves," she wrote, "a family of adventurers, as far West as it is possible for Americans to go under the present circumstances, and yet I can find nothing to regret—but the distance which separates us from so many near and dear friends."[26]

In 1824 Martha Gaston, a fairly recent emigrant to Wilcox County, Alabama, wrote to her cousin Jane Gaston, back in Chester District, South Carolina, with news regarding her family's good health ("Father I think is a goodeal fleshier since he came here"), her parents' apparent pleasure with their move, and her own delight at the extent of church activity in the area. Martha then turned to eliciting, rather than reporting, gossip. In her questions she humorously acknowledged both the passion and pragmatism characteristic of many marriage relations at the same time as she gave playful voice to how much the blending of marriage and movement in southern society found metaphorical recognition in its everyday language. "But you never said a word about your trip," she quizzed her cousin, "whether you were traveling to the land of matrimony or not. . . . I hope at least you are traveling to the land of happiness. If you are in the land of matrimony I want you to let me know, and how you are pleased with the country." [27] Gaston echoed in eastward jest the words of a thousand serious westward inquiries. Just as moving was central to the society, so metaphors of movement became an appropriate part of the language people used to discuss the related affairs of heart and household. Gaston gave illustrative voice to the reality of lives lived in different states and worlds, often separated from one another by great distance and fragmentary knowledge yet discussed in a shared language rooted in what those worlds held in common. In Georgia and in Mississippi, in dresses and in breeches, in marriage and in bachelorhood, however much the spoken parts differed, the language remained the same.

Emigration, then, was encouraged by the priorities of the plantation household as well as by the values and assumptions bred by those priorities. Most planters understood that emigration was one means to meet legitimate obligations and expectations. That does not mean that private discussions of emigration avoided the critical and apprehensive tones that characterized so much of the public debate. Like their critics, emigrants and their kinfolk often questioned the motives and abilities of particular emigrants. For many planters emigration remained an anxious, often wrenching, experience precisely because of its uncertain impact on existing family relations and the distribution of family power and property.

Relations between the generations, especially between fathers and sons, were often strained by emigration or talk of emigration. Not all parents behaved in the way William Gilmore Simms suggested was commonplace, eagerly pushing sons from the parental household in search of western fortune. Anne Horry Dent, who managed to keep her other son, George, close to home until her death in 1856, was content enough to see John be independent on his own plantation as long as he remained nearby. But she bitterly opposed John and Mary's plan to settle in "the wilds of Alabama." Later she would complain that if he had not been so eager to pursue greater wealth, "we might yet have been enjoying family union, instead of being so widely scattered and unavailingly lamenting our mistake." Fathers too could oppose their children's departure. Some saw emigration as a challenge to their power or as an indication of ingratitude or desertion. Plantation patriarch David Leech, for example, complained that his five sons all left him "to shift for myself in old age." Leech punished their desertion by shutting them out of his will.[28]

Even if they did not respond as aggressively as Anne Dent or David Leech, many parents proved ambivalent about the departure of their children (especially sons). The loss of a son was not, as it often was in nonslaveholding households, the loss of a laborer. Sons of the plantation were rather masters-in-waiting. Some already played a valuable role in managing their parents' plantations. Thus the more a son, like John Dent, had proved himself capable of taking on the management of his own plantation, the more a parent might regret his determination to leave for the West in order to do so. David Johnson's respect for his son's planting abilities and his awareness of how much Edward had contributed to the success of the family plantation only seemed to fuel his resentment at the son's decision to employ those skills on his own place. The elder Johnson wrote to Edward in somewhat grudging, formal terms of his having "received the announcement of your determination to leave my employment." However pleased the father would have been had his son "found it to your interest to continue," he declared that "I can't complain," sounding a lot like he was complaining. In Johnson's case regret at one son's departure was fueled by his doubts that his remaining sons could adequately fill the vacancy. Thus the emigration of the most responsible could increase fears regarding the immaturity of those who stayed behind.[29]

At other times doubts about the emigrant's ability to succeed could shape the views of fathers or other family members. In words not exactly oozing paternal encouragement, Thomas Harrison told his son James of his fear that his "change of residence" from South Carolina to Mississippi would "not be advantageous." "A new settled place is not likely to afford much business for lawyers," Harrison believed; "but of these matters you must judge for yourself." He went on, "Steadiness, sobriety and attention to business together with strict integrity will insure success. Every thing depends on yourself. If you fail it will be your own fault." James Henry Hammond, one of whose sons wished to buy a plantation in Mississippi, thought little of his children's ambitions and even less about their expectations as to how much he should do to assist in their fulfillment. "My children and myself differ so as to what I am to do for them and they for me that an abyss separates us and there is no ground on which we can meet," he told his brother. "Each," he complained, "requires to be set up in precise conformity with his imagination and in the mean time will only pretend and play at work, mope and piddle." Paternal anxiety could be generated for fathers, like David Leech or David Johnson, by fears about their own ability to cope or for those, like Thomas Harrison and James Henry Hammond, who worried about their sons' capacity to deal with new responsibilities in new, unsupervised settings.[30]

However different their personal circumstances, parental expressions of doubt about emigration shared a common character. Privately expressed resistance focused on the perceived consequences of emigration for individuals, families, and households. Private correspondence seldom gives any indication that family members resisted their relatives' departure because they feared its consequences for the wider society. Thus William H. Crawford, an enthusiast for emigration and expansion, could worry that James Tait, the son of his friend and political ally Charles Tait, "was going too far South," beyond the point where "a reasonable degree of health can be calculated upon" and, therefore, household preservation could be depended upon. Telling Charles Tait what he already knew, that "where health is not to be enjoyed happiness cannot be found," Crawford declared himself "fearful that James has set his affections too strongly upon the acquisition of pelf." Although "a competency is indispensable to the dignity of man," Crawford acknowledged, "the love of acquisition alone . . . is sordid avarice." Charles Tait seemed to share his old friend's doubts about his son's motives, and he linked them to a longer-running concern that his son lacked the right kind of ambition. In a later letter to another friend, he grumbled that "James, who has never yet risen higher than to be a militia captain, requests me to present his good wishes to you and to remind you that he has the honor, at least, to have been your and Mr. Calhoun's schoolmate." Instead of pursuing public glory, the father explained, his son was "busy in preparing for a crop of cotton" and wanted to plant two hundred acres. "He will, I dare say, get rich," sniffed Charles Tait, "but what is this miserable trash without consideration, without refined society, without intellectual pleasures? But some will say give me that solid pudding and you

may have the empty praise." Crawford and Charles Tait feared that the love
of money was overwhelming James Tait's obligations to personal honor
and family preservation. James Tait, it seems, preferred the pudding to the
praise. Charles Tait, it seems, did not approve of his son's choice.[31]

At other times, however, Charles Tait himself appeared to recognize the
importance, even the primacy, of moneymaking. He could also write to
his dear James of having "little now to wish for in this world but to look
on and witness your prosperity and the rise & progress of your family."
He hoped he had done his part in giving his son "the means of beginning the world with good auspices," means which used prudently and with
"the blessing of God" would ensure that he could not "fail of doing great
things" for his family. "Ten years ought," the father hoped, to "make you
as rich as you should wish to be." Tait was not being so much hypocritical,
or even just contradictory, as he was articulating a tension at the heart of
the plantation elite's efforts to define and sustain its place in society.[32]

Not even the severest of the emigrants' critics would have denied that
ultimately profit and honor were mutually reinforcing aspects of planter
life. It may be too simple to say, as one story had it, that "if a man could sit
on his porch and see fifty niggrahs ride his mules in from work—*that was
aristocracy*. But if he went broke and had to sell a niggrah . . . his reputa-
tion was gone and he could not borrow a dollah." But this anecdote does
lay open the essence of the relationship between profit and position, ownership and honor, that most planters would have recognized.[33]

The tensions arising from the intertwined ambitions and priorities of
these extending plantation households can be seen in the letters that criss-
crossed the Deep South bearing messages of advice and explanation, exhortation and justification. They reveal the anxiety and uncertainty of
elders even as they further stoked the fires of ambition and deepened the
dread of failure in the hearts of young men like James Tait and James
Harrison. Emigration intensified the intrinsic tensions between conflict
and cooperation, independence and dependence, self-expression and self-
abasement, that characterized the relations among all members of the
planter class, but perhaps especially those between fathers and sons.[34]

James Tait heard his father's doubts. In a letter from Alabama to his father, his new circumstances led him "to reflect on the vast difference" between his situation and his father's. The son sat in his "humble cabbin on
cane creek, entirely alone, in a wilderness," writing a "few poor lines" to a
father at "the centre of every thing that is the result of well-organized and

dense population." While the father was "engaged in the noble business of legislating for a great nation," the son's business was merely "the obscure one of preparing a few acres for the cultivation of indian corn."[35]

Tait's overly modest exaggeration of the distance between his new world and his father's world served to reinforce his claim that he was unsuited for the public world in which his father felt so at home. "Howsoever enviable your situation may be," James Tait confessed, "I have not ambition enough to envy it." "I was not born to be great," Tait insisted; "nature did not vouchsafe to bestow upon me that *vitium propium virtute* which is so necessary an ingredient in the composition of one destined to be illustrious." It would "ever be a painful reflection to me that I could not be what you wished me to be, and what, for ought I know, you may have expected I could be." In order "to make some attonement for this," the son would "endeavour to be among the foremost in renown, for the less conspicuous virtues. I will try and be a good citizen, and useful in my sphere." The distance James Tait spoke of represented a gulf between the ambitions of the father and the son. When James Tait wrote to his wife Caroline, he emphasized the reunion in independence that emigration would eventually bring. When he wrote to his father, he stressed the isolation of the canebrake, reflecting in his view of space his efforts to legitimate the distance between his own ambitions and his father's expectations.[36]

As a son James Tait was far from alone in his efforts to distance himself from a father whose support and approbation he nevertheless continued to need. Charles Tait, for his part, was a familiar kind of father figure, seeking to maintain power and influence over his extended household even as he encouraged his son to increase his own private power and public prestige. Intergenerational, transregional discussions show how much more than just practical considerations were at work in a parent's evaluation of the meaning of a child's, especially a son's, departure. Emigration could further intensify the tensions inevitably generated by matters of generational succession and family expansion in all plantation households regardless of location.[37]

Frequently, then, discussions of particular moves did not lack for contention and questioning. Particular members of the planter class often expressed doubts about how and why particular people were moving west. What they seldom did was question the legitimacy of emigration in a general way. William Crawford and Charles Tait feared that James Tait was going too much for the money and too far south for the health and safety of his household. They did not question his household's departure as such, and indeed both were enthusiasts for what they viewed as the right kind of emigration. Particular emigrants might have the wrong motives for leaving, but leaving, in and of itself, was not evidence for malign intent toward either family or community. Thus Charles Tait's assessment of his son's motives appeared to draw the same distinctions made by the critics of emigration: moderation versus materialism, public service versus personal interest, honor versus profit, praise versus pudding. Yet Tait did not add to these dichotomous distinctions another one central to public criticism of emigration: East versus West. For the public critics of emigration, the very act of moving was itself evidence of skewed priorities. It was evidence for a planter's failure to strike the right balance between profit and honor. This was not the case for emigrant families like the Taits. For them, emigration could certainly be the means to destructive ends if carried out by planters with the wrong motives. But undertaken by the right people it was an entirely legitimate means to the most important ends that a successful and honorable planter could pursue.

This distinction is further clarified when we see how many of those who were skeptical about the departure of others chose, or at least contemplated, emigration for themselves. Thomas Harrison, unhappy with his affairs in South Carolina, was actively considering joining his son and brother in Mississippi. Even as he expressed doubts about his son's motives for moving, Charles Tait was himself planning a move to Alabama that he believed would benefit his political career. James Lide was sixty-five years old when he eventually left Society Hill, South Carolina, for Alabama, after years of resisting his family's emigration. Indeed, when Caleb Coker, a local businessman, had sought Hannah Lide's hand in marriage, James Lide had made his permission conditional on Coker promising never to take his daughter westward. Nevertheless, James Lide at last was talked into moving by his son Eli Hugh Lide, who wanted them to settle at Pleasant Hill, Alabama, where a nephew, Robert Pugh Lide, had already relocated from South Carolina. Thus James Lide, a prosperous planter, son of a father, Robert, who had been a major under Revolutionary War hero General Francis Marion, set off for Alabama at the age of sixty-five, a pioneer patriarch leading his sick wife, Jane Holloway Lide, six of their twelve children, and six grandchildren, as well as an overseer and dozens of slaves, into the West.[38]

As with the younger emigrants, family and household priorities often prompted departure or thoughts of departure among older slaveholders. Indeed the sense of responsibility for younger generations so evident in the correspondence of men like Charles Tait was itself a major motivation for older planters to consider moving themselves. How to provide for posterity was a central question for the planter class. For many, emigration to the West was one possible answer. Charles Tait was not the only older member of his family considering a move westward. Discussing the possibility of his "continuing in Georgia," his brother James M. Tait could "only say" to Charles that he was "deeply impressed with a desire to leave it." As the head of "a growing family," James felt it his "duty to try and provide for them at least a decent compatancy." Believing this to be something he could not "well do in this country," he felt that he "must look out for a new one." By the 1830s William Tait of De Kalb County, Georgia, was "getting old" but was nevertheless considering a move "to the province of Texas." He explained to his brother Charles that he was motivated not by his "own individual interest but . . . the good of posterity." Texas, he felt, offered "greater inducements . . . than any country I ever [k]new to the head of a family." Samuel Townes understood that his sister and brother-in-law had "a large family of children to provide for & settle in life" and so reluctantly concluded that they were right to move to a "new country" where "the facilities" for doing so were "tenfold greater than those afforded by an old country." A planter writing from Alabama in 1818 argued that emigration undertaken later in life showed how "old people lives for their children & not themselves." [39]

Sometimes the limits of home prompted resentment on the part of those who contemplated leaving. James Henry Hammond was among the planters who linked thoughts of moving to worries about meeting future obligations such as the education of his six sons. In 1841 the South Carolinian noted his earlier reluctance "to remove from my native state and carry a family into the semi-barbarous west," but he wondered if now was not a good time for a change of heart. In part this change was prompted by the fact that he felt surrounded by barbarism where he was. In the supposedly civilized Southeast, he complained that his "life is wearing out in improving poor lands among unimprovable savages, to whose society a wilderness would be preferable." Hammond "look[ed] forward with anguish . . . at the prospect of my children living in such a place and among such people."[40] William Brickell was another father who appeared to blend his concern for posterity with resentment toward his native state. He recalled how he had seen "the necessity of transplanting my scions (now rapidly shooting up) into a new and open field, where there was no monopoly of honors, offices and places by a few old and influential families, by all manner of tricks of legerdemain." Having purchased land in Mississippi, Brickell "bade adieu to my native land" in the fall of 1835. He remembered turning and speaking as he crossed the Savannah River, "Carolina! 'I am thy never weaned / Though not thy favored son.'" His resentment directed against the place driving him out, Brickell presented a picture of himself very different from the greedy "Western Emigrant" that William Gilmore Simms blamed for leaving a state that had given him everything.[41]

Thus many looked to emigration as one means to meet parental responsibilities. For many parents age did nothing to dim their belief that their children's interests should come before their own ease and comfort. Mary Laura Springs was "astonished" to hear that Mrs. Mecham was among the many people in her part of South Carolina who had "taken a great notion of emigrating." Springs could not "conceive the least inducement" for "a person so far advanced in life as she is to make a removal (with this exception, a desire to remain with her children)." "The others," Springs assumed, "move chiefly on account or in hopes of ameliorating the station of their progeny."[42] Despite her incredulity Mary Laura Springs could indeed quickly conceive of two important reasons why older members of her class might decide to emigrate. Some, perhaps like James Lide, only moved when mass departure offered less separation from his family than would staying put. Others viewed the West as the place best suited to meet demands of planter responsibility that transcended age and time as surely as they did place.

The experiences of these various families illuminate how much the tensions and demands endemic to the elite slaveholding family recognized no generational barriers. The demands of family and business in a society both qualitatively agricultural and chronically anxious pressed on people of all ages and abilities. In some cases they could fall all the more onerously on those who sought responsibly to meet the new obligations that advancing years could bring. In some ways the younger men of families like the Taits, Dents, Townes, and Lides seemed more at ease with the idea of emigration as a means to meeting plantation responsibilities than did anxious elders like Charles Tait and Thomas Harrison. Younger members of the elite showed little inclination to depart from existing understandings of how slaveholders should live. Yet they seemed more fully to embrace emigration as a means to achieve what more of their elders had achieved by staying where they were. Younger people's willingness to emigrate underscored their desire to be planters by showing the geographical lengths to which they were prepared to go in order to establish their own households. Starting out in new places was psychologically easier than starting again in unfamiliar territory. This was perhaps especially so when those starting out could call on their elders for practical and material support in their endeavors. Older people, on the other hand, often felt a double anxiety. Expected to help the younger generation in taking new steps in the West, they themselves often had to take that step as part of their commitment to posterity.

Private deliberations, then, could be infused with anxieties every bit as intense as those that shaped public discussion of emigration. Yet whereas public anxiety stemmed from a fear that plantation society was in crisis, private anxieties grew from circumstances that the participants recognized as familiar, whatever their difficulties and tensions. The private papers of emigrant households offer little evidence that their free inhabitants shared their critics' understanding of either the motives for or the consequences of departure. Emigrants and their kinfolk judged the causes and consequences of emigration primarily in terms of their own family, not the broader society, and in terms of its impact on their slaveholding households, not on slaveholding society as a whole.

Reformers added family and household to the list of emigration's victims. Those who observed emigration from within those families and households came to a very different understanding of the relation between westward movement and household health. The view of emigration from within the household was neither uncomplicated nor uncritical. Yet it did tend to see the household not as a victim of emigration but as an engine of the ambition that drove its members onward and, often, westward. As with all engines, smoothness and friction, heat and fluidity, were complementary rather than contrary elements in its successful operation. In such a setting efforts to achieve independence, build a family, and guarantee the security of future generations often proved as difficult to reconcile with present desires as they were essential to meeting future demands. That these ambitions themselves grew from the same kinds of family imperatives—order and progress, success and succession, profit and honor—that some felt emigration threatened to undermine generated unavoidable tensions in a setting defined by complex ties of kinship, power, and property. Emigration certainly could complicate relations and add to household anxieties. But it could also smooth relations and ease tensions by offering one more potential pathway toward goals that, in their various ways, most members of the planter class accepted as legitimate.

Whatever their age or sex, planter emigrants' expectations were both created and constrained by their household situation and their role within it. Even when individuals seemed most intent on breaking free from expected forms of behavior, they seldom succeeded in breaking the web of relations and pressures created and generated by the plantation household. Most had no such intention. Most women knew that being a mistress in their own right did not mean being their own person, yet such recognition did not crush the desire to achieve the most their society allowed. Few young men, however ambitious their search for independence, looked to the North where a world of commercial opportunity and social fluidity was said to await the entrepreneurial and the individualistic venturer. Instead they went west to make money and create households in the certain ways of their mothers and fathers.

For their part, those mothers and fathers knew that the pursuit of those certain ways was for life, and therefore that the possibility of having to emigrate to follow them could become a part of life at any time. Indeed the desire to make money in a certain way was itself further stimulus for moving rather than staying, heading westward instead of northward. For many elite southerners, going west may have been the best, even the only, way to pursue the merged aims of profit and honor that their class valued. Emigration was inextricably bound up with other intrinsic and inescapable aspects and responsibilities of elite family circumstances and thus itself became an intrinsic and inescapable element in the life of the southern planter class as a whole.

Thus the mobility that, to the agrarian republican, appeared cause for anxious, even apocalyptic, analysis looked very different to planters who did not share their vision of the ideal household. Critics of emigration granted too much freedom of action—for good or ill—to the male planters whose behavior they sought to explain. The planters who led their caravans of kin and capital into the West surely would have been surprised to hear that they were out of touch with those around them or out of place in a modern world that hungrily demanded the cotton their slaves' labor produced. If the men of the planter class were isolated on their plantations, then it was a curious kind of isolation. What those critics saw, from a public perspective, as isolation from the important relations of agricultural life, male planters themselves, from the private perspective of their "paternal acres," saw as enmeshment in the essential relations of slaveholding life. These were precisely the relations—of ownership and kinship—that public debate of emigration's causes and cures neglected. Thus the critics' focus on the relations that male emigrants appeared to be breaking inevitably led to a neglect of those that continued to bind them.

The planter family portraits that emerge from the private words and thoughts of slaveholding emigrants did combine the new with the familiar, but not in the ways that the critics' public indictments claimed. Behind the urge to emigrate, the critics saw a reactionary streak in agricultural habits combine with an irresponsible attraction to the habits of modern life most calculated to encourage estrangement among people and alienation from place. For the movers themselves, however, their embrace of emigration was not a symbol of their surrender to the worst that the modern world had to offer. Rather it was one modern means by which to meet the demands, and confront the dangers, made upon them by that world. Mass movement offered the means to meet the demands of a world as crazy for cotton as its producers were for new places in which to grow it. Mobility served as the means to the long-established ends of preserving and strengthening the central human relations of the region's slaveholding society, the very kinds of relations (strictly hierarchical, inescapably reciprocal) seemingly melting into air in other parts of that same modern world. The fever for movement did not, as emigration's critics maintained, have its source in a rejection of the character and relations of plantation society. Rather, as its participants' own accounts illustrate, its roots were to be found in the anxious yet ordered qualities and characteristics at the very heart of plantation life. Even in such a swiftly moving world, staying put undoubtedly best served the interests of many individual planters and their households. For the planters as a class, however, standing still would have been the truly reactionary, even suicidal, response to a modern world that threatened to consume them even as it nourished their growth and fed their expansion.

5 The Land around Us: Southwestern Sights

But then it was only Goose Creek, Williamsburg, and
St. Stephens', and perhaps, here and there, some other spots,
while the progress of the back and middle country seemed
amply to compensate for these partial instances of decay.
Now, the disease is, it appears, universal, and South-Carolina,
excepting the old parish country, is to be abandoned like a
steppe in Mongolia or Tartary! And this, too, remark if you
please, is the condition of the whole South,—the new States
will soon be exhausted in their turn,—and Alabama and
Mississippi to be deserted by their migratory possessors
for Texas.
—Hugh Swinton Legaré

IN 1844 SAMUEL TOWNES PUBLISHED A *HISTORY OF Marion, Alabama.* Townes began by locating his adopted home in space: "32 28′ North latitude, and about half a degree South of Charleston, S. C." Townes's main purpose, however, was to locate his new home in time and to trace its progress "from a period of savage occupancy, through all the intermediate grades of society, to its present condition of elegance, refinement and social happiness." Townes sought to record its advance "from the stillness of solitude to the busy hum of happy and rewarded industry—from the yell of—the red man to the joyful acclamations and adoring hymns of the christian worshiper." The "fervent prayer" of the "humble historian" was that the town's inhabitants would "prove worthy of our happy location and peculiar privileges—that we may practice the virtues which will make us good and happy here, and enable us, after death, to rise high and yet higher, until we see the spires of the new Jerusalem glitter in the distance." [1]

In his desire to give public voice to his understanding of his community's historical significance, Samuel Townes was among those who sought to chronicle and interpret the rise of the Southwest as a whole. Some, like Townes, were residents of the region. Others found continued residence in the Southeast no barrier to expressing their views of this new entity on the American landscape. Some of them, like Samuel Townes, wrote history. Others offered their understanding of events for public perusal in sketches and stories, journals and newspapers. Whether as emigrants, travelers, or observers from afar, elite southerners participated not only in making the Southwest but in creating the images through which they and others gave meaning to its creation.

Better-known observers of the Southwest, such as William Gilmore Simms and Alexander Meek, shared Samuel Townes's understanding of how to measure progress: as upward movement through clearly defined stages of "civilization." Simms divided American history into periods. The present one encompassed the "transition from the colonial to the republican condition," the "progress of interior discovery and settlement . . . and the final and complete conversion to the purposes of civilized man, of that wild tract, that 'Boundless contiguity of shade,' spreading away from Altamaha to the Rio Bravo." Simms believed that temporal tracing of this kind was essential to understanding "the moral steps by which we attain the several successive epochs in our national career." In an image suggestive of his understanding of the historical interrelation of the spatial and the temporal, Simms called these periods "tracts of time." [2]

William Gilmore Simms and Samuel Townes were among the many "inquirers" into the material and moral development of the Southwest who assumed an intimate connection between the planters' progress and the progress of civilization. Townes and Simms had something else in common. At times both could be as scathing as they were congratulatory about the course of southwestern development. In these moments both writers could reflect a much gloomier perspective on the Southwest, one which spoke of degeneration and decline rather than progress and prosperity. In the seesawing southwestern analysis of observers like Simms and Townes can be seen the tensions and contradictions between the ideal understanding of life and history they embraced in theory and the "facts on the ground" they encountered in daily life. These tensions of thought and habit remained unresolved in the pages of Simms and Townes, as well as most others. It is necessary to explore how and why this was so, before turning, in the following chapter, to whether such anxious contradiction found any fuller resolution in the daily lives of the Southwest's slaveholders.

In the first half of the nineteenth century, judgments of slaveholding society's journey through space could not be separated from opinions regarding its historical movement through time. Whether being encouraged or decried, the demographic mobility and fluidity swirling around the southwestern states provoked elite southerners to a rich discourse of imagery and argument as they struggled to make cultural and historical sense of the anxious, ambivalent world that the slaveholders were making in the Southwest.

Alexander Meek was among the leading contributors to this discourse. Meek was a small child when he and his parents set off from Columbia, South Carolina, probably in that fate-freighted year of 1819. He grew up in Tuscaloosa, where he graduated from the University of Alabama in 1833. He served as a noncommissioned officer fighting the Indians in Florida and was later appointed attorney general of Alabama. In describing southwestern civilization Meek did two things that many other observers did. Like Simms and Townes he placed the region's present in the midst of a long, unfolding historical narrative stretching forward as well as back. Second, he infused his descriptions and analysis of the southwestern landscape and its inhabitants with religious allusion and utopian imagery.

Around about the time that the young Meek was making his own journey to Alabama, another emigrant, William Bibb, who became Alabama's governor during the territorial period and early statehood, declared Alabama "the Eden of the Nation." Twenty years of movement and settlement later, Meek showed that enthusiasm for analogies to biblical abundance remained high. In December 1839 he offered the gentlemen of his alma mater's Erosophic Society "some reflections upon the History, Character, and Prospect of the South West." Meek first thought back to a time "when the rapt prophet of olden time was led by the hand of Divinity, to the summit of the sacred mountain," from there to look out over the Promised Land, "all spread out like some great breathing picture." Meek then moved forward in time, to only one hundred years earlier, and imagined "an intelligent spectator" "placed upon some eminence overlooking the whole South West" and able to view that land in "all its magnificence, its fertility, its serene beauty," and, of course, "its conveniences for the purposes of civilized man." Meek felt sure that the earlier scene "could not have been widely different, or more inspiring" to the eye and heart.[3]

Alabama, Meek explained on another occasion, had all the "natural" ingredients necessary "to make a State great and flourishing," including fertile soil, "hills abound[ing] in mineral wealth," and an "atmosphere . . . as pure as the sky of Italy!" "Her rivers," he went on, "roil in magnificent beauty and grandeur" while "stretching their long arms, wherever the wants of agriculture, or commerce demand!" All this, and beautiful scenery "of the most pleasing and picturesque character" too.[4] Texas also had its boosters. A note reprinted from the *Natchez Herald* in the *Southern Agriculturist*, normally a bastion of the cautionary word when it came to things western, told of plantations on the Colorado River where cotton grew in quantities of 1,600 to 2,000 pounds per acre. What made these figures especially arresting was that the cotton flourished where "not a blow had been struck this year by the hoe or plough, and where not a single seed had been thrown into the ground." Rather this crop had grown untended only from what had "remained on the ground, of last year's crop.[5] The implications for those who actually worked the land were clear.

These kinds of reports fueled a view of the Southwest as a place of otherworldly abundance. Mary Austin Holley, a cousin of Stephen F. Austin, captured the marvel of it all when she described Texas as "a new island, as it were, [that] has been discovered in these latter days, at our very doors, apparently fresh from the hands of the Maker." In their wonder at the untouched abundance of the Southwest, writers like Meek and Holley seemed to suggest that such a new country demanded nothing less than a new creation story.[6]

Yet observers like Meek and Holley also saw clearly what at other times their rhetoric of untouched utopias masked. The lands of the Southwest had long been occupied by other people who first had to be displaced before civilization could take root. Texas had not been "settled" earlier, Holley argued, because of "the jealous policy of the old Spanish government" and the "uncommonly ferocious" character of the "Carancahua Indians, who inhabited the coast." Because of this the area had "remained for ages unknown to the world. Instead of being converted into an abode of industrious and happy freemen," it had been "doomed by the selfishness of men, to continue a howling wilderness." However pleasant it was to think of Texas, shiny and new, "apparently" being delivered "fresh from the hands of the Maker," Holley knew better. First it had to be wrested from the dead hand of failed and anachronistic civilizations. In a southwestern "Eden" moral ascent rather than decline would follow from the expulsion from paradise of its first inhabitants.[7]

If the civilizers were to make of this wilderness a paradise, they first would have to make it a battleground. Alexander Meek frankly recognized as much. He insisted that a serious study of his state's history—a task he considered essential and urgent—would show what was "most generally overlooked": Alabama's "foundations . . . were not effected by the tranquil course of peaceful emigration, but were wrought and consecrated through a bitter sacrament of blood." For Meek "the numerous and terrible wars, by which the intercourse" between the native population and white settlers "has ever been marked," "diffuse along all the lines of our progress the shadows and stains of blood."[8]

By the time of the Cherokees' Trail of Tears, the tragic, symbiotic patterns of clearance and occupation, swindle and sale, had become very familiar. Andrew Jackson, as soldier and as president, remained at the center of policy concerning the original inhabitants of the lands coveted by white settlers. That policy was well summarized in the 1830 legislation that gave it further impetus. The Indian Removal Act appropriated funds for the purchase of the land held by the Creek, Seminoles, Chickasaw, and Choctaw, as well as the Cherokee, who remained east of the Mississippi. It also earmarked moneys for the purchase of lands west of the Mississippi on which to settle those removed. President Jackson employed these legislative powers not only to pressure the Cherokee into leaving Georgia and Alabama but to compel the Creek, Chickasaw, and Choctaw into moving west of the Mississippi River. In September 1830 Choctaw chiefs signed a treaty ceding their lands in Mississippi and Alabama; two years later the Chickasaw also agreed to go, trading their lands east of the Mississippi for new territory in Arkansas. That same year some Creeks, tired of white settlers encroaching on their eastern Alabama home, ceded their lands in exchange for new ones west of the Mississippi. Following the Second Creek War in 1836, the remaining Creeks were forcibly removed from their lands, and in the fall of that year, accompanied by military escort, they began their trek west.[9] If talk of Eden and the Promised Land spoke to dreams of a place abundant in all its aspects, it nevertheless intimated potentially different experiences of movement to and from that place. Mixed images of Eden and the Promised Land spoke to mixed experiences: of expulsion and expropriation, departure and discovery, search and surrender, journeying to and journeying from, final peace and endless anxiety.

Alexander Meek stood in a Tuscaloosa street and watched this changing of the historical guard. "The dynasty of the Red Man is over!" he recorded. "Slowly, and sadly the Ænigma of the western world . . . bent his footsteps to the sinking sun! . . . driven before the progress of the white man, like a storm shattered barque, before an ocean wave!" This "melancholy pilgrimage of the stern, but spirit broken Creeks,—the last remnant of a once mighty race—to their occidental home" constituted, Meek believed, "an important era" in the history both of "'the simple children of the forest,' and of our young flourishing State." It showed, he thought, "with what rapidity events are progressing around us," as well as Alabama's "rapid strides" in population growth "and in the arts and sciences, consequent thereon." In sum, it "unfolds to the eye of anticipation, brilliant visions of her coming greatness and glory." For Meek there was nothing personal in this process. It was strictly history. The "children of the forest" were simply fulfilling their historically ordained role, departing the scene in order that new occupants could arrive, carrying with them the contagion of civilization in their calculating hearts and dreaming heads.[10]

Writers like Meek and Holley obviously sought to stimulate this process, exhorting new emigrants and encouraging those already there. While Alexander Meek addressed himself to those he hoped would lead Alabama into the future, Mary Austin Holley explicitly hoped that her book might be useful "to the emigrant, rather than the general reader, by assisting him to locate his ideas as well as his land." The West's boosters knew that however otherworldly their descriptions of the new country's bounty, their accounts also had to be sufficiently down-to-earth to appeal to the practical desires of prospective movers. Even the enthralled Holley cautioned that "a soil that yields the fruit of nearly every latitude, almost spontaneously," must still "have a seed-time and a harvest. Though the land be, literally, flowing with milk and honey, yet, the cows must be milked, and the honey must be gathered." Even in so generous a country there was no "exemption" from "the primeval curse, that, in the sweat of his brow, man shall eat bread." Holley warned that "the emigrant should bear in mind, that in a new community, labour is to be performed; that if he cannot work himself, he must take with him those who can." As the American settlement of Texas suggests, many took Holley's hint and brought with them enslaved laborers to do their sweating for them.[11]

In describing the Southwest's progress and potential, writers like Holley and Meek intermingled the romantic and the sublime with the practical and the social. Nature was to be valued for its magnificence and evaluated for its productive promise. Rivers were "noble and navigable." Majestic mountains took one's breath away, and in return one could take their mineral wealth away. Holley described "the country lying west of the Sabine river" as "an enchanting spot," a "fairy land," "a tract of surpassing beauty," but also one "exceeding even our best western lands in productiveness, with a climate perfectly salubrious, and of a temperature, at all seasons of the year, most delightful." Even as they sought to keep one eye on the scenery and the other on history, they tried to keep their readers' full attention on the main chance.[12]

Although such descriptions were obviously works of calculated persuasion, they also revealed a broader vision of history and progress. Prettiness and practicality intermingled in language and image, joined by the uncomplicated "ands" and "withs" of the imperialist rather than the querulous, qualifying "buts" of the conservationist or the reformer. To its admirers the Southwest represented an almost limitless world of opportunity, a place "adapted, beyond most lands, both to delight the senses, and to enrich the pockets, of those who are disposed to accept its bounties." It was a place where destinies—both personal and historical—would be fulfilled.[13]

Many emigrants, whether or not they read guides like Holley's, continued to head for the Southwest, intent on accepting its bounties and taking with them the laborers who would help them to do so. Histories and memoirs of the Southwest in this time tell of a land, as Mississippian H. S. Fulkerson expressed it, "aglow with speculation." With "emigrants . . . flocking in from all quarters of the Union, especially from the slaveholding States," the "new country" looked to Georgia writer Joseph Baldwin like "a reservoir, and every road leading to it a vagrant stream of enterprise and adventure." Especially in the 1830s, planters and their human property occupied a central place among those filling up the Black Belt of the Deep South amid the economic fluctuations, Indian clearances, and land speculations of the region's flush times.[14]

There was growing evidence across the region that the stable foundations of advanced "civilization" were indeed emerging from all this westward flocking and flowing. Educational interests were served by the opening of universities from Tuscaloosa to Texas.[15] The spirituality essential to civilization's spread was also apparent. Reporting to the Mission Board of the Methodist Episcopal Church from Nacogdoches, Texas, in 1838, the Reverend Littleton Fowler felt confident that "the soil, the government, language and climate will invite thousands annually to emigrate to our new and interesting Republic." His pleasing discovery that "the people are hospitable and intelligent and generally receive the ministers with pleasure and delight" encouraged Fowler to claim that "Texas is now, perhaps, the most inviting and interesting missionary field that has existed since the days of the apostles."[16] Other accounts focused on the architectural and institutional structures being built upon such evangelical hopes. Declaring Marion, Alabama, the "Athens [Greece, not Georgia, one presumes] of the State—the seat of learning, and abode of religion and sound morality," Samuel Townes cited as supporting evidence the Presbyterians' "large, convenient and handsome church." Not to be outdone, the Baptists had also built a "most elegant and tasty" house of worship in 1837, at a cost of seven thousand dollars. Townes credited this progress to "the public spirit" and "noble liberality" of both the town's citizens and "many of the planters who reside in its vicinity."[17] Many planter men and women did continue to complain about the lack of regular preaching and satisfactory church buildings in their new neighborhoods. Many continued to send their children east and north to schools and universities. Nevertheless the schools, colleges, and churches gradually dotting the social landscape of the Southwest did much to expand educational opportunity and to ease spiritual isolation.

This institutional development also added to a sense of the Southwest as developing a certain social fullness to complement its natural abundance. When William Gilmore Simms addressed the Erosophic Society of the University of Alabama in December 1842 he declared himself "forcibly impressed with those wondrous effects of time, which we never so clearly understand as when they are somewhat associated with our individual experience." "Little did I imagine," he said, recalling an earlier visit to Tuscaloosa, "that the rude and scattered hamlet which I then surveyed,—a fragmentary form, not half made up,—was, in so short a space of time, to become so eminent a city;—her dwellings informed by intellect and enlivened by society."[18] Simms's personal testimony to Tuscaloosa's rapid transformation seemed to place the Alabama town firmly within larger patterns of social and historical progress. At such times, then, it seemed that the Southwest, fueled by a rich blend of natural abundance and appropriate human activity, was indeed accelerating rapidly from "savage occupancy" to "social happiness" through those "intermediate grades of society" that Samuel Townes set out.

Not everyone was so sure. As the images of Fulkerson and Baldwin suggest, many observers were struck by the feverish, almost disordered character of the new region. Images of recklessness, disorder, and fluidity were also plentiful in descriptions of the Southwest. Many accounts of the region's inhabitants suggested they were a long way from answering Samuel Townes's "fervent prayer" that they "prove worthy of our happy location and peculiar privileges." Not all those social gradations to be worked through had to do with the native inhabitants. It seemed to some that the Southwest still had to slough off a layer or two of white skin before taking on the full colorings of civilization.

Southwesterners could react defensively when "foreign travelers" and "the Press in other sections of the Union" reminded them that, as Alexander Meek put it, the "peculiarities" of their society were "numerous, and very prominent." Yet even boosters like Meek acknowledged that the "excellencies" of the new residents' character were "qualified by attendant evils." They could also be found, at times, among their region's most unsparing critics, perhaps in part because their hopes for it had been the highest. Meek acknowledged the "roughness of manner" and the "improper haughtiness of spirit" that prompted "frequent violence and crime; a disregard of the laws and of any restraint; neglect of the charities and courtesies of social life, as effeminate and unbecoming; and a general deterioration of the moral feelings." The snootiest southeasterner could not have put it better.[19]

Yet Meek often qualified his concessions. The characteristics he enumerated were, "in a new and backwoods community, most usually, the shadows of the [pioneer] virtues." Mary Holley also acknowledged, even in the case of Texas, the inevitability of certain "inconveniences which unavoidably pertain to every country in the incipient stages of its settlement." Yet such character flaws constituted the ephemeral shadows of southwestern society (and of new societies generally) in the making, not its enduring substance. In recognizing the present significance of such "evils" and "inconveniences," Meek placed them within the narrative of progressive advance that framed his wider discussion of the region. "The evils of a very early state of society have measurably passed from among us," he insisted in 1839. "Their effects to some extent yet linger, but are daily diminishing, while the beneficial effects of emigration exist in their full force." Meek assured his readers that such wildness was a passing phase within greater and more significant movements through space and time: a mere subplot in a grand narrative of advance.[20]

Most observers of southwestern society and culture shared Meek and Holley's assumptions about how social and historical advance should proceed. Not all agreed that it was going as smoothly as the optimists believed. As southwestern development continued apace, its paradoxical blending of materialism and impermanence looked less like growing pains and more like the fully formed features of a social monstrosity. Finding its wildness neither comic nor ephemeral, they wondered if the region really was shedding those rough, uncivilized skins. Rather than being discarded, perhaps they were hardening into a permanent cultural shell, increasingly impervious to superior influences from without and hopelessly inhospitable to their indigenous development.

Many of those who criticized the Southwest's failure to develop were the same people who had placed much of the blame for the Southeast's decline on the emigrant slaveholders who had deserted one and were now busy despoiling the other. Indeed for many it was their awareness of the connections between the regions—a connection embodied by the emigrants themselves—that made them fear so much for the Southwest. In light of the perceived connection between southeastern decline and southwestern disorder, it was not surprising that the "charm" and pleasure afforded by Edenic tales of the Southwest soon dissipated. "Few now will find in 'the West!'" wrote R. of Orangeburg in 1836, "the source of fanciful associations which used to invest with such interest each legend of the wilderness, which found its way to our quiet homes. Different, far different, is the feeling now produced." That different feeling was one of suspicion regarding the truthfulness and integrity of those images.[21]

Critics attacked "the extravagant reports" and "the imperfect representations of travelers." A writer who condemned "the too partial accounts of our own friends who have settled upon the soil, and wish to have us as neighbours," also reflected the concern that most of what was known "of the great cotton growing section of the South-West" came from the unreliable reports of tourists, settlers, and, worst of all, speculators.[22] Critics like Thomas Spalding did not deny the great fertility of parts of the Southwest. But they did insist that reports of its abundance were greatly exaggerated.[23] One skeptic complained of "the spirit of generalising in descriptions, or of drawing general conclusions from particular facts," which he considered "the prevailing deception of the age." This deception meant that "all new countries . . . (if one favorable agricultural result be exhibited) are El Dorados, though they may contain as many swamps and marshes as the Carolinas, and not yield to Georgia in the extent of her pine barrens."[24] Some, like Patrick Noble of Abbeville, South Carolina, claimed that exposure to "the actual view" of the Southwest—containing its "many disadvantages and deprivations" as well as its admitted benefits—"dispels the illusion" of the region as an El Dorado.[25] But Noble was too sanguine regarding the power of "reality" to undermine fanciful or exaggerated images of southwestern fertility and abundance. Just as they had largely ignored the rational remedies of agricultural science that would have rendered emigration unnecessary, the emigrants seemed to take little interest in accepting more balanced accounts of southwestern promise.

And as they did in explaining the emigrants' resistance to agricultural reform, the critics located one source of the Southwest's social turbulence in the unsettled minds of those who led the way in settling it. As Spalding put it, the agriculturist's "expectations are excited to an extravagant degree," and "feverish inclinations are generated in his mind to flee to this land of promise."[26] Exaggerated claims for the Southwest found welcome refuge in planter minds already primed for delusion. Suspect reports of the Southwest were insistently linked to the suspect character of those who responded to them.

Critics sought to counter the unreliable and the utopian with analysis and imagery that focused on the minds of the emigrants and settlers more than on the places to which they moved. Words like *enchanting* took on a sinister tone; *splendid* was likely to appear beside *delusion* rather than *view* in debates that addressed the febrile nature of the emigrants' mental state rather than the fertile character of their destinations. Many critics of emigration and southwestern settlement peppered their complaints with comparisons of the Southwest to El Dorado. Where the imagery of Eden or the Promised Land suggested an actual place so awe-inspiring that only heavenly analogies could describe it, critics selected as their favorite comparative image a place that existed only as the figment of fevered minds.

Judge John Belton O'Neall complained of emigrants who saw the West as a place where "they expected to find the *el dorado*," while Patrick Noble believed that "the glowing descriptions given of these new countries have acted like a spell and men have imagined that they have at last discovered the true El Dorado."[27] The unrequited hopes of men like Noble that the "actual view" would dispel this dream landscape simply reinforced the power of the spell's hold. In describing the Southwest as El Dorado, these observers said less about the destination than about those who traveled toward it blinded to reality by their greed and gullibility. The imagery of choice remained otherworldly, but it spoke of chimerical quests rather than promised lands, of delusion and deception rather than productivity and progress, of El Dorado not Eden.

The critics' suspicion that the planters' southwestern dream was a mirage could not be separated from their appraisal of the planter emigrants themselves. Like the region's boosters these observers stressed the role of emigration in shaping the developing character of the southwestern landscape. Few elite southerners would have denied that geographic mobility had a role to play in human progress, especially in modern and dynamic societies such as those of the Deep South. What worried some observers was that mobility had replaced rather than merely preceded stability as southwestern society's defining characteristic. Movement for movement's sake was a sign of historic failure. A society lost in space was, necessarily, a society lost in time.

These fears found expression in images and allusions that, again, spoke of endless wanderings rather than final destinations. "No man is settled in the West," thundered William Gilmore Simms. "People build houses, and buy plantations, and make improvements, not to live in them or upon them, not to enjoy them, but to sell at a profit." [28] Simms criticized the "wild and destructive system, by which even they have sunk under embarrassment and ruin, with all their advantages of soil and climate." Many shared his fears that such persistent restlessness would make the journey from fertility to sterility as rapid in the West as it had been in the East. [29] Clearly, those who had despoiled, then deserted, soil moistened by the blood of heroic Revolutionary forebears were capable of any abuse toward the new lands and societies they now occupied.

Thus images of El Dorado spoke to the destructive as well as the delusional nature of southwestern settlers who, "first, by butchery and then murder" had "ruined one of the best portions of the habitable globe" and now headed west with their heedless disregard for soil and society as strong as ever. [30] A "Middle Georgian" correspondent of the *Southern Cultivator* likened the practices of the "Georgia *land-flayers*" to the Spaniards on the pampas of South America who "slaughter, annually, hundreds and thousands of the finest, fattest cattle in the world, purely for the sake of the hide alone." South Carolinian William Ellison raged against the "successful cotton planter" who "slaughters the forest, and murders the soil" at home before marching off "to a new country to recommence the same process." [31] "Like the discoverers of America," Judge O'Neall complained, " 'gold, more gold,' has been the unceasing demand of our people . . . and like the

Indian pointing his Spanish conquerors to the interior for the richer mines, so cupidity pointed our people to the richer fields and prairies of the southwest." [32] In their restlessness and rapacity, the planters embodied the impulses (such urges could not be dignified with the term *values*) of the gold seeker and the conquistador: lesser peoples of lesser times and places.

More conquistador than capitalist, closer to the madhouse than the countinghouse, planter settlers stripped southwestern places of their spiritual value and society-nurturing potential by reducing them to nothing more than items of exchange and sites of exploitation. Even the reprieve afforded by virgin fertility would prove fleeting. The eventual consequences were clear: initial success, measured only in money, would give way to ultimate failure, measured by the standards of civilization. "They will run our race!" insisted William Gilmore Simms. "Their products will whiten the frequent earth to the banks of the Sabine—they will grow rich for a season, exhaust the soil, and, in its barrenness, realize their own." [33] Southwestern land and society were joined in a destructive Saint Vitus's dance, grotesquely whirling and spiraling toward mutual death. As their images of conquistadors and El Dorado make clear, theirs was a Southwest defined by the futile and destructive quest for a chimerical fantasy, not by the steady, settled pursuit of a new Eden. [34]

Even worse, some feared that the Southwest represented the future of the South, a future in which mobility would be an intrinsic, unceasing, and disruptive feature of society. South Carolinian Hugh Legaré was among those who offered a deeply pessimistic counterimage to the view that whatever its initial drawbacks, movement over space inevitably would bring progress in time. Legaré recalled how his horror at seeing nature's reclamation of low-country places like Goose Creek, Williamsburg, and St. Stephen was tempered by the thought that "the progress of the back and middle country seemed amply to compensate for these partial instances of decay." By 1835, however, Legaré feared that "the disease" of mobility was "universal, and South-Carolina, excepting the old parish country, is to be abandoned like a *steppe* in Mongolia or Tartary!" Nor would this retrograde progression stop there. For "this, too, remark if you please, is the condition of the whole *South*,—the new States will soon be exhausted in their turn,—and Alabama and Mississippi to be deserted by their migratory possessors for *Texas*." [35] However deep their disdain, critics of southwestern settlers and society reflected much more than the mere assertion of the superiority of East over West, of settled civilization over disordered wilderness. On the contrary, they emphasized the connections between the two. After all, who had bred the people who were now despoiling the West?

Horror at the planters' failure to nurture appropriate relations with land and place (whether in the East or the West) could not be separated from fears that they were abdicating from their responsibilities toward history. Far from being agents of civilized advance, the planters appeared to some to be replicating the most retrograde characteristics of the peoples they were supposed to be displacing. Again, such fears found expression in telling analogies and images. The corollary to Hugh Legaré's portrayal of southern lands as abandoned steppes was that those doing the abandoning were akin to, as Thomas Spalding put it, the "Tartar of the Steppes." Critics frequently likened their peers' behavior to that of the most incorrigibly nomadic cultures. A contributor to the *Southern Cultivator* described the planters' movements as "Arab-like," while in 1845 a "Notice of New Books" in the same journal claimed that "one of the greatest . . . objections" to annexing Texas was that it would "tend to increase this Tartar spirit." Summing it all up by mixing it all up, the Reverend George F. Pierce told an 1844 meeting of the Alumni Society of Franklin College, in Athens, Georgia, that "the local affections have scarcely had a name, much less a habitation. . . . The homestead has been as the tent of the Ishmaelite—a lodge for a night, and the occupants wayfarers on pilgrimage to an El Dorado long sought but never found."[36] These were not images of mobility as the means to reaching final destinations but of mobility as the directionless wanderings of a doomed culture.

To think it appropriate to compare the planter class of the slaveholding states to such peoples was to call into question the most deeply embedded assumptions about the place of that class in the modern world. For the reformers, as for many other educated slaveholders, nomadic peoples epitomized backward social relations and the inhumane treatment of the natural environment. A distinction between nomadic life (unsettled, savage, ephemeral) and civilized society (rooted, cultured, enduring) was the foundation of the claims made by Alexander Meek and many others that in replacing the Creek and the Choctaw, people like him were no mere grabbers of land but truly agents of history.[37] The people they were replacing, on the other hand, understood as little about the workings of time as they did about the proper nurturing of place. As Governor William Crawford of Georgia expressed the matter, "The savage is careless of the morrow, so long as the necessities of the moment are supplied." In contrast, "the civilized man connects the future with the present, and is unhappy if not permitted to live in both." For the savage, indifference to place wandered alongside ignorance of time. For the civilized, attachment to place marched in step with an understanding of history.[38]

Such assumptions proved increasingly problematic as the planters' fondness for mobility showed little sign of diminishing. That "a wandering people is more or less a barbarous one" remained clear to William Gilmore Simms. So too did the conclusion that "the fate of the North American savage" would be "that of every nomadic nation." Pursuing the logic of his own assumptions, Simms acknowledged that "what is true of them is true of every civilized people that adopts, in whatever degree, their habits."[39] For planters who were supposed to be agents of advance, this adoption of backward ways was as inexcusable as it was inexplicable. Observers like Simms fretted that their own westering ambassadors were not so much replacing savage backwardness as replicating it, not so much progressing to a new age but regressing to a past one.

By the 1840s even Alexander Meek's Italian skies had grown cloudy. The ceaseless greed that so many linked to the settlers' endless restlessness now dominated the view. Driven to explain the bad as well as the good, expansive even in his pessimism, Meek began with the world. Sadly it was no longer, "as it was some six centuries ago, spotted all over, like a tessellated pavement, by a thousand contrarieties of color; by every diversity of purpose and ambition." Now, "from the quays of Liverpool to the cabins on the Oregon, the passion for pelf" had become "the arch monopolist,—the insatiable Neptune that eats up all other Gods." Worse still, the "creeping autocrat" of materialism stalking Meek's new global village found "its firmest home" in the United States. And nowhere more than in Meek's own "proud Southwest." For "do we not find that she is thoroughly engrossed in the paltry passion for pounds and pence," and that the country's people are at their most proficient when displaying "the limited philosophy of the ploughshare and the jackplane, or the degraded cunning of the yardstick and the packing screw?" Meek regretted "how deeply this spirit of utilitarianism, as by courtesy of speech it is called, is ingrained in the very constitution" of the society for which he had such strong feelings and stronger hopes. Samuel Townes's tale of progress also had its darker passages, reflecting his disillusionment with the seeming triumph of the material over matters of the mind and the spirit. In his hope that his study would "serve future readers and historians" can be read his expectation that "the present 'knowing generation'" of "busy currency tinkers, cotton growers, and negro purchasers" would greet it with indifference.[40]

Even the works of the writer who devoted more energy than any other to reconciling mobility and stability often revealed continuing anxieties as much as they offered resolution. The difficulties of merging the defense of land with the defense of slavery, traditional notions of social stability with the levels of mobility required by a modern society, are wonderfully, if inadvertently, illuminated in both the social analysis and historical romances of William Gilmore Simms. At times no one was more forthright than Simms in expressing the fear that Americans in general and southerners in particular lacked the guiding "social principle" and "spirit of place" so necessary to civilized stability and progress.[41] Without them, Simms worried that there could be no hope that emigration would bring forth stable society. Instead, "every remove, of whatever kind, is injurious to social progress; and every remove into the wilderness, lessens the hold which refinement and society have hitherto held up to the individual man." Simms went on to demand "the proofs that we are nobler, gentler, purer, wiser than our ancestors,—for, let me remark—no civilized people can continue stationary!" "The law of civilization," Simms continued, "is a law of progress; to fail in reporting which is a sure sign of retrograde, fatal to all our pretensions, and terrible in its consequences to posterity! These are questions to be answered."[42] If stability in space was a prerequisite of progressive movement through time, what was to be said about such a mobile agricultural elite? Furthermore, what did such restlessness say about those who claimed to be the guardians not only of a civilization but of a "civilizing" civilization. If the temptations of his environment proved no more resistible to the white man than they supposedly did to chattel or Choctaw, where did that leave the planters' claims for a culture built on the exercise of measured control over oneself and others? Like Thomas Spalding in the 1820s, Simms did not sound like a man who expected to find encouraging answers to these questions in the new societies of the Southwest.

Yet Simms was, after all, addressing an audience in Tuscaloosa, Alabama. In ways that suggested something more than the desire to please his hosts, he praised the cultural progress he had witnessed.[43] Indeed it was the energetic and dynamic transforming power of elite emigration that had carved the campus of the University of Alabama from the frontier in so short a time and had made possible the literary society now so eager to honor the region's leading writer. Who was to say that further westward movement to, or from, Alabama might not be productive of more, not less, progress? Was this not the spreading rather than the ebbing of civilization? Nor was Simms's pleasure confined to the demonstrably desirable cultural progress. When it came to economic advance, there too Simms was too much of the modern to disdain the incredible material advance that emigration had also fueled. In this he shared an attitude with many others who over the years had expressed their ambivalence about or antagonism toward elite emigration, yet who had hardly been blind to its creative potential. In his analysis of the evils of emigration and their relation to the extreme individual liberty enjoyed by the planters, Thomas Spalding had long since recognized the revolutionary implications of the freedom his class enjoyed. Spalding might have likened planters' "roving disposition" to that of "the Tartar of the Steppes," but he knew that such an Old World analogy soon lost its force when one looked at the consequences of their mobility. "Without this roving propensity," he believed, "centuries could not have produced the effect that twenty years have accomplished" in spreading a world-serving cotton kingdom across the continent. Spalding, like Simms, had no illusions regarding the revolutionary power of the southern planters' "almost mysterious love" of changing situation and the leadership it afforded them in the transformation of the modern world.[44] That observers from Townes to Meek, Spalding to Simms, found this power so troubling in some of its consequences did not immunize them from the seductive appeal of its revolutionary creativity.

Simms's hope that material dynamism need not mean moral declension, that the willful energy of a youthful society could eventually be tamed to enduring cultural ends, is suggested in another tale of Alabama. In *Richard Hurdis*, one in his series of Border Romances, Simms assigns to his eponymous hero many of the rash characteristics commonly associated with those leaving more easterly locations and attachments. "I was true to the nature and the temperament of my countrymen," claims Richard Hurdis. "The place in which I was born could not keep me always. With manhood—ay, long before I was a man came the desire to range." Hurdis's "thoughts craved freedom, my dreams prompted the same desire, and the wandering spirit of our people, perpetually stimulated by the continual opening of new regions and more promising abodes, was working in my heart with all the volume of a volcano. Manhood came and I burst my shackles." Hurdis's mother is also given a familiar part as she expresses uncomprehending, indignant resistance to her son's wanderlust, demanding to know if "the place you were born in, and the parents who bred you, and the people whom you have lived with all your life" were "not good enough" for the son determined to look for a "better place." Hurdis does indeed leave but after a series of adventures, eventually returns home having also found a greater sense of responsibility on his travels. In the character of Richard Hurdis, Simms revealed his hope that wandering ways might ultimately serve the cause of stationary stability, that the difficulties in reconciling his ideal southern civilization with ubiquitous southern roving would themselves dissolve with the disappearance or diminution of the latter. Yet that this was as much Simms's hope as expectation is perhaps suggested by the extent to which Hurdis's reckless wandering is transformed into rational stability by events rather than intent. In his desire that mobility will not prove intrinsic, Simms also suggests the fear that it will.[45]

Thus the most anxious estimates of the South's future could flow from the pens and lips of those who also proved most bullish about its superior society and boundless prospects. To some extent shifting and contradictory perceptions of mobility and its relation to social change reflected the contradictions and complexities of southwestern society itself. Was mobility a necessary precondition for stable and orderly social progress? Was mobility the sign and source of a reactionary retreat into savage backwardness? Was mobility the outlaw ally of a hypermaterialism that threatened to destroy all that was best in modern civilization as remorselessly and thoroughly as it had overwhelmed native nations and cultures? With mobility so obviously bound up with so many other developments, whether welcome or worrying, whose ultimate consequences remained unknowable, the ambivalence of observers like William Gilmore Simms was perhaps inevitable.

Yet the troubled consciousness of Simms, and of many of his fellow observers, also suggests the inadequacy of the universal assumptions that many elite southerners brought to the task of viewing a society that did not fit those assumptions. It was not the Southwest that was failing to progress. It was the ideas of progress and history employed by Meek, Townes, and others that had failed to come to terms with the particular circumstances of the expanding Cotton Kingdom. As trapped by the narrowness of their understanding of history and progress as their fellow slaveholders appeared to be constrained by their materialistic mania for "cotton and niggers," people like Simms and Meek made foreign by their use of language what should have appeared to them quite familiar and ultimately unthreatening.

Southwest was becoming like Southeast and was no more following the universal laws of history and progress in doing so than the older states of the region had. At the time, however, the contradictory and sometimes confused efforts of the region's analysts to understand southwestern society reflected their doubts about the subject, not about the images and ideas they employed in interpreting it. For many elite southerners the worrying possibility persisted that it was in the figure of the endlessly restless planter that the true "Ænigma" of the southern landscape was to be found.

As a historian, Samuel Townes sought to show that history, understood as progress, should ultimately have only one direction. His private life proved to be anything but reassuringly linear in its direction. Faced with declining wealth and health and finding his frantic efforts to reverse failing fortunes all to no avail, eventually Samuel and Joanna had to face the prospect of moving back to South Carolina. The main stumbling block, as older brother Henry Townes saw it, was Joanna's "reluctance to place herself in an entirely dependent situation." Yet if she was "not soon relieved," Henry believed, Joanna would "die of a broken heart!" Samuel and Joanna Townes eventually admitted defeat. "Our dear afflicted brother," Henry reported to another brother in the summer of 1847, "has at last given up. He & Joanna have struggled on as long as they could with poverty & disease & blindness & when they could no longer help themselves, they turn to us." As Henry called on the family to welcome them with sympathy and magnanimity, he also calculated the cost of their return. It would be "ten times as cheap" to support Samuel and his family in South Carolina as in Alabama, Henry believed, and he sent Samuel thirty dollars to pay for the journey. Two wagons would be best, Henry thought, one for the white family and one "for the servants, with the former also having "a top like a pedlars waggon. This is a very common way of traveling & many worthy families move to town first in such style." [46]

By January 1848 Samuel and Joanna Townes were back in South Carolina, "snug" in their new home and seemingly unperturbed by the recent killing of a neighbor by three slaves who had gone to the gallows "impenitent to the last hour," "cheerfully" convinced that they had struck a blow for liberty, and sure in the faith that they would still find Heaven at their journey's end. As a new year began, Henry Townes wrote to Samuel with the counsel the older brother loved to give, suggesting that Samuel "write a novel & beat Gilmore Simms, which would not be hard to do." [47] Henry Townes was perhaps too busy enjoying his little joke to recognize that his brother's writings already had much in common with those of his more prolific and famous countryman.

In his book Townes seemed both smitten and sickened by the society he had helped to create. Certainly his ambivalence in print reflected a private life that had an ample share of anxiety, anguish, and unfulfilled expectations to go with the pleasures and privileges that elite status brought to him and his family. In private, however, Townes and others tended not to talk much of history and progress when thinking of family and household matters. They found different ideas and other categories through which to enjoy and endure the equally conflicted and contradictory nature of life viewed from more circumscribed perspectives than the panoramic vistas of the social analyst. It is to that language and those beliefs that we now turn, and to the question of whether they proved any more successful in bringing the slaveholding elite to a fuller understanding either of the anxious and fractious society they were creating or of mobility's ubiquitous and ambiguous role in that creation.

6 A Household with a View: The Social Landscape

In memory of William Lumpkin who died December 17th, 1840, aged 60 years. Virginia gave him life, Georgia, wealth, honor, and friends, Mississippi a grave. Blessed are the dead who die in the Lord for their end is peace.
— Gravestone epitaph in the Lumpkin family cemetery, Athenia plantation, Mississippi

IN 1855 J. S. LITTLE WROTE TO JAMES MILLING FROM Rakepocket, Texas, with a picture postcard in words of the countryside through which he had been journeying. Little and Milling had met on their travels and, before separating at Waco, had agreed to write one another with accounts of their further adventures. On his "tour" through Texas, Little was especially struck by "the most beautiful landscape scene" he encountered at "the junction" of the Brazos and "Noulands" (probably the Nolan, a small tributary of the Brazos) Rivers. The Brazos was "red with the recent rise—wending its way around spurs of mountains & through valleys of greenest verdure," while walls of "massive rock" rose on either side of the other stream "to a sublime height, like huge Cyclopian battlements of olden story." In "the awe and ectasy of my soul," Little asked God if his works were "so grand & magnificent" in "derision of man's boasted monuments, his fortress & his towers." Little acknowledged that his "graphic powers" fell back "prostrate" before a scene that would require "the discriptive fancy of a Scott or the graphic genius of an Osian" to give the reader "the slightest touch of an idea off its sublimity."[1]

But Little was brought back to earth by more than modesty. For if the countless men who traveled the Southwest in these decades did so as individuals, they often journeyed as the explorer-emissaries of eastern households. Recognizing that it was not "the wandering vageries of a visionary enthusiast" that Milling wanted but the "common sense description of a passing observer," Little also provided a detailed account of the country's suitability for settlement. He told not only of places where "the valleys are too narrow & timber too scarce" and lands "as desolate & drear as shahara" but also of prairie land that, even if unsuited to "large cotton planters," would make "a poor man's paradise."[2] Even as this transported traveler viewed the Southwest as the creation of God, he journeyed with a practical eye for the places where humans like himself might dwell, surveying as he went the pathways and barriers to the region's transformation at the hands of earthly masters.

Little allowed himself the luxury of thoughts appropriate to the solitary romantic wanderer, but he also echoed the masters' mantra of household priority articulated by Charles Tait back in the 1810s: "Have in mind at all times the unity of Fertility, Salubrity, & Navigation."[3] These were categories dictated by the requirements of staple agriculture for a soil able to nourish cotton or sugar; a climate to assist in their cultivation while not incapacitating or killing too many of their cultivators, black and white; and waterways to facilitate their transportation to the wider world. But these were more than agricultural categories. The search for fertility, salubrity, and navigation spoke also to the emigrants' intermingled desires for comfort, health, family growth, and social connectedness.

Just as their households shaped the planters' understanding of their departure, so too did they provide the ideological observation platform from which the travelers formed their impressions of their new environment. The view from the household could be very different from those offered by the storyteller, booster, or critic. If truth be told, it often came closer to "common sense description" than to the "wandering vageries of a visionary enthusiast." Yet as Little's words suggest, such accounts in their own way could blend the poetic and the practical to create images of a region both otherworldly and yet eminently suitable for human settlement.

Views from the household were also more varied, for the female voices to be heard in the pages of private correspondence far outnumbered the occasional published words of a Mary Holley. In private communications slaveholding women and girls wrote countless words from and to the Southwest. The plantation household's diverse composition made for a variety of observations that tell of new places and new lives but also speak of the existing habits and beliefs that infused those observations. A similar vantage point did not necessarily make for similar responses to new surroundings. Particularly between men and women there were important differences of emphasis when it came to weighing up the pitfalls and possibilities of new surroundings. Ultimately, however, different impressions of the landscape spoke to a shared understanding of how it must be transformed. The different ways in which male and female planters responded to new lands revealed a shared commitment to transforming place in the cause of establishing the familiar relations of kinship and ownership at the heart of the plantation household and plantation society.

For those arriving in the Southwest, especially in relatively unsettled areas, first thoughts were often of how the landscape might transform them. That such thoughts could inspire both hope and trepidation is suggested by the vivid early impressions of Alabama left by various members of the Lide family. James Lide had left his plantation on the Pee Dee River in South Carolina and arrived in Carlowville, Alabama, in the winter of 1835, with numerous members of his household drawn from three generations of families, black and white. Maria Lide, sixteen years old, liked her new environment "better than any place" she had seen. She enjoyed being "surrounded by very tall trees, mostly oaks and chesnuts" but also "a few pines." She was also glad that her new home was nevertheless quite close to the Montgomery-to-Mobile road. Maria thought it "a right pretty place," while the strawberry plants growing wild around her new home suggested "what a rich country it is." Maria's niece Frances Jane Lide told not only of the "strawberrys . . . growing all over the woods" but also of last year's peaches that new neighbors said were as large as two fists, all to be washed down with the "delicious water" to be found in the neighborhood's springs. Impressed with its abundance and grandeur, Frances found that she too "like[d] the country a great deal better than I expected . . . the hills are almost like mountains you can stand on the top and look over and every thing looks blue you can see a great way off." Frances also told of having "learnt pretty well how to ride on horse back since we have been out here. I can ride on a mans saddle and go down a steep hill as well as I could on a side saddle in South Carolina."[4]

Her widowed aunt, Sarah Lide Fountain, saw Nubbin Ridge through dimmer, more careworn eyes, feeling "very much confined," what "with the cotton field on one side and a very thick woods up to the fence on the other." There was "no shade except some peach and apple trees around the houses, (which are loaded with fruit) but they afford very little shade. We have a pretty good spring convenient, but rather a steep hill to rise." For the older woman Nubbin Ridge was a place of sacrifice and constraint rather than a field of indulgence or adventure. Fountain emphasized not the hill's panoramic potential but its challenge to those who had to carry, not just taste, the sweet water of its springs. The bountiful fruit so astonishing to the young girls was a mere aside to one in need of the shade the fruit trees proved less generous in providing. She found the forest depths confining rather than awe-inspiring, the lack of settled society an isolating experience rather than a welcome opportunity to ride like the boys. Like many women Sarah Fountain feared she would "never become reconciled to my move unless a considerable change should take place, but I wish to be resigned, and try and content myself as well as possible, hoping that it will turn out for good in the end."[5]

Eli Lide seemed closer to the girls than the women in his estimation of the new country. After some grumbling about an incompetent overseer, Lide offered his brother-in-law a "peep at what I call the bright side." He excitedly informed Caleb Coker back in South Carolina of the "natural scenery which is grand and sublime, entirely superior to anything I saw on the Blue Ridge," and of soil so rich "it would do your heart good to look at it." In insisting that "our society here is fully equal to yours," Lide also emphasized those aspects of the new country—"better health and infinitely better water, together with greater facilities of navigation"—most conducive to its transformation in the interests of household productivity.[6]

Such images and responses were recorded all across the Deep South during the first half of the century. Those with the fewest responsibilities, like Maria Lide, could afford the most expansive of horizons. Household duties lowered the gaze of adults. Yet as women's tales of spartan living vied with men's reports of fertile soils, the words of settlers like Eli Lide and Sarah Fountain suggest different perspectives on the places that had drawn them west. The outer boundaries of these diverging opinions are revealed in responses from within another family. Henry and Maria Marshall moved west in 1837, drawn from the quiet civilization of Society Hill, South Carolina, where perhaps they had known Caleb and Hannah Coker, to the silent isolation of northern Louisiana. For Henry Marshall the attraction was the land and its future promise. "So much rich land," the young man believed, "must make a society." Maria Marshall's mother, who, with her husband, had traveled west to help the young couple set up home, saw things a little differently. "You have brought us to the end of the land!" Mary Taylor is reported to have told her son-in-law.[7] Whether describing a new world or the edge of the world, initial appraisals of abundance and emptiness spoke of the different temporal perspectives that men and women brought to their expectations of southwestern transformation. Men looked to an unbounded future of profit and honor. Women saw the restricting surroundings of the here and now.

Men hoped to see familiar society re-created on a higher plane, a possibility held out by a fertile land of opportunity. Those who operated the "business" side of the household understood that nature's abundance was initially a barrier to planting, especially in the early stages of settling unimproved lands. But that same abundance was the source of planter men's hopes that they could eventually live the planting ideal in ways denied them by declining eastern soils. Abner Nash, an emigrant from Georgia, eagerly acknowledged the pleasures afforded him by his new Louisiana sugar plantation. He told Salem, Georgia, resident William Graham that "if I ware to attempt to give you all the advantages of this country it would take two much time and if I ware to attempt to speeke of its disadvantages I doant know what I should say." Nash marveled at the country's "vast quantities of Horses, Cattle, and Sheepe that raise without being ever fed" and have "their young at all seasons of the year." He described the always abundant orange groves and the "fine Fishing creeks" filled with turtles and oysters, where he could catch "more fish in one day than would supply Salem for a weeke." The fishing news from Alabama, where catfish weighing from twenty to sixty pounds were reportedly to be found, was equally promising, as it was from western Florida, where Robert Charles found "rivers bursting out full grown at their source . . . & streams so transparent that the fish at the greatest depths could not conceal themselves, but appeared sporting in such numbers as I have never before seen except in dreams of angling." J. J. Seibels of Montgomery told his father, John, in Columbia, South Carolina, of a hog in the neighborhood "that weighs the enormous & almost incredible amount of 1311 pounds . . . it is the greatest sight I ever saw; the legs are perceptible only when lying down, & the whole body seems to drag along on the ground." Perhaps it was hardly surprising that the hog could "scarcely walk," having been raised on a constant diet of "ginger-bread & milk." The West, it seemed, was truly a land of milk and honey, even for the pigs.[8]

Similar reports reverberated around the South, communicating the prevailing sense that elite travelers and emigrants had happened upon a land where the normal rules of nature had been suspended. Even better, natural abundance could easily be transformed into a source of agricultural wealth. Describing the eastern bank of the Mississippi River as "the richest section of country" he had ever seen, John Sims told his cousin in Union District, South Carolina, of the locals' claims that they could "make two crops of corn, in one year off of the same field." And with cotton "as high as I can reach," Sims thought it "the greatest country for making money I *ever* saw." In western fields many men like Sims hoped to translate nature's riches into household wealth. In assessing the potential for doing so, western settlers and visitors often drew comparisons with the East (especially, of course, when communicating with those who toiled in more unyielding fields). Abner Nash told his Georgia friend William Graham of land that could be cultivated for a hundred years and still "be as good as ever." Such land could make its owner more money in three Louisiana years than in twenty years of toil in Georgia.[9]

For those accustomed to long years of making Carolina and Georgia money, here indeed appeared to be a new life in the fullest sense of that term. According to his son Eli, the sixty-five-year-old James Lide believed that he had "better prospects before him *now*, than he ever had, and that a man might live here clear and above board." The father was "fully as well pleased with the country" as the son, who in turn was "very much diverted" by observing its impact on the older man. "Father . . . is indeed the most busy man you ever saw, . . . all the time among his negroes in the field and . . . as active about his business as he could be at eighteen," marveled the younger Lide. "He seems to have forgotten that he is old."[10]

Many observers believed it was the prospect of riches that put the spring in the step of men like James Lide. And few planters would have denied the importance of profit as a central standard by which to take the new land's measure. Yet in many ways men's responses to the land reflected awestruck appreciation as well as heedless avarice. When Eli Lide saw the years fall from his father as he toiled among his slaves or when Abner Nash looked out on fields that could not fail for a hundred years, they saw the opportunity not only for profit but for the honor so often linked to it in planter rhetoric. This was not so much the public honor of duels fought or offices won but rather the reassurance and respect derived from meeting the objectives and obligations expected of successful planters. Meeting these expectations did not preclude making a profit. Indeed, as the planters' own frequent twinning of profit and honor shows, the two were inseparable.

As with the planters' reasons for moving in the first place, then, a clear desire to make a good living was shaped by a certain vision of the good life that economic success would allow. Men were absorbed both by the effort to meet new planting and professional duties and by the prospect that success in those endeavors promised a more authentic adherence to planting as a way of life as well as a way of making a living. Blending desire for profit and honor, feelings of greed and gratitude, emigrant men focused on the transforming effect of land as a key to the success they envisioned. Planter men would prove to be misguided in their expectation that new lands would allow them to make a reality of their own particular agricultural ideal. Their very success in re-creating the human relations of plantation slavery would ensure that hopes of a closer, longer-lasting attachment to land and place would not develop.

In the first flush of early-settlement enthusiasm, however, many planter men hoped that place would transform people. For their part, planter women could only hope that one day people would transform place. If men believed nature's bounty would never be exhausted, women feared that it would never be mastered. From a starting point of social emptiness, women considered the re-creation of basic domestic comforts a distant goal. Few women were as blunt in their estimation of southwestern places as Mary Taylor, who described northern Louisiana's leading urban center as "that *rathole* Shreveport." [11] Many did express their concern that making the places of the Southwest fit for civilized habitation would be a work of long duration.

The Lides' initial impressions reveal the discrepancy between the potent land and the puny structures they raised upon it. The Lides lived at first in "a double log house with a very narrow passage and but one chimney." Maria Lide reported that although the dwelling was "considered quite a comfortable one for this country," it had "a great many air holes." Inside there was no table, requiring the family to take the door down at mealtimes and set it up in the passageway. Although there were beds, they were made "out of little saplins" by the Lide menfolk. Sarah Lide Fountain supported her sister's account of the basic conditions of their early home, telling their sister Hannah Coker that "the rooms are small and open, there are cracks where the joists go in almost large enough for a dog to go through but they answer for windows as we have no others." The absence of regular windows made it "almost impossible to see to sew" when it was cloudy. Sarah Fountain could report that "we have pretty good out-buildings except negrohouses and Pa is making preparations to build them." Meanwhile the slaves were "still in their tents." [12]

In Texas, English emigrant Anne Coleman had to sleep in the same bed with the couple she was visiting, even though they were wealthy enough to put thirty enslaved hands in the fields surrounding their rough cabin. Propriety was maintained at least to some extent by the wife's sleeping in the middle. Nevertheless, for Coleman the scene offered striking evidence for how absorption in the business of the household had eclipsed concern for its inner comforts. There could only be one explanation for such unbalanced priorities: "To make money was their chief object, all things else were subsidiary to it." [13] For many women such physically unfamiliar and demanding circumstances could only have compounded familiar anxieties about their ability to meet the responsibilities of a plantation mistress.

Yet women's sadness at leaving behind much of what they valued only fueled their desire to rebuild the structures of slaveholding life and society, however unpropitious the ground might initially appear. Their efforts took many forms. Women's ability to alter their physical environment was limited. Not usually directly involved in refashioning forests into fields, women concentrated on smaller areas closer to home in their efforts to remake the wilderness. Some tried to re-create part of their surroundings with transplanted cuttings from back east. Sarah Gayle told her uncle she would "like greatly to have mulberry trees from those in Grandpah's yard" and "should feel a sad pleasure in planting over pah's grave, some of the trees under which he played in childhood." Serena Lea planted cedar seedlings and iris bulbs from Virginia around her Alabama home.[14] Such efforts might suggest a psychological desire to cordon off their own horticultural havens in the heartless, market-driven maelstrom whipped up by their menfolk. But Gayle's and Lea's small efforts to transform place spoke to larger desires to transcend space through investing new places with the feel and the presence of people separated from them by death or distance.

Living conditions usually improved over time, allowing women like Sarah Gayle of Alabama to look back to frontier conditions with something like nostalgia. In remembering "the dear little log cabins, thro' the openings of which the very birds might fly," now being rapidly replaced by "comfortable brick and framed dwellings," [15] Gayle showed more affection than most women for the rough-and-ready circumstances of early settlement. Yet other women's diaries and letters suggest that many women were less troubled by the physical discomfort of the frontier than by the psychological and social isolation that often lasted long past early settlement. For emigrants like Sarah Fountain, who believed there was "still a breach and ever will be unless yours our dear brothers and uncles families were here," the greatest distress was felt in the silences created by separation from family members who had not moved. Like many women, Martha Gaston measured her growing attachment to western lands by counting the increasing numbers of relatives who shared it with her. Gaston found herself becoming "pretty much attached" to Alabama and "more attached to my brothers and sisters than ever I felt before." Gaston believed she "would be willing to make it the place of my residence if my parents and other brothers were here." Conversely, back in Elbert County, Georgia, Lucy Clark wrote to her departed friend Caroline Tait that "since you have all left me, I can assure you Georgia has but few charms." Clark thought that she would "be very happy to be a close neighbor to you, in the Alabama, provided I could have my children all with me." Old places no longer seemed like home in the absence of the people who had given them meaning.[16] The more that new places became inhabited by familiar people, in person or in spirit, the more they resembled places that could be called home.

Isolation was always relative. All women at least could expect to travel with their own immediate family, and many, like the Lides, traveled in much larger intergenerational groups. Others chose points of settlement in part because of the prior settlement of friends or relatives. Samuel and Joanna Townes settled only five miles from his sister Eliza despite, or perhaps because of, Samuel's hatred for his abusive brother-in-law. Yet family was only one aspect of women's search for community. Planter women also felt the absence of the other collectives—of schoolmates for their children and fellow congregants for themselves—that formed the social fabric and carried women's lives beyond their own households. Although there was no "school in reach," Sarah Fountain hoped one would be established by the spring of 1836. She thought, too, that her South Carolina relatives would "be astonished" to hear "that we have not been to preaching since we have been here." Her father and brother had gone out in search of some preaching "last Sabbath" but "in vain." On the other hand, itinerant preachers sometimes searched with little success for worshipers. James L. Sloss reported in 1818 to the Presbytery of South Carolina that he was uncertain as to whether his "missionary labours" in the West had "been very useful." He had usually preached to "small but serious congregations"; most of the people in the area were "new settlers, and they seemed to think it necessary that every hour should be employed in preparing for next year's crop." To many, the priorities of planting were stunting the growth of the wider associations considered central to a settled society.[17] As they looked to a future Southwest defined by the quality of its relations rather than the level of its luxuries, Gayle, Fountain, and Gaston spoke for women whose priority was the knitting together of the webs of practical and psychological support that had surrounded them in the East.

In words describing new places, the men and women of the planter class revealed their expectations and anxieties regarding the impact of movement on relations between people. Differing emphases on absence and abundance, kin and commerce, domesticity and dominion, were frequently on display. A letter of advice from Sarah Gayle, for example, written to relatives considering emigration, followed a common pattern. Gayle's advice for her aunt Elizabeth Haynsworth was brief. She "must prepare to meet very different fare to that to which she has been accustomed," Gayle cautioned her uncle to tell her. "Our country is new yet, and has the wildness, with the freshness of youth about it," admitted Gayle, warning that her aunt would "find but little polish, little style, and where pretensions are made to it, it does appear to me to be awkward." In contrast, her response to William Haynsworth's request for advice on "the best spot" to settle proved far more expansive. Prefacing her comments with the disclaimer that her uncle "could not possibly have applied to one who could give you less information," Gayle then entered into a lengthy and informed discussion of the opportunities for professional and planting advancement open to him. Gayle had "little doubt" that her uncle would do well pursuing the profession of the law in a state with "few leading members of the bar." But no matter the lawyering opportunities, Gayle insisted that Haynsworth should also acquire a plantation. She even had "a place in view" for her uncle on the Alabama River. A proposed railroad terminus promised business opportunity, while the location could also "boast having the celebrated cane brake for a neighbor . . . full of rich planters." Information for the woman was presented in terms of narrowed access to what she would recognize as civilized standards. Information for the man was couched in terms of expanded opportunity compared to the East. Talk of her expectations stressed the hard struggle for domestic development in unpromising circumstances. Talk of his prospects emphasized the ongoing conquest of space.[18]

Whatever her professed modesty, Gayle clearly took a keen and informed interest in the affairs of "the man's world" on which she advised her uncle. Indeed her knowledge of the "other" sphere contradicts her assumption that her aunt would, or should, only be interested in the difficulties of domesticity rather than the possibilities of public life. Numerous letters like Gayle's show that at least when it came to interest rather than action, public and private spheres were far from impermeable. Joanna Townes looked forward to household success in what the planters understood as the public realm. Townes anticipated that her husband's first appearance at Bibb County Courthouse would offer "evidence of the station he will one day (& not far distant) fill in the world's estimation. That it will be *all* that even *we* could wish, *I will answer for.*" Never having seen her husband "in better health & spirits" or participating as "actively" in "the business of life & his profession," Townes felt sure her husband would "be the *Patrick Henry* of Alabama." Reporting to her father-in-law, Farish Carter, on the progress of his relatives in Union Springs, Alabama, Mary Carter also divided her discussion of household affairs into male and female spheres while nevertheless revealing her close knowledge of both. She reported on a cotton crop that appeared, according to her husband, James Carter, and her father, N. B. Powell, "unusually fine." She expressed concern about the cold weather and reported on recent news from Montgomery that told of already falling cotton prices expected to go lower still. Women like Carter, Townes, and Gayle ordered household news into different spheres of expertise and responsibility. At the same time they revealed their familiarity with the affairs of both. Women knew about public and business affairs because they heard of and discussed elections and sales and bales per slave at the dinner table, on the porch, in bed, in their correspondence.[19]

Women's interest in planting and politics derived from their awareness that the kinds of household progress for which they were primarily responsible depended in great part on how well the master met his responsibilities both within and beyond the household. Differing male and female perspectives and priorities in the present nevertheless made for a shared vision of future domestic and social development. This was especially true for those who were among the first to settle in a new place. In those circumstances untrammeled and abundant nature stood, physically and figuratively, as a wall between planter women and their idea of civilization. If that wall was to come down, female desires and male priorities would have to pull together. The remaking of the landscape in the interests of growing and selling cotton would also mean its remaking in the image of the eastern communities characterized by the kinds of human relations that planter women valued above all else. Women pursued their own visions of transformation no less implacably for their main means of doing so being other people: their men and their slaves. Yet the horticultural efforts of women like Sarah Gayle and Serena Lea to make western gardens with carefully nurtured cuttings from distant locations possessed a symbolism that far exceeded their physical impact. These efforts represented neither a desire to live in harmony with the wilderness nor the need to carve from it a domesticated retreat. Rather than an attempted rapprochement with nature, far less any kind of innate affinity with it, such efforts can be seen as part of planter women's wish to shape new places in the interests of establishing the kinds of relations between people upon which the power and prosperity of their class depended. Indeed it is difficult to imagine a more quietly impressive statement of imperialist intent than the carrying of one's own plants and trees into an already luxuriant western "wilderness."[20]

If women were acutely mindful that plantation households had to be successful centers of labor and trade, many men acknowledged that households had to grow as homes and that towns had to develop as social, and not just commercial, centers. Whatever their initial priorities, most men hoped that domestic comfort and social advance would come to accompany planting and professional success. They did so in part because they understood that their own public standing was affected by perceptions of their private circumstances. They also understood the importance of such progress to the women of the household and, therefore, to the ultimate success of the household.

Samuel Townes regretted the lack of progress in his domestic situation. Although Joanna "goes with me to a boarding house with cheerfulness," she did so "above all bouyed up with the hope that we shall soon have a house of our own and all those little comforts which constitute the charm of life and can only be found in one's own home."[21] Less apologetically perhaps, Henry Marshall wryly suggested that his mother-in-law, Mary Taylor, "would scarcely recognize Ratborough," such had been the rapidity of Shreveport's "improvement."[22] The hint of regional pride in Marshall's words sounded more loudly in the descriptions offered by other men. In the early days of settlement, Eli Lide had focused on the natural benefits afforded by his new neighborhood. A few years later he could take pride in the advancing institutions of the state, going so far as to suggest that his Carolinian relatives should send their children to Alabama to be educated.[23] Benjamin Hormon in Rochester, Louisiana, told Zachary Meriwether that "our country is becoming literly filled up with good citizens and many of them wealthy so that facilities of all kinds are accumulating around us."[24] Men certainly understood that "good citizens" could also be economic competitors. But they too looked to a time when southwestern settlement would be dense enough to provide the pleasures as well as the necessities of plantation society.

Blended together, the diverse priorities of planter men and women reveal their shared understanding of what a developed plantation society would look like. As ruling civilizations go, it was a conception modest enough to win awards for asceticism in most other times and places. An accurate, and appropriate, composite sketch of this society is to be found in a plantation-for-sale advertisement placed in the *Christian Index* of Washington, Georgia, by James Burke of Amsterdam, Mississippi. Burke lauded the "very superior" soil of his eight-hundred-acre plantation, its proximity to water (in the shape of Baker's Creek and "many fine springs") and to transportation (half a mile from the Vicksburg-to-Clinton railroad), and, of course, the "remarkably healthy" nature of the area. Burke also emphasized the proximity of the religious centers so important to a class with Christian principles and responsibilities. There were Baptist, Methodist, and Presbyterian churches within reasonable distance, in all of which "the Black population is favored with the preaching of the Gospel." That there were three temperance societies "in the vicinity" and "no grog shop within several miles," certainly "none sufficiently convenient to contaminate the morals and injure the negroes," was a bonus for those seeking to make a world safe for slavery.[25]

The description of James Burke's plantation reveals a social ideal in which the natural is brought into the service of a community built upon ordered relations among people and allowing for the harmonious blending of personal and public interest and of material and spiritual progress. Surely less ideal in action than in advertising, plantations like Burke's nevertheless increasingly dotted the southwestern landscape by the time he wrote in 1836. They represented, in the minds of many recent settlers, the successful transformation of social ideal into facts on the southwestern ground.

Eli Lide boasted of social advance as well as agricultural abundance as soon as circumstances allowed. Many emigrants followed his example. Even those most impressed with the social emptiness of new places were quick to comment on signs of social advance. Sarah Fountain felt the isolation from kin and congregation, but she also welcomed secular progress in the shape of the "steam-saw-mill" that would "be a great acquisition to the neighbourhood." And "if old cousin Nancy Lide," the wife of Eli, "would help us to some of her cash (as she has it so plenty) we could soon have a good Church." [26] A pleasant edifice for regular worship would be nice, but it would have greater significance as the sign of a congregation now sufficiently large to warrant a house of worship. A sawmill was source and symbol of greater levels of domestic comfort and architectural attractiveness. Churches, however, were centers of spiritual support and indicators of social consolidation.

Often these descriptions were intended to encourage easterners to visit or to remove permanently. Henry and Serena Lea were among the many emigrants who wrote frequent letters encouraging relatives to join them, as settlers themselves or at least as visitors. Much epistolary energy was given to allaying fears that a western visit would be one of danger and discomfort. Henry Lea jokingly asked if his relatives felt the need of protection or if they feared falling sick. If so, Alabama had doctors trained in America and Europe. Yet Lea also acknowledged that he might not be entirely free from the tendency to exaggerate that seemed endemic to the new regions, especially at that expectant time of year when "crops are now ripe and fine as fancy can make them." Just like the published works of the boosters, then, private letters needed to be read with significant skepticism. [27]

Often, however, vivid portrayals of daily life seemed to speak of genuine contentment. Samuel Townes, for example, offered an especially idyllic portrait of pastoral bliss and tranquil retreat in a letter he wrote in the spring of 1843. On a Sunday morning, with everyone else at church, Townes undertook the no less sacred duty of writing to his mother. Not knowing when he had "felt so homeish," he described to Rachel Townes "the balmy breath of Spring, the joyous birds, the budding trees, the gay flowers and my little Sam in full and eager chase of butter flies." Townes compared his son's play to that of his father and grandfather in "years and years gone by, in the days of their childhood and innocence" when they too "amused themselves, careless of the morrow and unconscious of the cares and pleasures that lie in store for him in the future." New children could give deeper meaning to new homes in the West by encouraging a sense of continuity with other childhoods spent in other times and places.[28] Samuel Townes's image of a happy, self-contained moment in an Alabama garden and James Burke's advertisement of the ideal plantation both spoke to the emigrants' success in replicating in the West the most desirable aspects of slaveholding life and society. The Burke place embodied the elevated circumstances that emigrating men and women of the planter class sought as well as the rapidity with which their efforts were bearing fruit.

Innumerable images in countless letters told of the growing cohesion and consolidation of plantation society in the Southwest. Such images were also among the many powerful connections continuing to bind Southwest and Southeast. These connections were about more than communication, about more than keeping in touch. They were essential to the creation of the kinds of households and communities that men and women like the Taits and the Gayles and the Burkes desired. Burke's plantation and Townes's garden were created by the efforts of the emigrants, certainly. But their creation must also be understood as a consequence of the continuing ties between eastern and western households and societies.[29]

Of great importance to this interregional cohesion was mobility of a different kind from emigration: the back-and-forth mobility of letters and mementos, of people and property. Emigrants sought to preserve ties by means of material objects of psychological and sentimental importance. Of all the presents sent to Marianne Gaillard in Alabama, "there is not one I prize so much as the precious relic" of her "brother's traveling journal." Mary Strother Means told her sister-in-law, Mary Hart Means, that her new baby "looks beautifully in all of the things" sent out from South Carolina and that "he looks sometimes like your family, sometimes like mine." As time and technology moved on, the daguerreotype image became a popular way to maintain contact across great distances. Martha Means was to tell her mother that "as soon as we can, we will have our little boys likeness taken and sent to her." After fourteen years apart from her brother, Marianne Gaillard was surprised to see that he "looked much older" in the portrait he had sent. Nevertheless she would "prize it very much," she assured him. "You could not have sent me anything that would have pleased me better."[30] In countless such cases visual images introduced new loves or "little strangers" to those far away or revealed the changes wrought by time on faces long unseen.

Among the most powerful points of contact and connection sustaining the planter class in places old and new were the very letters that now provide such rich resources for those who would know something of the slaveholders' thoughts and lives. People like the Townes family filled pages with powerful images of everything from child's play to the agonizing death throes of distant loved ones. Such sketches intimately captured moments otherwise quickly passing or preserved by mere memory alone, but now made timeless by the decision to render them in words for other people in other places.

Nothing short of the permanent settlement of friends and family, of course, could outdo visits from actual people. Appeals for visits, news of them when they took place, and regret when, as was often the case, they failed to take place filled the letters that passed back and forth across the Deep South states. Many women found the joy they hoped for in the arrival of friends and relatives. The arrival of long-known people could help to ameliorate anxious perceptions of new places. A visit, especially a first one, could invest homes in the West with greater significance, conferring legitimacy or generating familiarity. Serena Lea thought she would be "better satisfied with my own home now those dear ones have been at it." Now that her Georgia relatives had visited, Lea felt that she would "like my friends better because they have seen them, and even the very rooms and chairs seem dearer to me because they have been occupied by them." [31] Visiting relatives could invest new places with greater meaning, providing emigrants with the reassuring knowledge that at least some in the East could now picture them as clearly in their new surroundings in Alabama or Mississippi as they themselves could imagine family and friends in South Carolina or Georgia.

The hope of a visit could itself connect people separated by space. In 1835 Robert Charles of Mount Meigs, Alabama, was in high and forward-looking spirits in the wake of his daughter's birth and some "advantageous" land purchases that had left him and his brother-in-law, Thomas Taylor, holding "two thousand or more acres of prairie land up on Line Creek." He also was pleased that an earlier visit to Alabama "had left so favourable an impression" on his correspondent, Peter Bacot of Darlington, South Carolina. Charles lived "constantly in the hope" that they would "again live in neighbouring juxtaposition drinking many a sparkling glass & smoking many a genuine Havanna together." At the very least, he hoped that frequent visits would be possible "when the mechanical genius of the age shall have achieved its last great triumph over opposing space" and "a continuous chain of Rail Road" would run between Montgomery and Columbia.[32]

As Charles's letter indicates, while visits were nice, there was nothing to beat having friends and family decide to become permanent neighbors. The desire for further emigration was especially strong among women. The same desires that fed regret at departure from familiar surroundings fueled planter women's determination to re-create similar surroundings as soon as possible. Nothing would contribute to this more than the steady arrival of more neighbors to visit, more friends to attend school with, more believers to worship with. Sarah Fountain was among many for whom the gloom of isolation lifted somewhat as she found it "cheering indeed to see so many of our friends and relatives coming to this country." Often resistant to their own removal, women became the stoutest advocates of the removal of others.[33]

The prospect of a close relative settling permanently nearby made Serena Lea, for example, almost frantic with anticipation. "In a state of nervous excitement ever since" hearing of her brother Jacqueline Rootes's arrival in Athens from Virginia, it was Serena's heartfelt hope that he would continue on to Marion, not only to visit but to settle there with his family. "I have always felt," she explained, "that we should be together." Nothing, she believed "would contribute so much to my happiness." Lea also felt sure that the presence of her brother and his family would "contribute more to the restoration of my health than all the Doctors I could have." Yet Lea felt that moving west would greatly benefit her brother too. She repeatedly insisted that Jacqueline could "do much better in Alabama than either in Virginia or Georgia," and that her husband would "exert himself to the uttermost" to help him. "Brother Jacqueline must come," she wrote. "It would almost kill me for him to return to Virginia."[34] Such appeals connected people across the distance even as they looked to a time when distance would no longer separate.

Continuing connections also could, of course, be sources of grief and pain. Familiar kinds of relations were maintained and restored for ill as well as good. Samuel Townes's pleasure at his son's youthful carelessness of adult tomorrows, for example, was clearly genuine. Yet even as he suggested his ability to establish a haven of respite within the garden, Townes set his son's play against the backdrop of the anxious, often callous world beyond it. In this world continuities were harder to cling to, adult pursuits more likely to end in unforeseen and unwanted outcomes. The problems and tensions inherent in continuing relations between Southwest and Southeast often proved just as important in preserving those connections.

Scenes from another Marion garden suggest the all-too-human reality that family bonds could be at their strongest when at their most distressing. One late summer night in the year 1840, Serena and Henry Lea watched the brother whose visits they had longed for wander drunkenly in the garden that his sister had planted with gentler eastern exports. Talking "incessantly & incoherently" and acting like a child, "vacant & wild," Jacqueline Rootes could rave "all blessed night" according to his disgruntled night watchman, Henry Lea. In the Leas' case emigrants' hopes that the arrival of familiar faces would transform place for the better proved tragically misplaced. From "the very moment of first seeing him," Henry Lea explained, "it was obvious that he was intemperate." Jacqueline Rootes's drinking problem brought many upsets and problems to the Lea household. His early appeals for medicinal "toddies" grew increasingly insistent, sometimes angry, intensifying a dilemma of both private and public dimensions for the family. If they met his demands, they would be contributing to the sickness and possible destruction of a loved one. Yet, as Henry Lea explained, "if he failed to get what he wanted here he would return with the evidence very soon of having had enough at some other place or tavern."[35] The public visibility of her family's anguish "mortified" Serena Lea. She now felt "ashamed to show my face" in front of the friends who had heard so much about the brother who at long last had arrived "only to render himself ridiculous."[36]

Far from adding love and productivity to the Lea household, Jacqueline would make only the customary contribution of the hopeless drunk: shame, disruption, pain, and doctor's bills. As he drank "up town" and at home, Jacqueline's mental and physical health declined; "his digestive powers were completely destroyed" and his bowels in a "desperate situation." His last lost weekend began with him "seeing" a man in his room on Thursday night. The following evening he felt well enough, with Henry Lea away on business, to go "up town." Not being "a child to be ruled by women," he dismissed his wife's and sister's offers to make toddies at home. He went out and "drank until he could scarcely get home." On Saturday night he raved in the garden while Henry Lea, back home again, watched. On Sunday "he appeared better" and "slept soundly" that night, waking only once to call for the lamp that had just gone out to be relit. He awoke the next morning, had some water, went back to bed, and asked for a julep. They made him one, and he drank it. A few hours later "he was gone . . . without struggle as easy as an infant going to sleep." Dr. Fletcher, who attended him in his last moments, said he had never seen a more complete wreck.[37]

His wife Emily proved to be the silver lining in the otherwise dark clouds brought west by Jacqueline Rootes. The never-before-seen sister-in-law stayed on in Marion to provide much of the aid, solace, and family feeling hoped for from the idealized Jacqueline. Her contributions to the household were as unforeseen as was Jacqueline's disruption of it. In time she would marry again and permanently join a community she might never have dreamed of, let alone visited, had it not been for the impatient entreaties of a lonely sister to a brother back in the East. She thus became another strand in the expanding web of southwestern society.[38]

Numerous letters and journeys back and forth told tales of human relations entangling in ways that were often unexpected, frequently unhappy, and at times violent. Sometimes it was the havens that were heartless, as the Townes family well knew. Their hopes that emigration to Alabama would improve their sister Eliza Blassingame's marital circumstances had proved fleeting. After a period of hope, her husband had returned to his alcoholic and abusive ways. Eventually some of the brothers still in South Carolina traveled west, where, with Samuel Townes, they gave "the Beast," as Townes called Blassingame, a severe beating. Afterwards, according to Townes, his "vagabond kin" was "disposed to be as friendly and fawning as . . . a newly-whiped dog." Blassingame's head was "as bare as a pumpkin in several places" as a result of the beating, while "one of his sores suppurates yet a little." "Are you not glad to hear it?" Samuel asked his brother Henry in South Carolina. Samuel felt it "unnecessary" to ask "whether mother approbates our conduct. I know she does." Henry Townes knew too. He was "particularly pleased to be informed that it is E.'s and your own opinion that the whipping you boys gave B. will add to the peace contentment & happiness of his family." This was family violence in the cause of family values. Mere physical distance did nothing to weaken the Townes family's commitment to those values, regardless of where different family members happened to be located.[39]

In myriad ways, then, the movement back and forth of men and women, materials and mementos, strengthened the enduring ties of kin and commerce that united slaveholding households across the South. Indeed, the strength of those continuing connections in such a mobile, malleable society casts doubt on the value of viewing these households as autonomous units or, indeed, of overdrawing the social and cultural differences between Southeast and Southwest when seeking to explain the society of either. Out of planter dispersion, in other words, emerged greater planter cohesion.

The strongest of all the connections binding households across the miles was the human property that moved between them. Soon after arriving in Perry County, Alabama, Serena Lea wrote to her "beloved sister" Martha in Athens, Georgia, with "sincere thanks" for all the things she had sent. "They are doubly valuable to me coming as they did from one so dear," she declared, insisting that "the quilt will indeed be prized highly by me." Nor would Serena lack for help in arranging the quilt and the other just-delivered possessions. On the same wagon "the negroes all arrived safely" too, and with the exception of Tom, "all appear well satisfied." Both quilts and slaves proved welcome sights to settlers eager to transform new households into places of domestic comfort and productive labor.[40] Whatever the physical and psychological warmth provided by quilts, there was no doubt which of the wagon's many forms of property provided the most important of the mobile links binding families and households together. The slaves' presence was an assumed element of the planters' southwestern ideal. If new land's productive potential was to be realized, familiar forms of labor would have to be brought to the task. James Burke concluded his advertisement with the information that along with the plantation's stock and tools, "between 10 and 25 working hands" would be available for sale. Burke also recorded that the sale would go through only "to a gentleman who would treat his slaves humanely."[41]

If slaves were not already in place, they could be brought from the East, either by their owners or by slave traders. Vast numbers of slaves were driven west in this period. On New Year's Day 1837 Robert Gage wrote of a recent sale in South Carolina in which "a lot of 30 boys, girls, &c," had been sold "for the mere song of 27,000." "Think of that," he told his brother. "Are not the people mad? Money, money is all they cry. Money here would almost get a man's wife, if she would bring enough to buy a negro." The pervasive desire for human property, whatever its source in the "rational" pursuit of profit, also came enveloped in a passion that seemed at times to eclipse all other considerations.[42]

As the mass movement of slaves thickened the networks of kinship and commerce that held the slaveholding class together, emigration intensified the dread and violence inherent in even the most stable of enslaved circumstances. The private correspondence of planters offers countless examples of how the shattering of enslaved families not only fueled the explosive westward expansion of slaveholding households but also ensured the continued coherence across great distances of those extended households. Even a few examples can suggest the brutal and banal ways in which the movement of slaves sustained family ties that were also business ties.[43]

Mary Wallace of Union, South Carolina, was one of many slaveholders in the East whose human property was deployed in the West. Her brother, John Wallace, looked after her slaves in Como, Mississippi, and kept his sister informed about their condition. In August 1852, for example, all were "well, and perfectly satisfied" with the exception of "one of Sarah's twins, which has been sick 2 months, teething." Although "Eliza has been nursing it night and day" and John Wallace hoped for the baby's recovery, he told his sister that she "need not be astonished to hear of its death." Sam's sore leg still limited his labors to hoeing the garden, as it had for the past three years, and Wallace was thinking of "putting him at the shoemakers' business in Memphis" if Mary consented. Wallace was also thinking about moving farther west and told his sister that "if you desire to attach your fortunes to mine, I will carry your negroes along also, but if you do not wish them to go, say so, and I will keep them here."[44] The Wallace siblings' correspondence suggests something of how the ownership of slaves connected plantation households across the South in ways that reinforced family ties.

In the case of the Wallace family, cross-country discussions of slave property seemed to run smoothly. In other cases the bonds embodied in human property could chafe even as they connected, as family discussion of the future of James Carter's slaves illustrates. For younger people marriage often meant not so much the loss of parents but the gaining of parents-in-law. Marriage and emigration to Alabama from Georgia brought James Carter a second father figure whose advice was less than welcome but no less freely offered for that. "If I were to advise James," N. B. Powell told James's father, Farish, "it would be to sell about half of his Negroes, those that are unfaithful" as well as "those women that pretend to be always sick." A "bad Negro" was "dangerous" and "poor property indeed," in Powell's view, and he praised Farish Carter's wisdom in giving his son similar advice.[45]

The immediate cause of the older men's concern was a near riot on James Carter's plantation in which "there was blood shed" but "no life lost," although that "was really a wonder as knives were used." Paris—"an outrageous desperate fellow"—apparently "took the whip out of the overseers hand & inflicted wounds upon him that he will probably carry to his grave." The slaves were almost "ungovernable" and "determined not to make anything for their master but to destroy his stock & waste & ruin every thing." This only increased Powell's rage at an "ungrateful set of poor wretches" incapable of recognizing that they could not expect to find "a better master . . . in the W[estern] States." His son-in-law's "kind and indulgent" demeanor led Powell to doubt that Carter would take his advice. Powell knew that he "hates to sell them," a determination encouraged by Carter's conviction that he could "reform them by adopting a rigid system of discipline."⁴⁶ Thus family opinions divided over the question of how to deal with the human property of the household. Was the sale of some slaves a prerequisite for success or a sign of failure? James Carter's reluctance to turn a difficult test of mastery into a quick profit suggests how much he saw his situation as a test of will in dealing with slaves and relatives alike. The outcome of the test would have much to say about his ability to be a plantation master in his own right. When it came to establishing his and his household's independence, clearly it was not just strong-willed slaves who presented a challenge. Feeling that he was still the right master for the job, James Carter must surely have resented the paternalistic dialogue being conducted not only above his head but between households led by men who clearly saw his circumstances as their concern.

Avarice and anxiety also combined in the Harrison households of South Carolina and Mississippi as their members negotiated the long-distance sale of almost fifty people. In 1836 Thomas Harrison of Pendleton District, South Carolina, decided to send some of his slaves west to be sold. He entrusted the task to his son and brother, both resident in Mississippi. After studying for four years with James L. Petigru in Charleston, James Harrison had moved to Mississippi to practice law in Macon. His uncle Isham Harrison, Thomas's older brother, was already there, having left South Carolina in 1816, then settling for a time in Alabama before moving on to Noxubee County, Mississippi, in 1832.⁴⁷ Not yet having decided whether to buy land in the West, Thomas Harrison had "broken up" Sylvania, his South Carolina plantation, and sent his slaves west to be disposed of as his relatives thought best. Like many patriarchs, however, he was not slow to offer advice. "There are but few children among them and they really make a very respectable appearance," Harrison explained in one of several letters filled with suggestions and instructions. He thought that such an "uncommonly likely" group might average as much as $600 to

$700 at sale. "The way to get a good price is to ask a good price," he declared in a January 1836 letter to his son. If they could bring a good price on favorable credit terms, then James was "by all means" to sell them, dividing them into families for the purpose if he wished. If not, he was to hire them out, but for a short term rather than the whole year. "Make them clean their teeth at all events," the elder Harrison advised. As for the white folks, "we are here all alone," Harrison remarked of himself, his wife, and his daughter, Rose. "The place looks desolate," he observed, "like it had been visited by a pestilence which had swept off the inhabitants." The forty-nine former inhabitants of Harrison's plantation swept off to an uncertain West eventually arrived safely at Isham Harrison's place in Mississippi. There they were promptly disposed of in "the best sale that has been made in our country."[48] In households like the Carters' and Harrisons', calculations regarding how best to maintain or increase the slaveholders' power and profit often added up to dislocation and separation for the black families who bore the brunt of household success and failure alike.

Whether in the fields or on the block, slaves were central to the households of the Southwest and to the ties that continued to bind those households to southeastern kin and creditor alike. Slaves bound white families together. They had little choice but to absorb the staggeringly high cost to their own family life that cementing white relations entailed. That owners were often chillingly oblivious to such considerations only reinforces how much the smashing of some relations strengthened the sinews of others. Pictured in the eyes of many observers as trailing behind the carriages and sulkies of their pioneering owners, these slaves actually were powering the westward-bound cavalcades. Slaves were carried west as property, like the quilts, nails, beds, and tools that also helped to make new households. Slaves traveled west as human beings, too, like the babies, children, men, and women who bought and sold and owned them. From beginning to end, east to west, slaves constituted the indispensable and ambiguous force at the heart of the region's extending households and expanding society.

For enslaved emigrants mobility brought none of the hope and continued connection that tempered the anxiety and separation experienced by free men and women. Black family members, as the abolitionist Frederick Douglass explained, could not give up their emigrating kin "with that cheerfulness with which friends and relations yield each other up, when they feel that it is for the good of the departing one that he is removed from his native place." For free emigrants there was, too, correspondence and "at least the hope of reunion, because reunion is possible. But, with the slave, all these mitigating circumstances are wanting. There is no improvement in his condition *probable,*—no correspondence *possible,*—no reunion attainable." In contrast to the many continuing connections that kept relations between free people alive, the slave's "going out into the world," Douglass concluded, "is like a living man going into the tomb, who, with open eyes, sees himself buried out of sight and hearing of wife, children, and friends of kindred tie." With great resilience and strong faith, many slaves did succeed in making more than a living death of their forced separation from beloved people and places. Yet as Douglass suggests, the comparison between death and separation came closer to the truth for many slaves than it ever did for their owners.[49]

Mobile human property embodied the many ties that continued to connect the geographically separated households of Southeast and Southwest. The inherent tensions of slave ownership that did so much to generate emigration remained central to maintaining the robust and enigmatic bonds of "blood and business" that kept the region's households close in all senses except the geographic. The stresses, tensions, affections, and responsibilities of slaveholding families continued to play themselves out across the miles. Questions of order and progress, success and succession, profit and honor, neither resolved themselves nor evaporated with the passage of miles or the crossing of rivers. The scent of financial and family obligation remained strong. Attenuated, strained, even broken in some instances, household ties more often proved as durable as the handmade quilts and human capital that embodied them. Indeed they did so to such an extent as to call into question the value of making such geographical distinctions in discussing household contacts, connections, and organization.

Slaves kept slaveholders connected. They also kept them moving. Emigrant planters had sought to re-create familiar forms of household and society in new southwestern places. Their continuing willingness to leave those places offers strong evidence of their success in this re-creation. The description of James Burke's Mississippi plantation may stand as symbol of the planters' success in creating the kind of plantation society that both men and women desired. But the description did appear, after all, in a sale notice.

Any number of reasons might explain any given sale, of course. Yet by the 1830s James Burke was only one among many planters selling recently formed plantations in Mississippi and Alabama. Many of them were moving farther to the west, with Texas increasingly the favored destination for many slaveholding households. A generation after they had prepared for their own move from Georgia to Alabama, Caroline and James Tait watched their eldest son, Charles William Tait, leave Alabama for Columbus, Texas. As he left he undertook the next step in his family's cross-generational journey across the continent. Charles Tait's household was one of many. In 1851, as Charles Tait himself put it (albeit with an inappropriate image of return rather than new venture), "immigrants" from other states and from Europe were "flocking to Texas, like Pigeons to their roost."[50]

Tait was among the many who recorded the magnetic appeal of Texas. Fifteen years earlier, in the wake of the Texas Revolution, Tait's relative Rebekah Goode reported that Suggsville, Alabama, was "getting to be very thin," with "almost every one . . . going to Texas." Caroline Tait's brother Sidney and other members of the Goode family were among the large numbers moving west in this period. In their case the destination was Kemper County, Mississippi. Although Texas gave its name to the new fever, it was only one of many western destinations. By midcentury Mississippi, Louisiana, and Arkansas had joined Texas as states filling up with emigrating planters.[51]

Emigrants had been flocking west in large enough numbers to make a noticeable difference to places and people left behind. Many other southern Suggsvilles, only recently points of destination, had become points of departure. By 1850 about one-quarter of Alabama's native-born free population already lived beyond its borders. In the following decade Alabama, along with Louisiana and Mississippi, saw more departures than arrivals. Nor did figures for the native-born include those who had once been emigrants to the state.[52] Alabama was not the only point of departure. Many of Mississippi's residents looked to a "far West" that increasingly seemed to be defined as anywhere west of the point one had already reached. Emigrants from Alabama and Mississippi mixed with those still departing from places farther to the East, as many movers now went straight to Texas or Arkansas. In turn, these movers were replaced to some extent by emigrants who continued to think of Alabama and Mississippi as desirable destinations. In the 1850s, 7,000 white and 70,000 black South Carolinians left their state for cotton lands to the West, and the decade also saw the heaviest emigration of Georgians to Texas and the far Southwest. New streams of human movement blended with old. By midcentury all the states between South Carolina and Texas had become significant points of departure as well as arrival.[53]

Texas Fever looked and felt a lot like Alabama Fever from the private perspective of household necessity and motivation. Households still remained very much connected across the distances. On Christmas Day 1849 Charles Tait wrote to his parents from Texas to express gratitude for the presents and property sent out from Alabama. Revealing the perennial priorities of blood and business, his words echoed those of countless slaveholding movers before him. Tait thanked his father, James, "for the negroes & gin" as well as for "the bible & hymn book" and "the daguerreotype likeness." This latter gift pleased the son so much that he requested "a lock of your hair . . . to accompany it." James Tait was also to "tell Ma and the girls Louisa and I thank them for the beautiful presents." Charles Tait's repeated hopes and plans for his family to visit would have sounded entirely familiar to numerous slaveholders regardless of location. In the fall of 1850, he sent news that his wife Louisa had been "safely delivered of a daughter" and that both were "doing well." Charles Tait hoped that "*this* grand-child will be some inducement for you to come out this fall." In the meantime, "we wish you or Ma to send a name for it." The son told his father that "if all your children are lucky in raising their offspring, I think you will be like the patriarchs of old, the father of nations." In these ways the familiar ties of people and property continued to bind households across the miles as well as the generations.[54]

Planters' motivations for movement also remained familiar. And as before, the engine of household necessity and ambition moved more than just the young in search of independence or the financially failing in search of a second chance. In 1844 a frustrated Maria Lide told her uncle that "I expect to spend the remainder of my days in moving about from place to place." He had "no idea how tired I am of hearing about moving," the inevitable "subject of conversation" on the frequent occasions when her father, Hugh, and brother Paul got together. She did not know the reason; indeed the good crops of recent times only seemed to make them more "anxious" to move. Maria was at a loss as to why "none of them are satisfied here" but thought that they would eventually be moving at least as far as the Red River. Her brother had recently visited there and had been "perfectly delighted" with a place he felt had no equal. Perhaps facetiously, Maria Lide told of "trying my best to get brother in the notion of going to California" on the grounds that he would "be obliged to stop then for he could go no farther." There, he might be "far enough away from society to be satisfied to settle himself permanently."[55] The attitudes of the men of the Lide household show how even the highest hopes for new land in the

Southwest nevertheless were expressed within a context of thought and habit that could only diminish attachment to that land. Whatever the reasons for any particular household's continued movement, planters as a class proved to be no more attached to place in the Southwest than they had been in the Southeast. Ultimately planter mobility spoke less of particular successes and failures than it did of just how much mobility itself was an integral feature of plantation society everywhere.

It was Maria Lide's Red River guess, not her California dream, that would come true, although not until ten years later would Eli Lide set off for Texas with his household, black and white. On 15 April 1854 the Lide household stopped for the night on the east bank of the Tombigbee River. As everyone else slept, and with "nothing to break the silence of the night but wind rustling in the trees and the rain pattering upon the tent," Eli Lide took time to write to his "Honored and Very Dear Parents" back in Carlowville, Alabama. "Through a merciful and kind Providence," they had made twenty-three miles that day. Lide thought they would stay there until they could ship the slaves' clothing because it was "difficult to travel over the bogs and red clay hills with such loads as we have and carry as many negroes as ought to ride." The health news was mostly good. Maggie was suffering from chills and "some little fever," but Lide felt she would soon get better. Among the slaves "good health and fine spirits" prevailed, "with the exception of big Joe who is a little hoarse but he does not appear the less lively. Henrietta and her children are quite well which I suppose Sambo would be glad to hear. Dilly's health improves and we often get milk for her children (the twins) both of whom are quite well." In contrast to this good news was Lide's anxiety about his parents. In particular, he worried that he had "pained" the "kind and affectionate Parents" who had "nourished strengthened and advised" him throughout his life by his "ingratitude in leaving them in their old age." Such a thought "almost breaks my heart," the son continued. Yet he hoped that he was not ungrateful and described the "tears of gratitude" that could "now flow in unrestrained silence when there is none to criticise my sincerity or impugne my motive." "I often think how can I do without my Father and Mother," Lide went on, answering his own question with an emphatic "I cannot I cannot do without them." Nevertheless, he had left them. "Something within me whispers onward onward and urges me on like a prisoner who has . . . idle[d] in his Lords vineyard and lived on his bounty and made no returns for the favors received." Lide wished that he could know more of his Savior and "feel more of the blessed influence of his spirit." Lide likened himself to Abraham "as I travel along the wearisome road, and often does the desire arise in my heart to know what the Lord intends to do with me." Eli Lide wrote this on his birthday. He was fifty-eight.

Approaching Texas with greater anxiety and much less excitement than J. S. Little would in the following summer of 1855, Lide nevertheless shared Little's desire to find the divine in earthly pursuits. In this they were far from alone among the many slaveholding men and women of their time who ventured west, heads filled with awe, avarice, and uncertainty. Although older than his anxious words (both self-justifying and self-seeking) suggest, Lide was nevertheless seven years younger than his father, James, had been when he moved west from South Carolina two decades earlier, as fully stricken by Alabama Fever as his son now was by the Texas strain of that virulent blend of the material and the mysterious. Unfortunately for Eli Lide, Texas Fever would prove to be more than a metaphor. He died, of cholera, soon after reaching the Red River. It had been scarcely a month since he had written from the banks of another river to the "kind and affectionate" parents who survived him, along with his wife, ten children, several grandchildren, and, of course, his many "Negroes."[56]

7　The Planters' Progress

This glance at our mutual past awakens many reflections,
the principal of which, as it relates to that strange
philosophical romance, the progress of society, may well
enchain our attention, and constitute the legitimate topic
of our present essay.
—William Gilmore Simms, *Social Principle*

IN MAY 1840, IN MARION, ALABAMA, MARGARET LEA
was married in the parlor of her brother Henry's house on Greensboro
Road. By then, Texas had enjoyed four years of independence, part of that
time under the leadership of Margaret Lea's groom, Samuel Houston, who
had gone from military glory to political office as the new republic's first
president. The Leas and their friends celebrated the union in verse and jest.
Margaret's friends sang an original ode (to the tune of "The Old Oaken
Bucket") to honor the new husband:

> Our Washington's name has been hallowed in story,
> As founder of Freedom's retreat West.
> Another has risen to share in his glory—
> —The Texas Patriot, our honored guest.[1]

At the public dinner held to honor the newlyweds, Samuel Townes, Henry
Lea's law partner, toasted "the Conqueress of the Conqueror—Mrs. Margaret M. Houston."[2] The happy couple soon removed to Texas. So too did
the bride's widowed mother, Nancy Lea, who wanted to be close to her
daughter and to her extensive real estate investments in the area.[3]

If the private meanings of journeys such as those of the new bride and
the new mother-in-law remained familiar, the public background to them
had been transformed, not least by the deeds of men like the new husband,
Samuel Houston. When James and Caroline Tait, for example, moved from
Georgia to Alabama in the wake of America's war against Great Britain,
Texas was part of the Spanish Empire and home, at best estimates, to no

more than three thousand people. The following year the United States gave up any claim to Texas in the Adams-Onís Treaty of 1819. But the emigration of Americans, allowed by the Spanish and encouraged by the Mexicans after they achieved independence in 1821, sowed the seeds of an American population that would sorely disappoint its hosts' assimilationist expectations.[4]

By the 1830s the American community's lively sense of its character and interests as "Texans" had developed to the point of revolution, confirming the Mexican government's foreboding that instead of a buffer against American expansion, their encouragement had helped to construct its bridgehead. Growing tensions in the 1830s culminated with Texas's declaration of independence on 2 March 1836 at Washington-on-the-Brazos. The convention named Samuel Houston, a former governor of Tennessee, commander-in-chief of the army. At the battle of San Jacinto, Houston crushed the army of Santa Anna in less than twenty minutes and turned proclamation into fact.[5]

Victory brought forth an unusual republic, one populated by citizens most of whom hoped that independence would be but a short-lived stepping-stone to incorporation into the United States of America. Texans eventually got their wish. On 29 December 1845 Texas became the twenty-eighth state (and fifteenth slave state) of the United States of America. Annexation of Texas exacerbated existing tensions between the United States and Mexico while doing little to dampen the expansionist appetites of those Americans who sought to turn an even larger slice of the Mexican North into the American West.

Prospects of war with Mexico and territorial expansion did not meet with universal approval within the United States. "Mexico will poison us," Ralph Waldo Emerson observed, implying that victory over others would merely set the stage for internal conflict that would end in the nation's destruction. Emerson's view was most widely shared in the North, where opposition to the nation's geographical expansion was frequently bound up with antagonism to the spread of what increasing numbers called "the slave power."[6]

Many in the southern states were happy to swallow up as much of Mexico as possible. In June 1844 it seemed to Thomas Gaillard of Claiborne, Alabama, "that the People of the South have taken up with one spirit the question of the Annexation of Texas." Two years later his wife noted similar enthusiasm for war with Mexico. Marianne Gaillard reported the widespread expectation that there would be "no difficulty in raising a company" of volunteers. Martial sentiment was running strong in the county that "a draft must not be permitted," she told her brother in Charleston District, South Carolina. Similar feelings were felt and expressed across the cotton states. Serena Lea's nephew Thomas R. R. Cobb described something of the atmosphere for war in Athens, Georgia. Cobb was also certain that raising a sufficient number of volunteers would not be a problem. He had never seen "the people more excited," he told his brother Howell. "It is Mexico and War." Expansionist demand eventually brought open war with Mexico. In 1846 Charles Tait followed in the martial as well as migratory footsteps of his soldier-settler father by serving as surgeon of the Texas cavalry in the Mexican War. Tait and his fellows won a crushing victory that brought vast new areas within the American orbit.[7]

Sectional divisions were no more neat or complete on the issue of expansion than they were on any other question of national significance. Neither, of course, were these divisions a new element in debates on the nation's westward progress. Sectional (or, more accurately, regional) perspectives were certainly evident in support for and opposition to the War of 1812. By the 1840s, however, such divisions were even more pronounced. When James Tait marched off with the Georgia militia, he did so in the midst of disputes over the advisability of fighting "Mr. Madison's War." He marched home again, however, in an atmosphere largely purged of New England Federalist pessimism and charged instead with a patriotic faith that expansion served the national interest as well as lesser interests, personal and local, within the nation. When Charles Tait rode with the Texas cavalry, thirty years further on and more than a thousand miles farther west, he returned with a victory that only intensified the full-blooded argument surrounding the future of the American republic.

Americans had long viewed national affairs from the perspective of interests and identities rooted in multiple sources, of which national allegiance was only one among many. For many Americans, nevertheless, the years following this latest war would be an especially intense period of reordering priorities and interests and of rethinking the sources of both personal and collective identities. As "the South" emerged as a ubiquitous entity in the thoughts and arguments of Americans on both sides of the Mason-Dixon Line, the idea of sectionalism became a constant and increasingly large presence in the discourse of slave society. As this new definition settled on the slave states, it did not eclipse other entities or interests. But as American nationalism had once done, "the South" seemed to offer a larger focus of loyalty that could support rather than threaten its component parts. Eventually the shouting would stop and the shooting would begin, as the heroes of Mexico City turned against one another in the name of ideals and interests and entities that most had recognized but few had considered paramount back in the autumn of 1847.

The changed political atmosphere influenced, and is revealed in, shifting public attitudes toward planter emigration and its social impact. Discussion of continuing westward movement remained interwoven with wider debates regarding the nature and future of plantation society. In the 1820s and 1830s, fears for elite emigration's deleterious consequences had been closely related to broader issues prompted by national expansion. Nevertheless public observers like Thomas Spalding and Joseph Jenkins tended to take as their focus local communities or particular states. Even when their concerns extended beyond state boundaries, they were more likely to focus on region rather than section: on the Southeast rather than the South. They worried, for example, that emigration was fueling decline in the seaboard states even as it created a powerful economic competitor and potential political opponent in the Southwest.

In the 1840s many elite southeasterners still worried about the future of their communities and their states. Perceptions of what most threatened them had, however, shifted significantly. As with the Nullification Crisis a generation earlier, planter emigration was linked to a crisis in sectional relations. Now, however, emigration was less likely to be feared as undermining community and state than it was to be welcomed as strengthening class and section. Notwithstanding continued undercurrents of anxiety and anger over Alabama Fever and "Mississippi madness," most elite southerners now believed that the greatest source of social deviance was to be found in "the insidious assaults of mad enthusiasts who under the guise of philanthropy and patriotism would tear up the very foundations of our social system."[8] As southern order was increasingly threatened by the expanding galaxy of antislavery interests and arguments to the north, the solidly slaveholding states of the Southwest looked more and more like economic and ideological allies. As their sense of class and sectional identity crystallized around the issue of the nation's transcontinental expansion, planters who stayed behind were more likely to view those who continued to leave as strengthening rather than undermining slavery's defenses. Once addressed largely in the context of the defense of land and locality, emigration now increasingly found its place as part of the defense of slavery and section. In public debate the emigration of slaveholders had become the expansion of slavery.

Enthusiasm for slavery's expansion was nevertheless much more than the paradoxical product of the desire to defend the system where it already existed. More than the demands of political conflict turned planter emigration into a positive public good in the eyes of so many slaveholders. Shifting views of planter mobility were bound up with broader philosophical shifts in the way planters and their public champions understood and justified their maturing social system. By midcentury the once understated acknowledgment of slavery's cultural as well as economic importance had given way to an unrepentant defense of slavery that trumpeted its progressive and benevolent impact on all classes of southern society. The geographical expansion of slavery was, then, paralleled by a changed public understanding of human bondage: an ideological shift from the shaky terrain of "necessary evil" to the solid rock of divinely ordained "positive good."

The combative tone that infused a great deal of proslavery exegesis leaves no doubt about the influence of external criticism in promoting its development. As John C. Calhoun acknowledged, the sectional "agitation" had "produced one happy effect at least," by "compell[ing] us to the South to look into the nature and character of this great institution [slavery], and to correct many false impressions that even we had entertained in relation to it."⁹ In such an atmosphere the cultural output of the slave states took on ever greater importance. "It is important that we should write our own books," George Fitzhugh pithily pointed out in the pages of *De Bow's Review*. "It matters little who makes our shoes." Fitzhugh's ranking of books over boots suggests his conviction that the South faced a threat that was not only economic and political but cultural too.¹⁰

Yet public thought and action in any society, even a threatened one, are never shaped by external pressures alone. As with any developing society, changes in ways of thinking also resulted from southern intellectuals' efforts at an internal coming-to-understanding of the kind of people they were and the kind of society they wanted to live in. Calhoun and others sought to convince slaveholders that if they truly were leading the way in creating a new kind of society, then it was simply not good enough for them to judge their creation by the standards and assumptions of other places. Perhaps little could be done about the cultural condescension now so prevalent in the North and in Europe. But surely the slaveholders themselves could resist embracing those same assumptions. Throughout the 1840s and 1850s, proslavery theorists called upon their peers to wear proudly the label of slaveholder and to tailor their beliefs to suit their own society, rather than to clothe themselves in the thoughts and habits of others.

In other words, proslavery theorists and orators called on their colleagues to turn the southern intellectual project on its head. Elite southerners had to stop trying to fit the slave states' developing life and culture into categories or narratives constructed in and for other times and places, whether ancient and agricultural or English ("old" and "new") and industrializing. Instead the slaveholders had to rethink these categories and assumptions in the light of the social and material realities of the new kind of society they were creating. They had to reject what seemed irrelevant or likely to mislead, and to reaffirm that which continued to give meaning and direction to present circumstances. Thus the proslavery argument also developed as a reexamination and a reimagining of familiar intellectual and cultural categories and assumptions in light of the particular conditions of southern society.

This rethinking of slaveholding society and ideology had an important impact on developing attitudes toward planter emigration and its place in wider public debates about the meaning and destiny of plantation society. Two elements were of particular importance. One was the relentless emphasis in proslavery discourse on the human relations of slavery. The other element was the centrality of Christianity as a crucial force in shaping the slaveholders' understanding and justification of slavery. These emphases on the relations of slavery and the beliefs of Christianity manifested themselves in different ways in the public and private realms. But in both realms they worked to change attitudes toward planter mobility. They fueled the eventual widespread endorsement of emigration as a publicly beneficial force. They eased emigration's impact within and between households by reducing attachment to place while strengthening attachments between people regardless of location.

The proslavery argument's emphasis on relations between people did much to mute public claims that geographic mobility, by severing ties between people and place, had an inevitably destructive impact on social stability. It did so, in part, by undermining the claim that immobility was a prerequisite of social stability. Remember that this was a key assumption of the agrarian republican's definition of good social order. Agrarian republicanism revolved around an understanding of land as both an agricultural and a cultural resource requiring the nurture of planter men meeting their responsibilities as educated, engaged cultivators and informed, active citizens. The proslavery theorists' arguments, taken together, offer a striking contrast to an ideal of order grounded in ties between people and place. Certainly, proslavery theorists also exalted order. "God breathes throughout his universe the beautiful law of order: certain beings to certain ends," insisted Louisa McCord. There was "no higher law in sublunary things, and stamped upon creation, its beautiful effects are daily more and more developing themselves. Herein consists the world's true progress." In important ways both visions appeared to share similar aims: the preservation and advancement of an ordered and harmonious society.[11]

The good order of slave society nevertheless had very different sanctions and sources than that of agricultural society. Centrally important in this regard was Christianity's eclipse of classical literature as a source of the images and assumptions shaping the planters' understanding of their lives and their society. McCord was among the many who sought the foundations of society in divine law rather than classical ideal. The good order of slave society was grounded first and foremost in God-ordained relations between people, not in those between people and place. Many proslavery theorists might have liked to contrast their "emphatically" agricultural society with the factories and slums of the industrializing North. But the core of their developing ideology had remarkably little to say about the cultural or spiritual significance of land in shaping the character of the planters and their society. The works of McCord and other proslavery advocates instead focused steadily on the primary human relations of slaveholding society and on the need to tend those relations if the order and progress of society were to be ensured.

Yet the proslavery discourse did not lack for its own brand of organic imagery and allusion. It abounded in metaphors fibrous, foundational, and familial, all intended to drive home the message that relations between humans were the stuff from which good societies were formed. Slavery's defenders emphasized its benefits for all the groups who combined to weave what Thomas Roderick Dew of Virginia called "the texture of the population of our country." Dew described a slave South in which "a race of people differing from us in colour and in habits, and vastly inferior in the scale of civilization, have been increasing and spreading—'growing, with our growth and strengthening with our strength'—until they have become intertwined with every fibre of society." William Harper of South Carolina insisted that slavery had "interwoven itself with every fibre of the body politic" and had "formed the habits of our society." Many joined Dew and Harper in pointing to the orderly patterns of social stability that derived from the inseparable bonds that slavery had formed between black and white, slave and free.[12]

The paternalist network of command and subordination extended beyond the master-slave relation to encompass the white women and children of the slaveholding household. As James Henley Thornwell, minister of the First Presbyterian Church in Columbia, South Carolina, and the South's leading theologian, explained, "The relation of master and slave stands on the same foot with the other relations of life." At the same time, white women and children held varying degrees of power over the slaves of the household. Overall the developing prescriptive ideal of plantation society suggested an ordered, hierarchical society lived out under the eye of the omniscient God who had ordained its rightness.[13]

The writings of the Thornwells and McCords of the slave states should not be read as a rejection of progress or modernity. Indeed in their conviction that a society, even an agricultural society, could be understood with little regard for its members' relationship to land and place the proslavery theorists proved themselves strikingly modern. In their preoccupation with human relations the planters shared a great deal with people in other modern places. There too intellectual and spiritual lives were increasingly given over to fathoming the transformation that progress had wrought in human relations more and more detached from traditional moorings in native soils and familiar localities.

But if the questions were the same, the answers were often profoundly different. Elite slaveholders increasingly parted ways with their northern peers in their fundamental emphasis on relations between individuals rather than on the (male) individual as an autonomous social actor endowed with the power to choose and shape his relations to others. From the proslavery perspective an idea of progress centered around extreme notions of individualism was no kind of progress at all. Instead it promised an end to order. In contrast, McCord's "beautiful law of order" was no reactionary euphemism for resistance to change or progress. It was rather progress's most essential precondition. Order and "true progress" marched together, or they marched not at all. Order required the preservation of God-ordained human relations, not the deification of a new kind of individual supposedly capable of transcending his social circumstances. Household, class, and community (relations between humans) rather than individualism (understood as growing freedom from the bonds of human relations not freely chosen) were the interconnected hubs at the heart of the planters' modern journey. The developing proslavery perspective combined a strikingly modern neglect of place with a profoundly conservative emphasis on preserving, rather than escaping from, orderly and hierarchical relations between people.[14]

The proslavery focus on the human relations of plantation society is evident in the developing view of the plantation itself. A positive view of the relations of slavery prompted a less ambiguous understanding of the place that embodied those relations. Agrarian republicans, and even observers like Simms who allowed far more for slavery's presence and importance, were often ambivalent about the plantation's influence on southern life. Many feared that the planters' isolation on his plantation helped to explain his antisocial behavior, including his propensity to emigrate. The defense of slavery, on the other hand, offered a ringing endorsement of the plantation. "Every plantation is a little community," explained John C. Calhoun, "with the master at its head, who concentrates in himself the united interests of capital and labor, of which he is the common representative." Calhoun here emphasized what the critics neglected: the planter's relations within his household.[15]

But Calhoun went further, to argue that each plantation fulfilled an essential public role. Indeed, for Calhoun it was "these small communities aggregated [that] make the State in all, whose action, labor, and capital is equally represented and perfectly harmonized." In such circumstances it made sense to think of the slave states themselves as "an aggregate, in fact, of communities, not of individuals." The idea that the planter related to the broader society not as an individual or simply as the head of a family but as the representative of a set of relations central to both private and public life offered a very different sense of the plantation from the one presented by many critics and agricultural reformers. Calhoun's plantation community, both self-contained and socially central, retained few of the connotations of isolation and retreat regularly criticized by those who lamented agricultural bad habits and white flight.[16]

This understanding of what made slave society tick encouraged a more positive view of emigration as a cultural force. As one would expect, and as anxieties about the nature of southwestern social development suggest, the view that emigration had become a positive good was not unanimous. Indeed, to some extent the agricultural reform movement, with its familiar issues and anxieties, also moved west with the emigrants.[17] Yet the belief that the plantation, endowed as it was with all the requirements of survival and civilization, was indispensable to social development went increasingly unchallenged. At the same time, the experience of countless emigrating households offered ample evidence that whatever its impact on less important attachments to place, emigration had done nothing to weaken planters' commitment to organizing their households along familiar lines. It followed that planter emigration threatened neither the human relations of slavery nor the social order woven from those relations. Furthermore, if the plantation household was the cutting edge of civilization, was it not desirable that it should move wherever it could move? With how rather than where people connected to each other the crucial issue, the defenders of land and locale found it difficult to argue that the migratory impulses of the planter class offered a serious threat to social order and progress.[18]

The changed place of planter emigration in public debate is perhaps best suggested by the way a leading southern thinker in the 1850s addressed its complex impact on the slave states. Thomas R. R. Cobb, in his 1858 *Inquiry into the Law of Negro Slavery in the United States of America,* twinned, like many before him, the planters' neglect of the land with their disposition to emigrate.[19] Unlike most before him, Cobb linked both to slavery. Cobb believed that "the natural result" of the planters' investing of their surplus income in slaves was "that lands are a secondary consideration. No surplus is left for their improvement." "His valuable property (his slaves) are easily removed to fresh lands; much more easily than to bring the fertilizing materials to the old." The planters' "withdrawal of all investments from the improvement of the lands," Cobb admitted, represented "another deleterious effect of slavery to the State." This conditional attachment to land as resource was mirrored by an even more limited sense of land as home. "The homestead is valued only so long as the adjacent lands are profitable for cultivation." This indifference was passed from generation to generation. Because the planter had "no local attachments, his children inherit none." Rather the parent "encourages in them a disposition to seek new lands." Among people who "as a class" were "never settled," indeed "almost nomadic," it was "useless to seek to excite patriotic emotions in behalf of the land of birth, when self-interest speaks so loudly. . . . Of course we speak of classes, not of individuals." In 1858, then, Thomas Cobb repeated many of the concerns regarding the planter's nomadic ways and his lack of "local attachment" spelled out by Thomas Spalding, his fellow Georgian, more than thirty years earlier and by numerous others in the intervening years.[20]

Yet there were crucial differences in Cobb's analysis. For one thing, Cobb may have seen the planters' lack of attachment to place as unfortunate, but it was far from being either a source or a symbol of social crisis. Whatever their consequences for places in particular, Cobb knew, by the 1850s, that countless individual decisions to emigrate had not destroyed class or community solidarity. Movement had helped to fuel a different sense and kind of class and community solidarity: one shaped not by sentimental attachment to particular patches of land but by common interests and experiences and by a shared commitment to particular forms of social thought, habit, and organization.[21]

Cobb also differed from many earlier observers of emigration in his willingness to identify slavery as a cause of the planters' embrace of emigration and their neglect of land and locality. He made causally central to his explanation of planter emigration just about the only thing that the reformers had not: the ownership of human, mobile capital. To Cobb and to most of his peers by that time, the planters were slaveholders who happened to be agriculturists. The fear that mobility had induced in those who defined them primarily as the latter had been replaced by acceptance, even indifference. Indeed the very taken-for-grantedness of Cobb's words demonstrates that nothing had done more to defuse anxieties about elite emigration than the explicit recognition of just how central and symbiotic human bondage and human movement had been to the creation of southern society and culture.

Thus whatever its disruptive influence in some respects, Cobb had no doubt that "politically slavery is a conservative institution." He had in mind how black slavery ensured that there was "no war of classes" among free white people but rather a condition of "republican equality."[22] Others argued that slavery's successful ordering of human relations—between capital and labor, for example—had bred a sense of order and harmony in southern society. Overall, as James Henley Thornwell estimated the situation in 1850, the slaveholders had "been eminently conservative in our influence upon the spirit of the age." By then, it did not occur to many elite southerners that there might be a problem with the mobility that had done so much to build a society which had so successfully blended freedom with order, progress with conservatism.[23]

Thomas Cobb gave public voice to the hard realities illuminated so vividly in the private papers of plantation households. The ownership of mobile, human property not only enhanced the planters' ability to move. It also increased their willingness to leave. Yet the slaves' role in fueling mobility was more tragic than Cobb realized or, perhaps, even considered thinking about. The slaves also made leaving easier for the planters for reasons, paradoxically, to do with their own sense of attachment to the places left behind. For one thing, it was the slaves who were the real agriculturists. It was they, or at least most of them, who experienced the daily communion with the soil that the agricultural reformers considered so essential to the spiritual development of the "Good Farmer." As one correspondent to the *Southern Agriculturist,* writing in another context, remarked, "The planters of the South are peculiarly situated. They are the lords of the soil, but seldom personally engaged in cultivating it." This dual reality spoke to more than a division of masterly duties; it highlighted a fundamental division of plantation labor itself. It was a division that profoundly shaped the respective relations of both slaveholder and slave to the land. As the actual cultivators, the slaves came between the slaveholders and the soil. In doing so, they helped to ensure that the planters would define themselves less in terms of the places they owned than of the people they possessed.[24]

For their part, enslaved human beings were understandably reluctant to define themselves in terms of their relations to the people who owned them. Perhaps many were just as reluctant to attach themselves to the places of their enslavement. It is difficult to know what balance, if any, was struck in the minds of individuals between the satisfactions of cultivation and the anguish of enslavement. It would be quite understandable if the prisoner showed as little affection for the jail as for the jailer. Yet Frederick Douglass, for one, argued that emigration did more than wrench enslaved people away from each other. It also separated them forever from places to which they were often strongly attached. "The people of the north, and free people generally," Douglass believed, had "less attachment to the places where they are born and brought up, than have the slaves. Their freedom to go and come, to be here and there, as they list, prevents any extravagant attachment to any one particular place in their case." The slave, in contrast, was "a fixture," according to Douglass, with "no choice, no goal, no destination." Rather the slave "is pegged down to a single spot, and must take root here, or nowhere." Generally understood as a "threat" or "punishment," the prospect of removal was "attended with fear and dread" by the slave who "looks upon separation from his native place, with none of the enthusiasm which animates the bosoms of young freemen, when they contemplate a life in the far west, or in some distant country where they intend to rise to wealth and distinction." The slaves then, in Douglass's view, felt deeply the pain of separation not only from people but also from place.[25]

The tragedy was even greater than Douglass described, for no class of free people was less attached to place than the free people who owned other people. The indifference to place that Douglass observed in free people was intensified in slaveholders by their ownership of mobile human property. Ownership of slaves eased emigration and settlement as practical matters. The ownership of slaves also bred a lack of attachment to place extreme even by American standards. By their presence the slaves not only facilitated movement; they helped to create the conditions in which the psychological and spiritual toll that movement might otherwise have taken on the planters was greatly diminished. Those same conditions made departure all the more intolerable for those with no control over where they were going and no means to return from beyond the grave that servitude and geography had dug for them.

As land continued to shrink as an intellectual and spiritual resource in the hearts and minds of the slaveholders, it nevertheless grew in importance as a prize and prerequisite of slaveholding society's continuing power. Land, in other words, retained its centrality in public discourse in precisely its most dangerous form from the antiemigration point of view: as a political as well as material enticement to further westward movement. Growing sectional conflict encouraged demand for new lands in the Southwest. At the same time, both the relations of slavery and the developing ideological defense of those relations diminished the spiritual and cultural significance of land by privileging human relations over ties to place. Land was the means to the end, the mere stage for the playing out of the paramount associations of the slaveholders' public and private lives.

For those who still lamented what they believed to be westward emigration's destructive consequences for land and society, this narrowing of focus was the worst possible outcome. Yet only ideas that really strike home are likely to take hold there over time. A vision of the slaveholding good life that had no place (however subordinate) for the women or slaves at the heart of its households had little chance of capturing imaginations or adherents. The humane vision of man united with land embraced by so many of emigration's critics required the inhumane reduction of women and slaves to invisibility or instrumentality. The everyday reality of running a plantation gave the men and women of the planter class no choice but to recognize the complexity of its human relations and their importance in shaping thought and behavior. The proslavery argument had the virtue of stressing the slaves' centrality to the plantation household and, in turn, the plantation household's centrality to society. Accordingly, it met with strong approval from the slaveholders who read it in their papers or heard it from their pulpits.

Of course, the plantation household was no more the harmonious home of the proslavery ideologues than it was the isolated island of the agricultural reformers. Slaveholders knew that too. Slaves were essential, but they could also be disruptive and threatening. As workers and humans they could be sources of conflict as well as profit. As capital and property they could be symbols of failure as well as success, no more so than when standing on the auction block whose importance to slaveholding society the public champions of slaveholding order tried so hard to obscure. The planter men and women who lived amid the chronic obsessions of the marketplace and the demanding intimacies of the household knew that the relations of slavery could be sources of anxiety and failure as well as profit and honor. So although closer to the hopes and realities of planters' lives, the new ideologues of the slaveholders' Christian Kingdom underplayed the anxieties that also existed at the heart of household circumstances.

Yet if the relations of slavery could be more troublesome than the proslavery argument generally allowed, religious faith could do more than underpin its ideal vision of how things should be. It could also help to ease the inevitable tensions and anxieties generated by how things really were. Many masters and mistresses nodded assent to Sunday morning assertions that "God's beautiful order" had found its ideal modern home in the slave states of America. They also drew heavily on a religious sensibility more suited to Monday mornings and to those dark nights of the soul that even the most blessed of people must sometimes endure. Private voices were more attuned to the inevitable daily failures of human relations lived face to face than to the eventual victory of those relations manifest as system against system. As such they were less likely to speak to the certainties of proslavery than of the mysteries of providence. Christianity as preached legitimated and idealized a stable social order rooted in the human relations of slavery. Christianity as practiced did much to assuage the anxieties and tensions that inevitably infused a highly mobile slave society.[26]

This was certainly the case when it came to planter emigration. The language and imagery of Christianity profoundly shaped planter men and women's understanding of all aspects of daily life. Especially important for emigrant households (and in the extended households of the expanding region that included those who stayed as well as those who moved) was evangelical Protestantism's understanding of life itself as a journey. Life was a journey, moreover, that the believer should expect to end at any time. Preparation for the next, eternal life rather than preoccupation with the anxieties of the present one should be the believer's fundamental concern. Martha Means of Louisiana spoke for many when she expressed the hope that her family would "all be ready to follow our children & friends who have gone before us. . . . I trust in God [that] we will all be prepared to meet in that blessed kingdom, where there will be neither pain nor sorrow & where there will be no parting." She worried, however, that her husband had not been saved, and she fervently hoped that the recent death of his brother Edward would bring William Means "to know & feel that this world is not our abiding place." The death of his brother had indeed caused William "to feel more that I have to die" and so to try "to feel the great necessity of being a Christian." Means admitted finding "the temtations of Satan & this world very hard to overcome," but he was praying that he would "be able to resist them" and so be ready to meet the "dear brother who has gone before me." Means expressed the hope, held dear by many, that "we all be prepared to meet in heaven when we are called from this troublesome world." The language and imagery of earthly impermanence suffused planter men and women's discussions of their families and their society.[27]

The responses of Edward Means's relatives to his death convey the importance of recognizing that the journey might well be a short one, liable to end at any moment. Discussing the recent death from fever of Mrs. Gerald, a "young, wealthy & beautiful" woman of her Montgomery neighborhood, Mary Ann Hutchinson believed that her "fate shows the emptiness of all earthly possessions." Committed Christians had to strive to embrace a spirit of voluntary alienation from the material things of this world. As it did for many, death also brought home to Hutchinson the importance of the command "Be ye also ready." When Eliza Kennedy, a recent emigrant to the "wilds" of Louisiana, commiserated with her cousin Sarah Jackson on a family death, she insisted that a Christian's faith should be strong enough to accept "the dispensations of providence however severe," knowing that "only a short time . . . is given to us to prepare for a better stage of existence." Such acceptance was hardly easy, even, as Hutchinson put it, for "those who profess to be strangers and pilgrims here." But to accept that this world was not one's abiding place and that the things of this world had little abiding value was the aim. Like planters who remained indifferent to the outward appearance of their homes because they knew their household would soon be on the move, so religious sojourners minimized the value of leaving earthly monuments along the way.[28]

Evangelical planters' belief that life was mere prelude to eternal joy was nowhere more evident than when they talked about their earthly journeys through southern space. This belief was perhaps especially strong among the women of elite emigrant families. The planter women who were mostly invisible in the antiemigration jeremiads of social fragmentation often proved the most poignant chroniclers of the costs that movement imposed on ties of kinship. The same women's words also best illuminate the power of faith to explain and ease the trials of mobility and separation. Letters back and forth across the developing region blended discussions of geographical movement with talk of spiritual journeys. Mary Boyd, a recent emigrant to Alabama, expressed her hopes in the form of a very common progression when she began by telling her cousin Jane Gaston, back in Fishing Creek, South Carolina, that she thought "often . . . of being separated from my earthly friends." Boyd believed that "if life and health permit I shall see you all once more in this world." But if that was not to be, she counseled, "let us all try to prepare to meet in the world above where we shall hurt no more." That such eternal reunion was possible was due to a God who "will be our guide even unto Death." [29]

If faith could bridge the chasm between worlds, it could surely diminish the distance between East and West. Martha Gaston, writing in 1822, beseeched her cousin to "let not the distance that is between us separate our affections." Instead she asked her to "keep in remembrance that every step we take is bringing us nearer to the end of our journey." Jane Gaston must have understood her cousin's appeal. In an 1860 letter Martha remarked that they had corresponded with each other nearly forty years, "but a short time to the eternity we hope to spend together." Separation, like other unwelcome aspects of life, was to be faced with stoicism and faith, not selfishness and fear. Faithfulness would shrink the space that formed an earthly barrier between people separated by geographical distance. Physical separation would one day be overcome, perhaps in this world but certainly in the next.[30] By putting earthly deprivation and separation in the context of eternal community, their faith also helped Christian women and men to remain connected across daunting distances. Such an understanding of Christian duty could seem forbidding, especially perhaps to those already separated from the church membership and rich spiritual life they had enjoyed in the seaboard states.[31] A faith that placed present circumstances in the context of future blessedness was nevertheless made-to-measure for sustaining people in turbulent times and uncertain places.

A constant presence in many emigrants' lives, evangelicalism shaped believers' understanding of their relation not only to God and to each other but also to place. Emigrants looked to their faith to help interpret their relation to the environment they journeyed across and settled upon. The evangelical Christianity embraced by so many emigrants was not a faith likely to provoke desire for communion with one's natural surroundings in the cause of creating heaven on earth. It was no accident that the agrarian republicans looked more to classical than to biblical literature in drawing their pseudo-pantheistic portraits of Man and Nature united. The Bible and the beliefs of evangelical slaveholding emigrants did not so much justify the exploitation of the physical environment as they encouraged its neglect as a force in thought and faith. A faith, furthermore, that encouraged disregard for all earthly places was unlikely to grant much significance to any particular place, not even South Carolina. Its definitive distinctions between the transience of this world and the permanence of the next worked in believers' hearts and minds to diminish attachment to land as an object of either secular nostalgia or spiritual veneration. Their restless spirituality almost guaranteed that no earthly place could really be home and further minimized the spiritual value of land already diminished by the household's agricultural practices, market circumstances, and human relations. Those seeking support for the "naturalness" of people's permanent attachment to place could hardly have found a less helpful ally in evangelical Christianity.[32]

It was in many ways fitting that the faith that did so much to ameliorate the private tensions and anxieties raised by emigration and westward settlement was so often best expressed by the women so often ignored in public explorations of those subjects. These were women like Mary Boyd who adhered passionately to a set of beliefs that cast earth as a testing ground and human existence as a short, precarious journey through it. When Boyd wrote of "this mazy wilderness," she was talking about life, not Wilcox County, Alabama.[33]

Whether in the countless private letters of women like Mary Boyd or in numerous published articles and public orations, elite southerners persistently mixed the material and the metaphorical in seeking to understand not only the meaning of emigration but also the development of the class and the society that emigration had done so much to shape. How they did so reflected persisting differences between private and public perceptions of the relations of slavery, the meaning of religion, and the experience of emigration. Mary Boyd's "mazy wilderness" could seem a long way from Louisa McCord's "beautiful law of order." The public view of the plantation household was not, then, the same as the view from those households. In crucial respects, however, public estimates and private understandings of emigration did grow closer as slave society grew wider. By midcentury both private and public understanding of emigration (and of most other aspects of slaveholding life) was profoundly shaped by the human relations at the heart of slavery and the religious faith at the core of the slaveholders' private thoughts and public discourse. In their own ways private and public discourses both made slavery and religion central to their explanations of the myriad journeys—private and public, secular and spiritual, in time and through eternity—that shaped the slaveholders' world.

In these changing, partially converging understandings of planter emigration can be seen broader changes in planter habit and thought. Partial convergence reflected the public debate's catching up with private discussion and making central there the slavery and religion that had long occupied the center ground of private thought. In this sense the developing public discourse of this time—as seen in the debate over emigration— disclosed not only the widening distance between North and South. It also announced a break with the past: with agrarian republicanism's traditional notions of stability, order, and progress. In their place stood more appropriate understandings of those concepts. These understandings emphasized relations between people at the expense of people's relation to place and so were better suited by far to the world the slaveholders were making.

Changing and converging attitudes also indicated elite slaveholders' recognition that the traditional pairing of social stability and demographic immobility did not apply to a modern slave society. Those who feared that the relations of slavery would be diminished by distance turned out to be wrong. These relations of kinship and commerce instead proved capable of entwining geographic mobility and social stability into section-strengthening cords of class solidarity. By the time this was clear, mobility had become so much part of the patterns of slaveholding life and society that its importance and value often went unexamined. Proslavery advocates spent a great deal of time extolling their system's superior capacity for harmonizing the various class interests of modern society, especially those of capital and labor. In proslavery discourse it went mostly unremarked how successfully the planters and their households had reconciled another apparently antagonistic pairing of an anxious modern age: geographic mobility and social stability.

Combining mobility and stability, the slave plantation was both the engine and the anchor of slave society, steadying and stabilizing the planters' surging progress westward. Thus the uprooted class that some still feared would never achieve stability and maturity had already done so, judged by the standards of a new world in which rootedness was much less a question of connection to place and much more a matter of relations among people.[34]

Mobility, then, was not simply a vehicle for the carrying of existing thoughts and habits across the continent. It was that of course, as the Southwest's growing similarity to the Southeast suggests. But mobility was more. It was itself a fundamental determinant of planter thought and habit; of, in other words, their identity as individuals, as households, and as a class. To recognize the power of mobility as a cultural force in plantation society is to understand better how an agricultural people could care little for land as either cultural or spiritual resource.

What was true of emigrant households was to a large extent true of those that never moved. Far from an aberrant presence in elite southern society, emigrants more closely resembled a glass held up to that society, one that both mirrored and magnified the nature and character of the southern elite as a whole. Together, both public and private responses to the slaveholders' westward movement reflect how mobility, slavery, and Christianity combined to encourage a way of looking at the world that magnified the significance of human relations (between owner and owned, men and women, past and present, the living and the dead), while minimizing the significance of space as a barrier to human connection and of place as a framework for those relations. The planters' responses to their journeys across space expose the essence of their travels through time, offering up a paradoxical portrait of an agricultural class for whom land meant less and less. In their increasing obsession with relations between people, pursued at the cost of alienation from land and place, the planters revealed themselves as profoundly modern. In the ways in which they sought to define themselves in terms of relations between people, under God, they reveal the lengths to which they would go to develop their own conservative pathway to progress and salvation.

Changes in geographical location did bring into sharper relief the continuities of spiritual and intellectual ties between family and friends. The very fact of separation produced the evidence that illustrates how much members of planter families continued to be connected by shared concerns and a shared language in which to discuss them, a language as comprehensible in the canebrake of Alabama or the bayous of Louisiana as on the streets of Charleston or the squares of Savannah. Living in different states, emigrants and their families continued to inhabit the same ideological world. It was a world of habit and thought both aggressive and reflective, imperious and doubting, expansive and constrained, an apt intermingling of characteristics for a class that came to maturity in plantation society's anxious atmosphere of inegalitarian interdependence and perpetual motion. It was a class whose life-giving roots lay not in the soil they owned, whether eroded or fertile, but in the relations they formed, both good and evil: a class whose place was on, but never truly of, the land of the South.

Notes

ABBREVIATIONS

ADAH   Alabama Department of Archives and History, Montgomery
Alabama W. S. Hoole Special Collections Library, University
         of Alabama, University
Auburn   Auburn University Archives, Auburn, Ala.
Duke   Manuscript Department, William R. Perkins Library,
         Duke University, Durham, N.C.
LSU   Louisiana State University, Baton Rouge
Montreat Presbyterian Church (USA) Department of History,
         Montreat, N.C.
UGA   Hargrett Rare Book and Manuscript Library, University
         of Georgia, Athens
UNC   Southern Historical Collection, University of North
         Carolina Library, Chapel Hill
USC   South Caroliniana Library, University of South Carolina,
         Columbia

I. WHEN PLANTERS ROAMED THE EARTH

1. Lyell, *Second Visit* 2:57.

2. Ibid., 64, 17–18, 66. Stanley Trimble, "Nature's Continent," in Conzen, *Making of the American Landscape,* suggests that perhaps no "other large area of the world" was "transformed more rapidly at the hands of people" as "near-primeval land . . . sprouted farms and cities" (9).

3. Power, *Impressions of America* 2:123–26.

4. According to Hodgson this family had not found New Orleans to their liking (Hodgson, "Letter VI," 22 March 1820, in *Letters from North America* 1:110, 114–15).

5. Samuel McDonald to Ann Brantley, 27 May 1817, Elizabeth Furman Talley Papers, UNC.

6. Tocqueville, *Democracy in America* 1:281. On migration in the North, see Atack and Bateman, *To Their Own Soil,* 71–85. On westward movement in the United States generally, see McClelland and Zeckhauser, *Demographic Dimensions*

of the New Republic; Billington, *Westward Expansion;* Kulikoff, *Agrarian Origins,* 208–25.

7. Kirkland, *Western Clearings,* 4. *Charleston Reporter,* 6 Aug. 1817, quoted in Charles Lowery, "The Great Migration to the Mississippi Territory, 1798–1819," in Gonzales, *Mississippi Reader,* 77; Huntsville *Alabama Republican,* 17 April 1819, quoted in Rohrbough, *Land Office Business,* 125. See Perry, *Boats against the Current,* 133, for Kirkland's own involvement in land speculation and settlement.

8. Rohrbough, *Land Office Business,* xii. Although some historians, Rohrbough for example, tend to use the term *migration,* I follow the planters themselves in preferring *emigration.* Both terms indicate movement, of course, but emigration carries with it a stronger sense of movement *from.* Among other benefits, it reminds us that many slaveholders and slaves did not just move out of their own community or state but often out of their country (into "territories" like Alabama or other nations such as Mexico or, later, the Republic of Texas).

9. William W. Bibb to Charles Tait, 19 Sept. 1818, Tait Family Papers, ADAH.

10. Charles Tait to James A. Tait, 20 Jan. 1819, ibid. See the biographical and genealogical material in same collection for the Goode family.

11. Ibid., 11 July, 26 Nov. 1818, 15 Jan. 1819, 29 Dec. 1818.

12. Ibid., 29 Dec. 1818, Tait Family Papers, Auburn. See also ibid., 7 Nov., 14 Oct. 1818, 15 Jan 1819. Although Charles Tait was not specific about how friends and family might help James, there was a great deal of collusion among buyers at the land sales, including among those whom the Fort Claiborne *Courier* called "gentlemen speculators" (Fort Claiborne *Courier,* rept. in the Huntsville *Alabama Republican,* 1 May 1819, quoted in Rohrbough, *Land Office Business,* 126). Government officials on the spot were largely powerless to prevent this kind of activity. As secretary of the treasury, William H. Crawford had ultimate responsibility for land. Crawford, who happened to be a close friend of Charles Tait, initially thought such activity required no attention. In 1820 he changed his mind and advised land officers to "counteract combinations by bidding" against them (127).

13. Charles Tait to James A. Tait, 26 Feb. 1819, 7 Nov. 1818, Tait Family Papers, ADAH. A few weeks earlier Charles Tait had expressed the hope that James would "find land . . . which unites fertility, health & commerce" (ibid., 14 Oct. 1818).

14. Charles Tait to Elizabeth Caroline Tait, [n.d.] 1818, 13 Dec. 1818, Elizabeth Caroline Tait to Charles Tait, 20 Jan. [1819], ibid.

15. Lyell, *Second Visit* 2:6; Power, *Impressions of America* 2:123–26; Hodgson, "Letter VI," in *Letters from North America* 1:114–15. On the slave trade in the nineteenth century, see Curtin, *Atlantic Slave Trade,* 231–64. The slave trade to the United States had, of course, slowed to an illegal trickle by this time, but movement of slaves within the country and its territories was rapidly growing. Kulikoff, *Agrarian Origins,* 263, estimates that "nearly a third of a million slaves had moved

southwestward by 1820," with more than 750,000 doing so between 1820 and 1860. Oakes, *Ruling Race,* 79, writes that "there was no period before the Civil War when this massive movement of slaveholders slowed down for long."

16. Moffatt, *Charles Tait,* 227–28.

17. Both Bibb and Tait had lost their Senate seats, in part as a consequence of their support for the Compensation Law or Salary Act of 1816. By greatly increasing politicians' income, the legislation ignited, in Charles Sellers's words, a "volcano of public indignation." It was subsequently repealed (Sellers, *Market Revolution,* 104–6). Governor Bibb died in 1820 not long after falling from his horse during a thunderstorm. See also Abernethy, *Formative Period,* 120–24; Thornton, *Politics and Power,* 10–14. For a discussion of Walker's life, times, and associates, see Bailey, *John Williams Walker* and "John Williams Walker," 179–95; Owsley, "John Williams Walker," 100–119. Sellers, *Market Revolution,* 169, also discusses the "Broad River men" who made up the "Georgia Machine."

18. James Oakes calculates that "even in the wealthiest areas of the cotton belt," the mobility of "the wealthiest—and presumably most stable—class" matched that of the poorest and most itinerant of "northern urbanites." The southern "master class," Oakes concludes, was "one of the most mobile in history" (Oakes, *Ruling Race,* 76–78). In *Slavery and Freedom,* 99, Oakes suggests that "only a small minority of planter families, as few as 20 percent, lived in the same place for more than two decades." Economic historian Gavin Wright also describes how the most-propertied residents of the South moved as much as the least-propertied inhabitants of the North. Wright emphasizes, not how typically American this made them, but how starkly it differentiated their behavior from "wealthy property holders" in the North. There "even home ownership significantly reduced the likelihood of moving," and "most of the very rich had stable long-term connections with an urban or regional business community" (Wright, *Old South, New South,* 26).

19. This study, then, is neither a demographic account of mobility nor a social history of settlement, although these are parts of the story. Many other works have focused on these, and other, aspects of westward emigration in the years following 1815. In addition to works cited elsewhere, the following are just a few of the important works on southern history that deal to a greater or lesser extent with westward expansion. Everett Dick offers a social history of what he calls "this ceaseless hegira" in his *Dixie Frontier.* For a recent study of emigration from the Upper South, see Fischer and Kelly, *Away, I'm Bound Away.* Works that focus on the demography of migration include Otto, *Southern Frontiers;* Lynch, "Westward Flow of Southern Colonists"; Lathrop, *Migration into East Texas;* Schaefer, "Statistical Profile." On emigration and southern agriculture and economy, see Ransom, *Conflict and Compromise,* 22–68; Wright, *Political Economy,* 10–42. For a consideration of yeomen and planter relations and their relative significance in the migration process, see Rohrbough, *Trans-Appalachian Frontier;* Foust, *Yeoman*

Farmer and Westward Expansion, chap. 1. Yeoman farmers and southern herders are also treated in Owsley, *Plain Folk,* 23–89, and his "Pattern of Migration and Settlement." More recently, Charles Bolton discussed the emigration of poor white people in his *Poor Whites,* 66–83. On the societies destroyed or displaced by the westward movement, see, for example, Hudson, *Southeastern Indians;* Rogin, *Fathers and Children;* Prucha, *Great Father,* 179–242.

20. Meinig, *Shaping of America,* 235, and 285–96 for differences between the upper and lower South and their relation to westward emigration. In making the case for the impact of latitudinal emigration on social, political, and cultural development in the Southwest, Meinig goes so far as to describe the region as "South Carolina extended" (285). The term highlights the unparalleled role played by South Carolinians in the settlement of the Southwest. Nevertheless it obscures, in my view, the contribution of the slaveholding Georgians who, along with their neighbors to the east, took the lead in shaping the new region's landscape and character. Taking Alabama as an example, by 1850, 48,663 of the young state's settlers had arrived from South Carolina while 58,997 had crossed the border from Georgia. A further 28,521 had arrived from North Carolina, 10,387 from Virginia, and 757 from Maryland.

21. On questions of planter motivation and on various other subjects sketched out in this introduction, this study both builds on and departs from existing works that explore the meaning of the westward movement and settlement of the slaveholders. Chief among these works are Oakes, *Ruling Race* and *Slavery and Freedom;* Fogel and Engerman, *Time on the Cross;* Cashin, *Family Venture;* Censer, *North Carolina Planters* and "Southwestern Migration"; Freehling, *Road to Disunion.*

22. Charles Tait to Elizabeth Caroline Tait, 13 Dec. 1818, Elizabeth Caroline Tait to Charles Tait, 20 Jan. [1819], Tait Family Papers, ADAH.

23. The argument that what divided these "many Souths" was at least as important as what united "the South" is made forcibly in Freehling, *Road to Disunion,* chap. 1.

24. Mel Bradford, for example, discusses the "agrarian republican theory" of John Taylor in his introduction to Taylor, *Arator,* 11–43. See also Grammer, *Pastoral and Politics.* I prefer Bradford's "agrarian" (or "hard pastoral") to Grammer's "pastoral" because it better suggests the agrarians' central emphasis on farming practices and agricultural experimentation and improvement. Grammer does, however, take full account of how writers like John Taylor combined the ideal and the practical, the material and the moral (33).

25. Freehling, *Road to Disunion,* 30, 7, for quotes and 25–36 for general discussion of the subject. See also Fogel and Engerman, *Time on the Cross,* 44–58; Oakes, *Ruling Race,* 69–95; Cashin, *Family Venture,* 32–49; Censer, *North Carolina Planters,* 127–34, and "Southwestern Migration."

26. Freehling, *Road to Disunion,* 28.

27. Fox-Genovese, "Social Order and the Female Self," 49–50. Lewis Simpson has carried a similar interpretation into the realm of southern letters. There he has analyzed the South's unique contribution to the cultural task of reconciling "freedom and community" and has tied it to their attempt to build "a modern society founded on chattel slavery" (Simpson, "Slavery and Modernism," *Brazen Face*, 80). See also Genovese, *Slaveholders' Dilemma*, 12–13. None of this is to deny that a central component of conservatism, for slaveholders and for others, is the attempt to ground modern claims for their values in a continuous cultural, religious, or intellectual tradition. See, for example, Marsden, *Fundamentalism and American Culture*.

2. THE SPIRIT OF EMIGRATION

1. John C. Calhoun to James E. Calhoun, 7 May 1820, in Meriwether, *Papers of John C. Calhoun* 5:96. Col. Andrew Pickens was related to John C. Calhoun through his mother, who was Calhoun's cousin. After his move to Alabama, Pickens, a former governor of South Carolina, remained in close contact with his Calhoun kin. According to Orville Vernon Burton, John C. Calhoun "sponsored" Pickens's son, Francis, when he returned to South Carolina later in the decade (Burton, *In My Father's House*, 66, 117).

2. Mrs. S. A. Robson to Mrs. Charles (Sophia Hughes) Hunt, 26 Jan. 1835, Hughes Family Collection, UNC; William Blanding to Rachel Blanding, 5 April 1834 (quoted portion written on 8 April), Blanding Family Papers, USC; Robert J. Gage to James M. Gage, 14 April, 12 Nov. 1835, James McKibbin Gage Papers, UNC. The Deas family referred to by William Blanding were the in-laws of doctor and proslavery writer Josiah Nott, who also moved to Mobile two years later with his wife, Sarah Deas Nott. See Horsman, *Josiah Nott*, 54–55.

3. Atack and Bateman, *To Their Own Soil*, 71–72, discuss the difficulties of gathering accurate figures on emigration in the period before 1850 when "evidence of internal migration . . . is much more sketchy." Yet there is no reason to disagree with Allan Kulikoff's view that "thousands of planters" moved to the Southwest in the 1820s and 1830s alone (Kulikoff, *Agrarian Origins*, 236).

4. Rogers, "Great Population Exodus," 14–15; David Moltke-Hansen, "The Expansion of Intellectual Life: A Prospectus," in O'Brien and Moltke-Hansen, *Intellectual Life*, 19. See also Smith, *Economic Readjustment*, 25–26. Rogers takes his estimate from Smith's figures. In the 1830s, the decade of peak migration from South Carolina, a total of 121,714 people left the state. In the same period its population increased by only 13,213, from 581,185 to 594,398. By 1850 more than 50,000 South Carolinians lived in Georgia, more than 45,000 in Alabama, and about 26,000 in Mississippi, and they accounted for over 30 percent of all emigrants to those states. Smith estimated the net migration from South Carolina in the period

1820–60 at 376,144 people, 202,527 of them white, 173,617 black. These figures from Smith, *Economic Readjustment*, 22; Foust, *Yeoman Farmer*, 16. Smith describes the movement out of South Carolina between 1820 and 1860 as "one of the largest ever experienced from so small an area in so short a period" (19). See also Ford, *Origins of Southern Radicalism*, 38–40, on population decline in South Carolina.

5. Y. Z., "Embanking and Draining Our Low Lands, to Prevent Emigration, &c.," *Southern Agriculturist* 11 (Jan. 1838): 14. Georgia's population grew from 340,987 in 1830 to 691,392 in 1840 and to 906,185 in 1850. See Bonner, "Agricultural Adjustment in Ante Bellum Georgia," in Bonner and Roberts, *Studies in Georgia History*, 123. See also Foust, *Yeoman Farmer*, 16; Billington, *Westward Expansion*, 317.

6. I follow the common practice of defining a planter as an owner of twenty or more slaves. According to the 1850 Federal Census, there were 25,596 slaveholders in South Carolina, of whom 4,674 (18.26%) owned twenty or more slaves. Of the 38,456 slaveholders in Georgia, 5,995 (15.59%) were classified as planters (De Bow, *Statistical View*, 95).

7. James Hemphill to Andrew Munro, 24 Dec. 1833, Hemphill Family Papers, Duke.

8. "Permanency of the American Union," *Niles' Weekly Register*, 7 June 1817, 229. This address was "part of an essay delivered before the Literary and Philosophical Society of Charleston in 1815" (229).

9. Simms, *Views and Reviews*, 16–17.

10. Quoted in Bartlett, *John C. Calhoun*, 83–84. Bartlett also discusses Calhoun's nationalism, suspicion of Great Britain, and early support for tariffs as a means to cementing national unity (82ff.). See also Freehling, *Prelude to Civil War*, 92–96; Freehling, *Road to Disunion*, 261.

11. Andrew Jackson to (Secretary of War) George Graham, 21 Dec. 1816, quoted in Roberts, "Politics and Public Land Disposal," 165.

12. Andrew Jackson, "Second Annual Message, 6 Dec. 1830," in Fred L. Israel, ed., *The State of the Union Messages of the Presidents*, vol. 1, *1790–1860* (New York, 1967), 335.

13. Andrew Jackson to (Secretary of War) George Graham, 21 Dec. 1816, quoted in Roberts, "Politics and Public Land Disposal," 165.

14. Editorial, *Savannah Daily Republican*, 31 May 1821.

15. John C. Calhoun quoted in Sellers, *Market Revolution*, 78. Sellers also discusses Calhoun's early support of internal improvements. For postwar opposition within South Carolina to the nationalist views and policies of Calhoun and his followers, see Ford, *Origins of Southern Radicalism*, 114ff.; Sellers, *Market Revolution*, 143ff.

16. William H. Crawford to Charles Tait, 12 July 1817, Tait Family Papers, ADAH. At this time Crawford was secretary of the treasury in James Monroe's

government, having served a term in the United States Senate, as America's minister to France, and as secretary of war.

17. Spalding, *Address of Hon. Thomas Spalding,* 6.

18. Hugh Swinton Legaré to Alfred Huger, in Legaré, *Writings of Hugh Swinton Legaré* 1:221–22.

19. On the Missouri controversy, see Freehling, *Road to Disunion,* 144ff.

20. Bartlett, *Calhoun,* 142; Sellers, *Market Revolution,* 136, and chap. 4 generally for an extensive discussion of "The Crisis of 1819." As Frederick Jackson Turner put it, "The price of cotton was in these years a barometer of Southern prosperity and of Southern discontent" (Turner, "Colonization of the West," 560).

21. Eldred Simkins, "Back Country Cultivation.— On Horizontal Ploughing in the Upper and Middle Country," *Southern Agriculturist* 2 (Sept. 1829): 387–88.

22. William Elliot, "A 4th of July Oration regarding the Tariff," 4 July [1830], 3–4, 11–12, Elliot-Gonzales Family Papers, UNC. William Elliot (1788–1863) was a planter, writer, legislator, and antitariff Unionist in the Charleston and Beaufort districts of South Carolina.

23. Ibid.

24. Thomas Fuller Hazzard, "The Culture of the White Poppy in the Southern States Recommended," *Southern Agriculturist* 4 (Aug. 1831): 410–13; William J. Alston, "An Address Delivered before the 'Anti-Tariff Agricultural Society of Broad River,' Fairfield District, (S.C.) on Its First Anniversary, in July, 1829," ibid., 3 (March 1830): 114–15. On the Nullification Crisis, see Freehling, *Prelude to Civil War.* Although tariffs and nullification were important issues in Georgia, they had not generated the levels of internal conflict or sense of external threat that had combined to create a pervasive atmosphere of social crisis in South Carolina. The Georgia legislature did pass a set of resolutions that condemned the "tariff of abominations" as "deceptive in its title, fraudulent in its pretexts, oppressive in its exactions, partial and unjust in its operations, unconstitutional in its well known objects, [and] ruinous to commerce and agriculture." Yet sentiment in favor of nullification as a remedy was far less strong in Georgia than in South Carolina; indeed many Georgians were as strongly opposed to nullification as they were to the tariffs. See Coulter, "Nullification Movement," 4.

25. John Berkeley Grimball Diary, 8 Oct. 1832, Grimball Family Papers, UNC. For the politics of this period, see Ford, *Origins of Southern Radicalism;* Bancroft, *Calhoun and the South Carolina Nullification Movement;* Freehling, *Prelude to Civil War* and *Road to Disunion.* On the beginning of elite emigration in South Carolina, see Smith, *Economic Readjustment,* 19ff.

26. Perhaps one reason why nullification proved less popular and controversial in Georgia was that emigration had been less prevalent there than in South Carolina during the 1820s. Georgia remained a destination as well as a starting point for emigrants, while many more of those who did move remained within the

state's boundaries, settling on lands that became available through appropriation from the Creeks and the Cherokees. Georgia, of course, had had its own quarrels with the federal government over its claims to Indian land. Indeed some South Carolinians argued for Georgian support for nullification on the grounds that Georgians had already had their own successful nullification movement. But in one sense the success of Georgia in "nullifying" Chief Justice Marshall's decision in *Worcester v. Georgia* (1832) had helped to limit emigration for the time being and, therefore, to limit its saliency as a public issue. See Coulter, "Nullification Movement," 9; and also Boles, *South through Time,* 236–38.

27. Judge John Belton O'Neall, "Address Delivered before the South Carolina State Agricultural Society," *Southern Cultivator* 1, no. 14 (1843): 108.

28. James Henry Hammond quoted in William Gilmore Simms, "Southern Agriculture," *Magnolia* 4 (March 1842): 132; Y. Z., "Embanking and Draining Our Low Lands, to Prevent Emigration, &c." For another example, among many, of this view, see Patrick Noble, "Effects of the Remarkable Prevalence of Cold in South-Carolina. Remarks on Emigration to the West," rept. from the *Farmer's Register* in *Southern Agriculturist* 9 (June 1836): 332–33.

29. Whitemarsh B. Seabrook, "Extract from an Address, Delivered before the United Agricultural Society of South-Carolina, in the Hall of the House of Representatives, on the 1st. of December, 1828," *Southern Agriculturist* 2 (April 1829): 173–74. See also Faust, "Rhetoric and Ritual," 33. Seabrook was governor 1848–50.

30. James Hemphill to Andrew Munro, 24 Dec. 1833, Hemphill Family Papers, Duke.

31. "James Hamilton, Jr.'s Speech at Walterborough, October 21, 1828," in Freehling, *Nullification Era,* 54. Outpourings in this vein of what Michael O'Brien calls "robust elegy, energetic melancholy" were common (O'Brien, *Rethinking the South,* 82). See also Ralph T. Eubanks, "The Rhetoric of the Nullifiers," in Braden, *Oratory in the Old South,* 19–72.

32. James L. Petigru to Hugh Legaré, 29 Oct. 1832, in Carson, *Life, Letters, and Speeches,* 104.

33. Sarah Gayle Journal, 26 Sept. 1832, and Sarah A. Gayle to William Haynsworth, 31 Dec. 1832, Alabama. Political conflict also played a part in James S. Deas's decision to emigrate. Embittered by his loss to James Chesnut in the South Carolina State Senate race of 1832, Deas and his family left for Alabama in 1834. See Horsman, *Josiah Nott,* 54–55.

34. William Gilmore Simms to James Lawson, 25 Nov. 1832, in Oliphant, *Letters of Simms* 1: 46–48. On the Nullification Ordinance, see Freehling, *Prelude to Civil War,* 261ff.

35. William Gilmore Simms to James Lawson, 19, 22 Jan., 27 Nov. 1833, 25 Nov. 1832, in Oliphant, *Letters of Simms* 1: 49–50, 52, 54, 46–48.

36. William Gilmore Simms to James Lawson, 25 Nov. 1832, 19, 22 Jan., 27 Nov. 1833, ibid., 46–48, 49–50, 52, 54.

37. Colleton [Joseph E. Jenkins], "Some of the Causes of the Decline and Fall of Most of the Agricultural Societies of South-Carolina," *Southern Agriculturist* 8 (March 1835): 115.

38. See Kovacik and Winberry, *South Carolina*, 92, who also provide figures that suggest how earlier destinations within the state had themselves become points of departure by the 1830s, and Barnwell, *Love of Order*, 12, for the statistics on Fairfield and Chester and for further discussion of their significance.

39. John Gage to James M. Gage, 15 Nov. 1835, James McKibbin Gage Papers, UNC; Colleton, "Some of the Causes," 115.

40. Colleton, "Some of the Causes," 115.

41. Ibid. For a later reference to South Carolina as a frontier state, politically speaking, see Edisto Island, "On the Establishment of an Agricultural Professorship," *Southern Agriculturist* 9 (May 1836): 244. Edisto Island argued, "South-Carolina will soon be prepared to occupy the important and hazardous station of a frontier State (in a few years she may be compelled to assume it,) in relation to the great question which now convulses the general community." See also Faust, "Rhetoric and Ritual," 44–45.

42. William Ellison, "On the Resources of South Carolina," *Southern Agriculturist* 3 (Feb. 1830): 82–84; William Ellison, "On the Cultivation of the Wild or Native Grape Vine," ibid., 2 (Jan. 1829): 13–15. Elsewhere, Ellison asked planters not to "flatter" themselves that an improvement in tariff rates would produce a rise in prices and argued that in some cases protectionist policies indirectly benefited cotton growers by subsidizing sugar planters who might otherwise turn to cotton (William Ellison, "Extracts from an Address Delivered before the Fairfield Agricultural Society," ibid., 3 [Jan. 1830]: 1–7).

43. William Gilmore Simms, "Spirit of Emigration," *Southern Literary Journal* 2 (June 1836): 259. Such debates, of course, also took place elsewhere. On those who stayed behind in New England, for example, see Barron, *Those Who Stayed Behind*. See also Faust, "Rhetoric and Ritual," 29–31. Faust prefaces her discussion of South Carolina with a brief discussion of agricultural orations elsewhere in the nation.

3. PUBLIC THOUGHTS

1. Dr. Joseph Johnson, "Communication to the Agricultural Society of South-Carolina, on the Improvement of Soils by Marl and Lime," *Southern Agriculturist* 11 (Nov. 1838): 578.

2. See Faust, "Rhetoric and Ritual," 29–31; Grammer, *Pastoral and Politics*.

3. The westward expansion of slavery, or of "the slave power," was, of course, a central issue in the 1850s. What is meant here is that westward expansion had ceased to be a major "internal" issue in the South in the sense of arousing fears that it was weakening slaveholding society or was somehow antithetical to slaveholding values. See chap. 7 below.

4. See Meyer Reinhold, "Survey of the Scholarship on Classical Traditions in Early America," in Eadie, *Classical Traditions,* 44. "The development of American society, based on an unstable, multi-dimensional pluralism and commitment to progress and change was," in Reinhold's view, "incompatible with the absolute models of antiquity with their emphasis on the universal, on order, stability, reason, balance. The unique, dynamic American society, revolutionary, disorderly, future-oriented, could not long continue to venerate antiquity as before. Even Jefferson could say 'I like the dreams of the future more than the history of the past.'" For the critics of emigration discussed here, the continuing effort to ground their "dreams of the future" in the "history of the past" lay at the very heart of their efforts to come to terms with elite emigration.

5. John Witherspoon to Shepard K. Kollock, 4 Sept. 1834, John Witherspoon Letters, Montreat, quoted in Deschamps, "Presbyterian Church," 184. On general concerns regarding spiritual decline and on the chronic problem of ministers' departures compounding already troublesome shortages of candidates for the ministry, see Loveland, *Southern Evangelicals,* 53.

6. Minutes, Hopewell Presbytery (Georgia), 13 Sept. 1837, Montreat; Rusticus, "Effects of Emigration on the Churches," *Southern Religious Telegraph,* 6 March 1835.

7. "History of Bethel Presbyterian Church, South Carolina, 1811–1828" (n.d.), quoted in Deschamps, "Presbyterian Church," 166.

8. See Deschamps, "Presbyterian Church," especially chap. 8, "The Church and Westward Migration," 163–64. Deschamps writes that "controversy over slavery and doctrine in the 1830's greatly hindered the expansion of the General Assembly of the Presbyterian Church, but nothing weakened synods of the South Atlantic states so much as the westward movement." Deschamps also discusses the church's missionary efforts and suggests that "interest in the spiritual needs of frontiersmen might have continued had not the westward movement assumed new proportions in the 1830's." Faced with "a mass exodus of ministers and members," the Presbyterians mounted "a vigorous campaign" against the departure they believed was breaking down both church and community life" in the South Atlantic states (163–64).

9. John Witherspoon to Shepard K. Kollock, 4 Sept. 1834, John Witherspoon Letters, Montreat. Quoted, ibid., 184.

10. A Pine Land Planter, "Emigration," *Southern Agriculturist* 12 (July 1839): 349.

11. Ibid.

12. Sinclair, "On Rural Buildings," ibid., 8 (April 1835): 175–78.

13. P., "Short Cotton on the Low Lands," ibid., 10 (Oct. 1837): 519.

14. Robert Roper, for example, stated that "South-Carolina is emphatically an Agricultural State" (Robert Roper, "Anniversary Address Delivered before the Agricultural Society of South Carolina, August 19, 1834," ibid., 7 [Nov. 1834]: 566–69). See also Faust, "Rhetoric and Ritual," 45, for an identical assertion from Whitemarsh B. Seabrook.

15. Well-Wisher to Agriculture, "On the Necessity of Agricultural Education, Being Bestowed on Those Intended for Superintendent of Plantations, and the Benefits Which Would Arise from Proper Encouragement Being Held Out to Respectable Youths, to Engage as Such," *Southern Agriculturist* 2 (Jan. 1829): 1. Such concern was not confined to South Carolina and Georgia. On agricultural reformers' critique of destructive and unpatriotic agricultural practices in Virginia, see Cashin, "Landscape and Memory," 477–500.

16. Thomas Spalding, "Brief Notes on the Cultivation of Cotton, Rice, Sugar Cane, and the Grape Vine," *Southern Agriculturist* 1 (Feb. 1828): 58.

17. Ellison, "Extracts from an Address," 6.

18. Ellison, "On the Resources of South Carolina," 82; Ellison, "Extracts from an Address," 6. See also Ellison, "On the Cultivation of the Wild or Native Grape Vine."

19. John D. Legaré, "Farewell Address of the Editor," *Southern Agriculturist* 7 (Dec. 1834): 660–61. Legaré's address is also a good example of an article that discusses many of the means and methods by which agricultural improvement would be achieved. See also Roper, "Anniversary Address," 561–69; B. R. Carroll, "A Few Hints for the Improvement of Our Agricultural Societies," *Southern Agriculturist* 8 (June 1835): 281–83; Ellison, "Extracts from an Address," 1–7. William Ellison argued that agricultural societies advanced knowledge and fostered "fraternity of feeling." See also Faust, "Rhetoric and Ritual," 29–53.

20. William Harper, "To the Honorable Speaker, and Other Members of the House of Representatives . . . on Behalf of the Monticello Planters' Society," *Southern Agriculturist* 12 (Feb. 1839): 60–61.

21. Hazzard, "Culture of the White Poppy," 410. Adopting a more secular tone, Hazzard also appealed to the spirit of 1776 in calling on planters to meet the challenges facing "the place of my nativity; the sepulchre of my ancestors" (413). For a general study of the agricultural journals and papers of this period, see Demaree, *American Agricultural Press,* and for the *Southern Agriculturist* in particular, see Theodore Rosengarten, "*The Southern Agriculturist* in an Age of Reform," in O'Brien and Moltke-Hansen, *Intellectual Life,* 279–94.

22. Harper, "To the Honorable Speaker," 60–61; Thomas Spalding, "Copy of a Letter to Mr. Crawford, on Legislative Patronage," *Southern Agriculturist* 1

(Oct. 1828): 433–35. See also Whitemarsh B. Seabrook, "Extract from an Address, Delivered before the United Agricultural Society of South-Carolina, in the Hall of the House of Representatives, on the 1st. of December, 1828," *Southern Agriculturist* 2 (March 1829): 111–15. Seabrook, president of the United Agricultural Society of South Carolina, believed that as "the perpetuity of" South Carolina's "domestic altars is inseparable from the reservation of the rights of her landed proprietors, I am satisfied that I shall not appeal in vain, when I ask the deputed guardians of an oppressed community for their patronage and support" (115).

23. Roper, "Anniversary Address," 567. On agricultural professorships and the importance of agricultural education generally, see also Seabrook, "Extract from an Address," 111–15; Senex, "On a Professorship of Agriculture," *Southern Agriculturist* 9 (March 1836): 122–24; Edisto Island, "On the Establishment of an Agricultural Professorship," 240–46; Neckar, "Knowledge and Agriculture: The Foundation of General Prosperity," *Southern Agriculturist* 11 (Oct. 1838): 521–25.

24. James Gregorie, "Interesting Letters, on the Cultivation of Sugar," *Southern Agriculturist* 2 (April 1829): 96–100. On the prospects of sugar production, see also A Small Planter, "On the Making of Raspberry and Strawberry Cordials, Cider, and Wine; Also, Observations on the Growing of the Sugar Cane, in the Lower Part of South Carolina," ibid., 6 (May 1833): 238–42. On the South's potential for opium production, see Hazzard, "Culture of the White Poppy." A brief survey of any of the region's various agricultural journals would provide numerous articles on all of these topics and many more besides. For examples, see Ellison, "On the Resources of South Carolina," 82–84; A Highlander, "The Culture of Silk and Vines, Recommended as Substitutes for That of Cotton in the Upper Part of Georgia and Carolina," *Southern Agriculturist* 4 (Feb. 1831): 60–61. A Georgian signing himself "No Emigrant" wrote of experiments in corn raising in Georgia, ibid., 10 (Jan. 1837): 12–13. "Early Silk Manufactures in This Country," ibid., 10 (March 1837): 153–56, discusses the benefits of silk cultivation. Even more articles discussed how crops should be grown and tended. See, among many, N. Herbemont, "On Manures," ibid., 9 (Jan. 1836): 7–18; Simkins, "Back Country Cultivation," 385–91; A Highlander, "On the Benefits Arising from Horizontal Ploughing and Ditching," *Southern Agriculturist* 4 (June 1831): 301–3; J. Hamilton Couper, "Essay on Rotation of Crops," ibid., 6 (Feb. 1833): 57–59. For an example of appeals to beautify plantations in order to encourage attachment to them, see "Agricultural Architecture," ibid., 10 (April 1837): 203–4.

25. N. Herbemont, "On Emigration to the Western Country," *Southern Agriculturist* 8 (May 1835): 242; Spalding, "Brief Notes," 58. Whether the planters were as destructive as their contemporary and later critics believed them to be is challenged by Earle, "Myth of the Southern Soil Miner," 175–210.

26. R., "The West!" *Southern Agriculturist* 9 (Jan. 1836): 5–7. See Chaplin, *Anxious Pursuit*, especially chap. 1, for a discussion of how the slaveholders of the

Atlantic seaboard linked ideas regarding progress and agriculture in the eighteenth and early nineteenth centuries.

27. Spalding, *Address,* 6–7.

28. Quoted in "Early Silk Manufactures in This Country," *Southern Agriculturist* 10 (March 1837): 153–56.

29. Simms, "The Good Farmer," *Ladies' Companion* 15 (Aug. 1841): 154–55.

30. Ibid., 156.

31. Seabrook, "Extract from an Address," 111.

32. Ibid.

33. Francis D. Quash, "An Address Delivered in Charleston, before the Agricultural Society of South Carolina, at Its Anniversary Meeting, on the 18th of August, 1831," *Southern Agriculturist* 4 (Oct. 1831): 510. John D. Legaré, "Farewell Address of the Editor," 660–61, expressed frustration that planters were "compelled to follow the tracks pursued by our ancestors, without knowing whether they are correct or not, and whether a small variation would not produce more happy results." See also N. Herbemont, "On the Culture of the Grape Vine, with Observations on the Practice Recommended by Various Writers," *Southern Agriculturist* 3 (June 1830): 304–6.

34. William Gilmore Simms to Charles L. Wheler, 9 May 1849, in Olpihant, *Letters of Simms* 2:516. Such views took on the pervasiveness of conventional wisdom among those who aspired to literary respect, even fame. John James Gresham, for example, in an 1831 oration to the sophomore class at Franklin College, Athens, Georgia (later the University of Georgia), lamented how "one of the most prominent obstructions to the advancement of literature" was the willingness of men "to relinquish all hopes of rising to eminence for the present gratification of their avaricious desires." Reinforcing this preference was the fact that "the wide extent of our territory and the alluring prospect of profitable speculations are continually inviting emigrants to the west" (Journal of John James Gresham, 33, John James Gresham Writings, UGA). See also Moltke-Hansen, "Expansion of Intellectual Life," 13.

35. W., "On Rice Threshers," *Southern Agriculturist* 7 (Nov. 1834): 579.

36. Roper, "Anniversary Address," 567.

37. Ibid.; Eldred Simkins, "The System of Horizontal Ploughing . . . Considered and Replied To," *Southern Agriculturist* 3 (July 1830): 343–44; James Gregorie, "On Upper Country Cultivation," ibid., 2 (July 1829): 327. Gregorie was editor of the *Southern Agriculturist* at this time. See also Herbemont, "On the Necessity of Acquiring a Knowledge of Agriculture," ibid., 4 (Aug. 1831): 393–98.

38. Simkins, "System of Horizontal Ploughing," 343–44.

39. Spalding, "Brief Notes," 58.

40. Ibid.; Thomas Spalding, "Cotton—Its Introduction and Progress of Its Culture, in the United States," *Southern Agriculturist* 8 (Feb. 1835): 82.

41. C. C. Pinckney, "Causes of Emigration," *Southern Agriculturist* 8 (March 1835): 128.

42. William Ellison, "On Horizontal Ploughing," ibid., 3 (April 1830): 178.

43. S. D. C., "Emigration," *Watchman of the South*, 22 Nov. 1838. As Margaret Deschamps notes, "Church papers joined in the effort to stay the tide of emigration" (Deschamps, "Presbyterian Church," 176).

44. "Thoughts for Emigrants," *Southern Religious Telegraph*, 13 Oct. 1837; review of *A Treatise on the Theory and Practice of Landscape Gardening, Adapted to North America, with a View to the Improvement of Country Residences*, by A. J. Downing, *Southern Cultivator* 3, no. 7 (1845): 109.

45. Alston, "An Address Delivered before the 'Anti-Tariff Agricultural Society of Broad River,'" 120.

46. A Rustic, "Observations on the Apathy Which Pervades the Community of the Southern States, relative to the Improvement of Agriculture," *Southern Agriculturist* 4 (March 1831): 125–26; "On the Improvement of Soils" by the Editor, ibid., 11 (Nov. 1838): 575. Historical geographer Yi-Fu Tuan discusses the relation of "patriotism and rootedness" and suggests that "love of country, or patriotism, was an intense emotion among the peoples of ancient Greece and Italy. Attachment to one's native land, the place of one's birth, the hearth in which one was nurtured, the domicile of the deified souls of departed ancestors *(manes)* and of the gods, was so strong that the ancients could scarcely conceive a fate worse than exile, unless it be the destruction of the country itself" (Tuan, "Geopiety: A Theme in Man's Attachment to Nature and Place," in Lowenthal and Bowden, *Geographies of the Mind*, 23–24).

47. Simms, "The Western Emigrants," in *Poems* 1:163–65. On the ambivalent attitude of Simms and others toward their society, see Faust, *Sacred Circle*. On Simms's ambivalent attitude toward the West, see John McCardell, "Poetry and the Practical: William Gilmore Simms," in O'Brien and Moltke-Hansen, *Intellectual Life*, 188.

48. Discussing his own earlier experiments growing sugarcane, Thomas Spalding noted the various encumbrances to their success, including the nonimportation act and the War of 1812. Spalding also acknowledged that in hard times "it was not for men who were in debt to risk any thing in experiment" (Spalding, "On the Cultivation of the Sugar Cane, Erecting of Proper Buildings, and Manufacturing of Sugar," *Southern Agriculturist* 2 [Feb. 1829]: 55ff.). For discussion of reform's failure to resonate with planters, see William M. Mathew's introduction to his *Agriculture, Geology, and Society*, 43–46; Genovese, *Political Economy of Slavery*, 124–53. Genovese writes that "the overwhelming burden of evidence suggests that the reform movement . . . met noteworthy success below Virginia only in a few localities" (124).

49. N. Herbemont, "Address to the President and Members of the United Agricultural Society of South Carolina, Columbia, Dec. 1, 1829," *Southern Agriculturist* 2 (July 1829): 296–97.

50. Some agricultural reformers did address the implications of slavery for the fulfillment of the agrarian ideal. Grammer, *Pastoral and Politics*, chaps. 1 and 2, discusses how Virginia agrarians John Taylor and John Randolph addressed the presence of slavery and its uncomfortable fit with the agrarian ideal. Farther south William Gilmore Simms's work was unusual in the extent that it acknowledged that the agriculturist was also a slaveholder. Yet the contradictions evident in Simms's efforts to reconcile the "good farmer" with the "good master" only serve to illuminate the difficulties involved in doing so. In "Stowe's Key to Uncle Tom's Cabin," *Southern Quarterly Review* 8 (1853): 249–552, Simms argued that "no real hardship" was suffered by either black or white as a consequence of the "sunderings" from place attendant on emigration to the West, "none, at least, which they feel very severely. In the case of the negro it is borne very lightly and with the greatest equanimity." Yet in the same review Simms was also of the "opinion that the slave should be *adscriptus glebae*—bound to the soil,—as we believe is even now the case in Russia—to be sold with it, never from it. It is no charity to the negro to have it otherwise. His moral improvement depends in great measure upon his being stationary." Simms's contradictory views regarding movement's impact on the slaves suggest a deeper difficulty in assessing the relative importance of connections to people and ties to place.

51. For an excellent discussion of the "absent slave" in republican thought, see Ashworth, *Slavery, Capitalism, and Politics*, 21ff.

52. Perry, *Boats against the Current*, 58, describes the period as "an age of widespread and ritualized nostalgia." Freehling, in *Road to Disunion*, 28–30, sees opposition to westward movement as further evidence for the backward, reactionary nature of the South Carolina gentry, but this hardly explains their enthusiasm for scientific reform. James Oakes, on the other hand, sees enthusiasm for reform as further evidence, with mobility, for the planters' commitment to modernity in general. Recognizing a conservative element to their efforts, on balance Oakes believes that "in their zeal to tout the profitable potential of the old slave states, reformers revealed what poor conservatives they were. For in resisting economic decline, they were not arguing for social stasis" (Oakes, *The Ruling Race*, 90). Both Oakes and Freehling overlook the extent to which the most enthusiastic proponents of scientific reform and progress were often the severest opponents of westward movement. The life of large slaveholder, scientific reformer, and railroad investor Thomas Spalding exemplifies how these were complementary as well as conflicting aspects of the same worldview and illuminates the analytical dangers of confusing conservatism with reaction.

53. See Faust, "Rhetoric and Ritual," for a discussion of the agricultural address as jeremiad. On the Puritan jeremiad's relation to rapid change, see Miller, *New England Mind,* 46–52. On the late nineteenth century, see Lears, *No Place of Grace,* who writes that "Puritan and republican jeremiads have often served to reinforce the dominant culture by reducing social conflicts to questions of individual morality and providing troubled Americans with an innocuous means of discharging half-conscious anxieties about the effects of expanding market capitalism." See also Bertram Wyatt-Brown, "Modernizing Southern Slavery: The Proslavery Argument Revisited," in Kousser and McPherson, *Region, Race, and Reconstruction,* 28–29. Wyatt-Brown writes that "nostalgia for lost virtues and hatred of modern cant and grubbiness were not themselves peculiar to plantation dreamers. British self-criticism . . . supplied them with ample means to catalogue the wrongs of industrialization. Thomas Carlyle, Charles Kingsley, Sir Walter Scott and other luminaries whom southern literati admired offered the same kinds of ambivalent responses to modernity and the overthrow of ancient custom that they themselves felt." Arguably, of course, the "hatred of modern cant" could itself be a form of modern cant.

4. MOVING HOME

1. Elizabeth Caroline Tait to Charles Tait, 12 Jan. 1818, James A. Tait to Charles Tait, 15 Dec. 1817, Tait Family Papers, ADAH. Elizabeth Caroline Tait is referred to throughout the family's correspondence as Caroline. See Owsley, *Struggle for the Gulf Borderlands,* chap. 16, for discussion of the continued conflict with the Creek Nation.

2. Charles Tait to James A. Tait, 25 Feb. 1814, Tait Family Papers, ADAH. Information regarding Tait's commission and swearing-in is contained in Tait family biographical and genealogical information in the same collection. See Owsley, *Struggle for the Gulf Borderlands,* 56ff., for an account of the Creek raid on the militia's fortified camp, which left Flood's troops "badly mauled, and their morale . . . low" (59).

3. Horsman, *War of 1812,* 183; Sellers, *Market Revolution,* 90. See Coulter, *Georgia,* 204–5, 212–13, for the 1802 agreement that settled Georgia's land claims and for the treaty. Georgia agreed to give up all claims to land west of the Chattahoochee in return for land previously claimed by South Carolina and the promise regarding Creek removal. See also Horsman, *Frontier in the Formative Years,* 54ff., on the various treaties and cessions of the period before 1815. As Horsman points out, the complexity of the circumstances made for uneven development of the region. See also Phillips, *Georgia and States' Rights.*

4. Rohrbough, *Land Office Business,* 71–88, 110, discusses the use of land bounties to encourage participation in the War of 1812, the problems in adminis-

tering them in the immediate postwar years, and the presence of veterans among the prospective purchasers of the public lands. See also Davis, *The Cotton Kingdom,* 11–45.

5. James A. Tait to Elizabeth Caroline Tait, 6 Feb. 1818, Tait Family Papers, ADAH; James A. Tait Diary, 10 Nov. 1824, Tait Papers, Auburn.

6. Elizabeth Caroline Tait to Charles Tait, 29 Dec. 1817, James A. Tait to Charles Tait, 15 Dec. 1817, Tait Family Papers, ADAH.

7. On the shift of production out of northern households, see, for example, Clark, *Roots of Rural Capitalism,* and Boydston, *Home and Work.* It is, of course, important to remember that much of the North remained agricultural and did not, therefore, conform to this pattern. Yet as far as the class whose social and political status most closely matched that of the southern elite, it was an increasingly accurate description. The following discussion of the distinctiveness of the plantation household is greatly influenced by Fox-Genovese, *Within the Plantation Household;* Fox-Genovese, "Antebellum Southern Households," and Johnston-Miller, "Heirs to Paternalism."

8. Fox-Genovese refers to the slave families as "truncated households" (Fox-Genovese, *Plantation Household,* 38; Fox-Genovese, "Antebellum Southern Households," 239). For a discussion of the slave family's lack of autonomy, see Kolchin, *Unfree Labor,* 110–20, 195–240.

9. See Johnston-Miller, "Heirs to Paternalism," 17.

10. Oakes, *Ruling Race,* chap. 3, very much sees the planters' willingness to move as further strong evidence for their commitment to the priorities and values of a world shaped by individualism, market forces, and liberal capitalism. The influence of the market on the slaveholders is undeniable, but to view the planters as, in essence, capitalists who happened to own other human beings is to obscure the extent to which the relations and circumstances of slavery in general and slaveholding households in particular profoundly shaped the planters' motives and mores. Oakes himself argues as much in his later *Slavery and Freedom.* There, slavery assumes a far more prominent role in Oakes's interpretation of how "the rationalizing force of capitalism fused with the irrational substance of slavery" (54) to shape the development of the slaveholders and the South.

11. James A. Tait to Elizabeth Caroline Tait, 6 Feb. 1818, Tait Family Papers, ADAH; John Horry Dent quoted in Mathis, *John Horry Dent,* 17–18. See Cashin, *Family Venture,* 32ff., for further examples of young men motivated to emigrate by their desire for "manly independence." I disagree with Cashin's view that this independence encompassed a desire on the part of young men to break with their families and with the paternalist practices and values of older slave states and older (and female) slaveholders. In Cashin's view it was only when forced to by the practical and financial challenges of building plantations in frontier conditions that young men turned reluctantly to their families for support. Jane Turner Censer

takes the opposite view. In *North Carolina Planters,* 128–34, and "Southwestern Migration," 413ff., Censer portrays younger planter men as imbued with the values of their parents and emigration as an essentially cooperative venture from the start. I agree with Censer that in most families cooperation was evident, and assumed, from the start, although in many cases much less consensual and harmonious than she argues. More generally, I find unconvincing Censer's interpretation of planter family relations, aims, and values as largely indistinguishable from those of successful nonslaveholding families and businesses anywhere else in America. Two articles that support Censer's portrayal of the emigrant venture as well planned and cooperative in nature are Jackson and Jackson, "Moving to Alabama," and Barrett, "Whitfields Move to Alabama."

12. Smith, "Farm Journal of John Horry Dent," 44–53.

13. John Horry Dent, quoted in Mathis, *John Horry Dent,* 17–18.

14. David Johnson Sr. to Edward Johnson, 5 Aug. 1836, David Johnson Papers, USC.

15. Thomas Harrison to James Harrison, 24 May 1835, James T. Harrison Papers, UNC. James Harrison would eventually wed an heiress, marrying Regina Blewett, the daughter of a wealthy cotton planter, Major Thomas G. Blewett, in 1840. The Blewetts were also emigrants, having moved from Chester District, South Carolina, to Columbus, Mississippi, in 1832 (Meynard, *Venturers,* 727).

16. Abner Benson to Dr. Elias Benson, 3 Sept. 1821, Perry County Collection, Alabama.

17. Rebecca Latimer Felton, *Country Life in Georgia in the Days of My Youth,* quoted in Scott, *Southern Lady,* 62–63; James A. Tait Diary, 10 Nov. 1824, Tait Papers, Auburn; Mathis, *John Horry Dent,* 17–18.

18. Henry Townes to George Franklin Townes, 16 Jan. 1834, Townes Family Papers, USC.

19. Charles Tait to James A. Tait, [1818], to Elizabeth Caroline Tait, 13 Dec. 1818, Tait Family Papers, ADAH.

20. Henry Townes to George Franklin Townes, 16 Jan. 1834, Townes Family Papers, USC.

21. In *Family Venture,* 44–49, Cashin argues that planter women were almost always opposed to emigration and almost always excluded from household decisions about whether to move or not. In *North Carolina Planters and Their Children,* 132, Censer discusses some women's successful opposition to emigration. In "Southwestern Migration among North Carolina Planter Families," 412, Censer argues for female involvement in, and support for, decisions to move. There is evidence for both positions. Many women clearly regretted the separation from kin that came with emigration. On the other hand, such was the scale of emigration that for some women movement may have appeared likely to reunite them with

more friends and family than it separated them from. This may have been the case with Polly Holt of Georgia. Her husband Hines informed Alabama friends that while he was confident that his trench plowing and manuring would produce as much corn to the acre "as the best Alabama low grounds," his wife Polly would nevertheless "be quite willing to move to the Alabama only give her one day to get ready" (Hines Holt to Bolling Hall, 18 June 1822, Bolling Hall Papers, ADAH). See also Farragher, *Women and Men,* 19–20, who discusses emigration's relation to other events in the "life cycle of families." Among midwestern emigrants to Oregon and California, Farragher notes, "honeymoon emigrations were a tradition." He suggests that "the willingness to pick up and leave the old farming life for a better one—the willingness to change—was so strong that it seemed almost institutionalized. The overland emigration was fundamentally bound up with family life." Given this evidence, Farragher believes that "we can be reasonably certain that emigration at these points was culturally sanctioned; the only question was where they would go."

22. Henry C. Lea to Henry Jackson, 9 Sept. 1828, Jackson and Prince Family Papers, UNC.

23. Nancy Gage to James Gage, 1 May 1835, James McKibbin Gage Papers, UNC; Martha Jackson to Sally R. Cobb, 19 March 1847, Jackson and Prince Family Papers, UNC.

24. John Moore to Richard Singleton, 14 June 1824, Singleton Family Papers, UNC.

25. Samuel A. Townes to George Franklin Townes, 22 June 1834, Townes Family Papers, USC.

26. Eliza Kennedy to Martha Jackson, 6 Jan. 1849, Jackson and Prince Family Papers, UNC; Mary Adams Maverick to her mother, 25 Aug. 1838, quoted in Marks, *Turn Your Eyes toward Texas,* 63.

27. Martha Gaston to Jane Gaston, 22 Nov. 1824, Gaston-Crawford Papers, USC.

28. Simms, *Social Principle,* 43–44; Anne Dent quoted in Mathis, *John Horry Dent,* 19, 21, 149; David Leech to Joseph Alexander Leech, 25 Jan. 1819, Leech Family Papers, Duke. On parental opposition to departure, see also Cashin, *Family Venture,* 39–49.

29. David Johnson Jr. to Edward Johnson, 7 May 1835, 5 Aug. 1836, David Johnson Papers, USC.

30. Thomas Harrison to James Harrison, 11 March 1834, James T. Harrison Papers, UNC; James Henry Hammond to Marcellus Hammond, 24 June 1859, in Bleser, *Hammonds of Redcliffe,* 58.

31. William H. Crawford to Charles Tait, 12 July 1817, Tait Family Papers, ADAH; Charles Tait to John Williams Walker, 5 Jan. 1820, Walker Papers, ADAH.

Tompkins, *Charles Tait,* 22, notes that the three men were probably schoolmates at Moses Waddell's Carmel Academy in Columbia County, Georgia, where both Walker and John C. Calhoun had been students. Walker shared his friends' concern regarding James's choice, in part because he wanted the Taits to settle near him (John Williams Walker to Charles Tait, 22 Sept. 1818, Tait Family Papers, ADAH).

32. Charles Tait to James A. Tait, [1818], Tait Family Papers, ADAH.

33. These words of "an old Georgian" are quoted by Bancroft, *Slave-Trading in the Old South,* 345. Historians too have pointed to the planters' own more realistic view of the relation of wealth and status. In *John Horry Dent,* 1, Gerald Ray Mathis suggests that John Horry Dent "knew by early manhood that his small ruling group held a position of authority and power by virtue of birth *and* wealth, and knew also that the first condition did not remove the need for the second." In other words, "legitimate birth into the ruling classes . . . provided no sure exemption from the necessity of maintaining one's upper-class status with a regular flow of profits from the marketplace. It was in this light that young John Horry Dent viewed himself as a child of privilege who needed a fortune." In "Planters and Patriarchy," 51–52, Michael P. Johnson justifiably generalizes on this point. "Planters understood," he writes, "that patrimonial riches were the foundation of patriarchal authority. Few would have agreed with the epigraph in a twentieth-century genealogy of the Heyward family: 'A Good Name is Rather to be Chosen than Great Riches.' Instead, the planters would have insisted on both a good name and great riches, and many would have pointed out that the former was not an alternative to but a consequence of the latter."

34. See Johnson, "Planters and Patriarchy," 45–72, for a discussion of the "paradoxical" tensions generated within the patriarchal family by the competing aims of its different members, especially those of fathers and sons.

35. James A. Tait to Charles Tait, 7 Feb. 1818, Tait Family Papers, ADAH.

36. Ibid. The Latin phrase should read *vitium propius virtutem;* it is taken from a sentence in Sallust's *Conspiracy of Catiline* 11.1, which reads: "Sed primo magis ambitio quam avaritia animos hominum exercebat, quod tamen vitium propius virtutem erat." In English: "At first, however, ambition more than greed fired men's souls, which, though a fault, was not very far from [i.e., closer to] virtue."

37. Johnson, "Planters and Patriarchy," 56.

38. Green, introduction to *Lides Go South,* v. Many of the Lides' letters are reprinted in this collection, and Fletcher Green's introduction provides detailed information about family members and their movements.

39. James M. Tait to Charles Tait, 20 Jan. 1818, William H. Tait to Charles Tait, 6 March 1835, Tait Family Papers, ADAH; Samuel A. Townes to George Franklin Townes, 3 Jan. 1832, Townes Family Papers, USC; Josiah Foster to Benjamin F.

Perry, 5 July 1818, Benjamin F. Perry Papers, ADAH, quoted in Wyatt-Brown, *Southern Honor,* 198.

40. James Henry Hammond Diary, 30 March 1841, in Bleser, *Secret and Sacred,* 49–50. See also entry for 22 Sept. 1848, ibid., 191–92.

41. William Brickell Sr. to Henry Ravenel, 8 Nov. 1858, Thomas Porcher Ravenel Papers, South Carolina Historical Society, Charleston.

42. Mary Laura Springs to John Springs, 3 April 1831, Springs Family Papers, UNC.

5. THE LAND AROUND US:
SOUTHWESTERN SIGHTS

1. Samuel A. Townes's book was originally published in 1844 in Marion, Alabama, as S. A. Townes, *The History of Marion: Sketches of Life, &c. in Perry County, Alabama.* According to Tom Skinner, one of the editors of the reprint edition of 1985, there are only two extant copies of the first printing, one at Duke University, Durham, North Carolina, and the other at Judson College in Marion, Alabama (Skinner, introduction to Townes, *History of Marion, Alabama,* xii-xiii). Townes's book was also reprinted as Townes, "History of Marion: Sketches of Life in Perry County, Alabama," 179, 215. All page references are to this 1952 edition.

2. Simms, *Views and Reviews,* 84, 76–77. The quote within the quote is from William Cowper's "The Task," bk. 2: "Oh for a lodge in some vast wilderness / Some boundless contiguity of shade" (William Cowper, *The Task and Selected Other Poems,* ed. James Sambrook [New York, 1994], 83). See also Guilds, *Simms,* 333–38. On the intellectual roots of this understanding of history and society, see McCoy, *Elusive Republic,* 13–47. For the southern elite specifically, see Chaplin, *Anxious Pursuit,* chap. 1.

3. William W. Bibb to John C. Calhoun, 23 Jan. 1818, in Meriwether, *Papers of John C. Calhoun* 2:89; Alexander Beaufort Meek, "The South-West," *Southern Ladies' Book* 1 (April 1840): 194–95. Meek's work was originally an oration given at the University of Alabama and later also published as "The South-West; Its History, Character, and Prospect: An Oration before the Erosophic Society of the University of Alabama, December 7, 1839," in Meek, *Romantic Passages,* 13–69. Biographical material from "Meek, Alexander Beaufort," *DAB.* See Shields, "Social History of Antebellum Alabama Writers," 168ff., for an analysis of this "most self-conscious man of letters among Alabama's writers," a "poet, historian, essayist, and perennial promoter of Southern literature" (168).

4. Alexander B. Meek, "An Oration Delivered before the Society of the Alumni of the University of Alabama, at Its First Anniversary, Dec. 17, 1836," *Southern Literary Journal* 4 (April 1837): 185.

5. "Cotton Crops in Texas," *Southern Agriculturist* 10 (April 1837): 222. Land that people had actually taken the trouble to plant, according to the same observer, was producing as much as 4,100 pounds to the acre. "The cotton of Texas," the report concluded, "is unsurpassed" (222). Richard G. Lowe and Randoph Campbell suggest that "there is good evidence that Texas soil did produce more cotton per acre than that of any other southern state." They estimate that "some alluvial soil along the larger rivers in southern Texas yielded as much as 2,000 pounds [of seed cotton] to the acre, but 1,200 to 1,400 pounds were more normal figures" (Lowe and Campbell, *Planters and Plain Folk,* 14).

6. Holley, *Texas,* 5. See Kolodny, *Land before Her,* chap. 5, for a discussion of Holley. For a broader discussion of guides to Texas, see Roff, "Visions of a New Frontier," 15–25.

7. Holley, *Texas,* 3–4.

8. Meek, "The South-West," 201, 204.

9. Wallace, *Long, Bitter Trail,* 63–66, 77–88.

10. Meek, "An Oration," 185.

11. Holley, *Texas,* vi, 8–9. Discussing the early literature of colonization in words appropriate to the work of men and women like Meek and Holley, Jackson Lears writes that such work is "both an advertisement and a religious document. It promotes the acquisition of a valuable piece of real estate but also preserves a genuine sense of wonder at the pulsating ripeness of the natural landscape" (Lears, *Fables of Abundance,* 26).

12. Alexander B. Meek Notebook, Alexander B. Meek Papers, ADAH; Meek, "The South-West," 195; Holley, *Texas,* 1–2. Meek's undated notebook contains a variety of notes on places and events in Alabama history, brief notes on general historical facts, descriptions of famous Americans, as well as the amounts paid to authors like Byron and Scott for their works.

13. Holley, *Texas,* 5.

14. Fulkerson, *Random Recollections,* 66; Baldwin, *Flush Times,* 60.

15. The University of Alabama, located in Tuscaloosa, opened in 1831. Both its physical layout and academic offerings were modeled on those of the University of Virginia. Baylor University, chartered by the Republic of Texas in 1845, opened in May of the following year in the town of Independence. Texas's oldest institution of higher learning, which would later move to Waco, admitted both men and women in its first class. The University of Mississippi in Oxford opened in 1848. From 1849 to 1856 Augustus Baldwin Longstreet of Georgia was its president (Sarah Woolfolk Wiggins, "Alabama, University of," in Wilson, *Encyclopedia of Southern Culture,* 269; Eugene W. Baker, "Baylor University," ibid., 272; David Sansing, "Mississippi, University of," ibid., 292–93).

16. Littleton Fowler quoted in Lytch, *Cradle of Texas Presbyterianism,* 16. According to Lytch, "the General Assembly of the Presbyterian Church assigned re-

sponsibility for the evangelization of Texas to the Synod of Mississippi. Well aware of the opportunity in Texas for planting churches, the synod commissioned four ministers in 1837 as missionaries to this new territory" (17).

17. Townes, "History of Marion," 199–200. Not a religious man himself, Samuel Townes appended a sardonic note to his catalog of religious advance stating that joined to the Methodists' "new and sightly temple, dedicated to the service of God" was "the Masonic Fraternity['s] . . . splendid hall, in which they do things that none but the initiated know of" (200). For Townes's attitude toward religion as well as much else about his character and life, see Allen, "Biographical Sketch of Townes," xxiv–xxv.

18. Simms, *Social Principle,* 5–6.

19. Townes, "History of Marion," 215; Meek, "The South-West," 206–7.

20. Meek, "The South-West," 206–7; Holley, *Texas,* 2.

21. R., "The West!" Once upon a time, of course, the lands of the East had themselves been the object of such otherworldly descriptions. See Louis B. Wright, "The Colonial Search for a Southern Eden," in Gerster and Cords, *Myth and Southern History,* 17–30.

22. Thomas Spalding, "On the Culture of Sugar and Indigo," *Southern Agriculturist* 1 (Nov. 1828): 483; review of *The South-West by a YANKEE,* ibid., 9 (Feb. 1836): 78.

23. In true reformer fashion Thomas Spalding presented rational, countervailing evidence in the form of some "memoranda" he had made on a visit of his own, in 1825, to the Louisiana sugar plantations of South Carolina emigrants of his acquaintance. He provided details of good but not "astronomical" yields but noted also the necessarily large scale required to achieve profits "purchased by great labour" and "by great expenditure upon land, and upon machinery" (Spalding, "On the Culture of Sugar and Indigo," 483).

24. "Notice of the Climate, Soil, and Production of Florida; by X.Y.Z.," *Southern Agriculturist* 7 (Jan. 1834): 23.

25. Noble, "Effects," 333.

26. Spalding, "On the Culture of Sugar and Indigo," 483.

27. O'Neall, "Address," 108; Noble, "Effects," 333.

28. Simms, "Spirit of Emigration," 264. See also McCardell, "Poetry and the Practical," 187–210; Ridgely, *William Gilmore Simms,* 67ff.

29. Simms, "Southern Agriculture," 138.

30. "Letter to the Editor," *Southern Cultivator* 1, no. 13 (1843): 101. The Reverend George F. Pierce put westward emigration in the context of an "idolatrous devotion to money-making" and "the prostration of every energy—the sacrifice of feeling—hope—all at the shrine of covetousness (the American Baal)" (Pierce, "Oration Delivered before the Alumni Society of Franklin College, at Athens, in August," ibid., 2, no. 25 [1844]: 194).

31. "A Letter to the Editor from a Middle Georgian (from Sparta)," ibid., no. 7, 108; William Ellison quoted in Smith, *Economic Readjustment,* 29–30.

32. O'Neall, "Address," 108.

33. Simms, "Southern Agriculture," 142.

34. Such imagery, and the differing meanings given to it, was hardly new, of course. Lears, in *Fables of Abundance,* 33, writes of the seventeenth century as a time when differing visions of America vied with one another, when "neither the New Atlantis nor the New Israel exhausted the imaginative possibilities of New World abundance. Alongside emergent strategies for containment, older utopian visions wallowed in abundance rather than keeping it at bay. Perhaps the most durable of these was El Dorado, the mythical Kingdom that fired the imaginations of Sir Walter Raleigh and other adventurers, the place (according to Raleigh's account) where men anointed their naked bodies with oil, covered themselves with gold dust, and cavorted in drunken ecstasy for six or seven days at a stretch. This was a far cry from God's New Israel; it was closer to the sensual exuberance of Carnival."

35. Hugh Swinton Legaré to Alfred Huger, 21 Nov. 1835, in Legaré, *Writings of Hugh Swinton Legaré* 1:221–22.

36. Spalding, "Cotton," 81–87; "Improve Your Lands, by a Planter," *Southern Cultivator* 3 (1845): 126; review of *A Treatise on the Theory and Practice of Landscape Gardening, Adapted to North America,* by A. J. Downey, ibid., no. 7, 109; Pierce, "Oration," 194.

37. For descriptions of the native population, see, for example, Simms, "Southern Agriculture," 132; William Gilmore Simms, "Agricultural Labor, as One of the First Conditions of a National Existence (from an Agricultural Oration Delivered in South-Carolina, in 1840)," *Magnolia,* n.s., 2 , no. 1 (1843): 16. See Drinnon, *Facing West,* 131–46, for a discussion of Simms's views in this regard. Chaplin, *Anxious Pursuit,* 61ff., discusses these stereotypical contrasts between "savage" nomadism and settled civilization. Cashin, "Landscape and Memory," 483, notes how Indians, among other "less privileged Virginians," were considered culprits in the mistreatment of the environment. As William McLoughlin notes, however, the 1825 census by the Cherokee Council revealed a very different picture of life in one native community, showing that the Cherokee living east of the Mississippi River consisted of 14,972 people in addition to the 1,038 slaves owned by the Cherokee elite. These slaves provided essential labor for the Cherokee's expanding cotton fields, as well as their increased hog and sheep production. As McLoughlin notes, the eastern Cherokee in 1825 were in possession of "7,628 horses and 22,405 cattle spread among 2,500 families. Virtually every family had a plough and a spinning wheel and one out of four had a loom and a wagon. There were 31 gristmills scattered around the nation, 14 sawmills, 6 powder mills, 9 saltpeter works, 18 ferries, and 19 schools. . . . No available figures are available for the number of miles of roads, but there were 62 blacksmith shops, and 55 silversmiths still practiced that

ancient Cherokee art" (McLoughlin, *Cherokees and Missionaries,* 125). As D. W. Meinig points out, such evidence actually made the Cherokees "living refutations of all those deeply ingrained and widely propagated European and American ideas of Indians as primitives, savages, footloose hunters—wild people" (Meinig, *Shaping of America,* 88).

38. Governor William Crawford, "An Address, Delivered before the Agricultural Association of the State of Georgia, at Sparta, on the 26th day of November, 1846," *Southern Cultivator* 5, no. 1 (1847): 1.

39. Simms, *Social Principle,* 36.

40. Alexander B. Meek, "Jack-Cadeism and the Fine Arts: An Oration before the Literary Societies of La-Grange College, Alabama, June 16, 1841," in Meek, *Romantic Passages in Southwestern History,* 149–50; Townes, "History of Marion," 179.

41. Simms, *Social Principle,* 22–23. David Moltke-Hansen, "The Expansion of Intellectual Life," 19, relates Simms's address to a broader context in which "social order was a constant preoccupation of Charleston. It seemed threatened on every hand—not just by ideas of class upheaval and racial equality but by the wild allure of the frontier, severe economic and demographic shifts, and the heat of politics. When Simms spoke of 'The Social Principle' in 1842, he was voicing a common concern, not only by defining the principle in terms of domesticity and deference but by assuming that this ideal of order was continually being undermined by America's pell-mell rush westward."

42. Simms, *Social Principle,* 36, 24.

43. Ibid., 25.

44. Spalding, "Cotton," 82, 81.

45. Simms, *Richard Hurdis,* 13–14, 17. Freehling, *Road to Disunion,* 238, 240, interprets this scene as an example of the attacks made by South Carolinians like Simms on "that most irresponsible Carolina aristocrat, the one who deserted Carolina." In this view, Hurdis "is the restless, hot-tempered, young Carolina blade who, when disappointed in love, wishes a 'better place' out West," while his mother laments his departure and insists that his "ancestral home is 'good enough.'" According to Freehling, "The only redeeming character amidst the 'license of the wilderness' is Colonel Grafton, an old friend of the Hurdis family, who has imposed a speck of order on disorderly frontiers." Arguably, however, by locating this familiar plantation household scene, not in South Carolina or Georgia, but in Marengo County, Alabama, Simms is not addressing the localized nature of the familiar cultural patterns and attitudes represented within the Hurdis household. Rather he is suggesting their geographical diffusion.

46. Samuel A. Townes to George Franklin Townes, 24 Nov. 1847, Henry H. Townes to George F. Townes, 24 Aug., 1 July 1847, Townes Family Papers, USC.

47. Henry H. Townes to Robert Townes, 15 Jan. 1848, to Samuel A. Townes, 28 Jan. 1848, ibid.

6. A HOUSEHOLD WITH A VIEW:
THE SOCIAL LANDSCAPE

1. J. S. Little to James S. Milling, 2 June [1855], James Milling Papers, UNC.
2. Ibid.
3. Charles Tait to James A. Tait, 7 Nov. 1818, Tait Family Papers, ADAH.
4. Maria Lide to Hannah L. Coker, 7 March 1836, Frances J. Lide to Hannah L. Coker, 20 May 1836, Lide-Coker Family Papers, USC.
5. Sarah L. Fountain to Caleb Coker, 25 May 1836, ibid. Sarah Fountain was thirty-seven years old when she moved to Alabama; she was the elder sister of Maria Lide, who was sixteen. Frances Lide, their niece, was the daughter of Eli Lide.
6. Eli H. Lide to Caleb Coker, 25 Oct. 1836, to Hannah L. Coker, 16 July 1840, ibid.
7. Henry Marshall to Maria Marshall, 1 Nov. 1833, Marshall-Furman Papers, LSU, quoted in Stuck, *End of the Land,* 25; Mary Taylor quoted, ibid., 46. Stuck writes that this moment was "celebrated in family lore," suggesting, perhaps, that the statement might never have actually been made, although the plantation was later named Land's End.
8. Abner Nash to William P. Graham, 4 July 1831, William R. Graham Papers, UNC; Robert F. Charles to Peter Bacot, 12 Aug. 1832, Bacot Family Papers, USC; J. J. Seibels to John T. Seibels, 7 Aug. 1843, Seibels Family Collection, ADAH.
9. John H. Sims to William Sims, 9 Oct. 1819, William Sims Papers, Duke; Abner Nash to William P. Graham, 4 July 1831, William R. Graham Papers, UNC.
10. Eli H. Lide to Caleb Coker, 24 March 1836, Lide-Coker Family Papers, USC.
11. Mary Taylor to Maria Marshall, 11 March 1838, Marshall-Furman Papers, LSU, quoted in Stuck, *End of the Land,* 48.
12. Maria Lide to Hannah L. Coker, 7 March 1836, Sarah L. Fountain to Hannah L. Coker, 10 Feb. 1836, Lide-Coker Family Papers, USC. The English naturalist Phillip Henry Gosse, who spent eight months of 1838 in Alabama, recorded that "very many of the houses, even of the wealthy and respectable planters, are built of rough and unhewn logs, and to an English taste are destitute of comfort to a surprising degree." Gosse contrasted these humble dwellings with the "inexpressive grandeur of the primeval forests" (quoted in William T. Going, "Gosse on the Frontier," in *Essays on Alabama Literature,* 169). See Abernethy, *Formative Period,* 36–37, for the ubiquity of such rudimentary accommodations in the early days of planter settlement in Alabama; Oakes, *Ruling Race,* 82–87.
13. Anne Coleman quoted in Exley, *Texas Tears and Texas Sunshine,* 31–32.
14. Sarah A. Gayle to William Haynsworth, 31 Dec. 1832, Gorgas Family Papers, Alabama; Seale, *Sam Houston's Wife,* 4.

15. Sarah A. Gayle to William Haynsworth, 31 Dec. 1832, Gorgas Family Papers, Alabama.

16. Sarah L. Fountain to Hannah L. Coker, 10 Feb. 1836, Lide-Coker Family Papers, USC; Martha Gaston to Jane Gaston, 17 April 1822, Gaston-Crawford Papers, USC; Lucy Clark to Elizabeth Caroline Tait, 19 June 1819, Tait Family Papers, ADAH.

17. Sarah Lide Fountain to Hannah L. Coker, 10 Feb. 1836, Lide-Coker Family Papers, USC; James L. Sloss to the Rev., the Moderator, and Members of the Presbytery of South Carolina, 30 Sept. 1818, Records of the Presbytery of South Carolina, Montreat.

18. Sarah A. Gayle to William Haynsworth, 31 Dec. 1832, Gorgas Family Papers, Alabama.

19. Henry Townes to George Franklin Townes, 16 Jan. 1834, Samuel Townes to John Townes, 18 Sept. 1834, to which Joanna Townes adds a note from which this quote is taken, Townes Family Papers, USC; Mary Carter to Farish Carter, 8 April 1846, Farish Carter Papers, UNC.

20. Lears, *Fables of Abundance,* 77, follows Annette Kolodny in interpreting the meaning of such activity. "When they confronted the American landscape, men and women often spoke different languages: if men feared a devouring Mother Nature or desired to possess a 'virgin land,' women were inclined to peaceful coexistence—they tended to be gardeners, in metaphor and actuality. The uprooted East Coast women described by Kolodny, preserving cuttings from their gardens en route to Missouri or California, embodied a nurturant alternative to the stance of domination." See also Kolodny, *Land before Her,* 35–54. As far as the South is concerned, this seems a less than satisfactory explanation. The most outspoken advocates of this kind of coexistence were men in the East, while women in the West commonly responded to not-yet-transformed landscapes with dread and antagonism. More generally, it seems a rather generous reading of the compatibility of horticulture and wilderness.

21. Samuel A. Townes to George Franklin Townes, 22 June 1834, Townes Family Papers, USC.

22. Henry Marshall to Maria Marshall, 18 Feb. 1839, Marshall-Furman Papers, LSU, quoted in Stuck, *End of the Land,* 63. Among the signs of Shreveport's advancing civilization had been a visit from Episcopal bishop Leonidas Polk.

23. Eli H. Lide to Caleb Coker, 25 Oct. 1836, to Hannah L. Coker, 16 July 1840, Lide-Coker Family Papers, USC.

24. Benjamin Hormon to Zachary Meriwether, 27 Jan. 1850, Zachary Meriwether Papers, Alabama.

25. "For Sale—Real Estate in Mississippi," advertisement in the Washington, Ga., *Christian Index* 4 (14 July 1836): 482.

26. Sarah L. Fountain to Caleb Coker, 25 May 1836, Lide-Coker Family Papers, USC.

27. Henry C. Lea to Henry Jackson, 12 July 1835, 23 Nov. 1834, Jackson and Prince Family Papers, UNC.

28. Samuel A. Townes to Rachel Townes, 9 April 1843, Townes Family Papers, USC. Samuel A. Townes III was born on 27 May 1840. See also Allen, "Biographical Sketch," xx.

29. Burton, *In My Father's House,* 117–18, discusses the region's "extended communities" and how "white kinship ties influenced the concept of community and extended that concept beyond geographical boundaries."

30. Marianne Gaillard to John S. Palmer, 19 Dec. 1844, 29 May 1846, Palmer Family Papers, USC; Mary Strother Means to Mary Hart Means, 17 Nov. 1858, Means Family Papers, USC.

31. Serena Lea to Martha Jackson, 2 Jan. 1840, Jackson and Prince Family Papers, UNC.

32. Robert F. Charles to Peter Bacot, 28 Sept. 1835, Bacot Family Papers, USC.

33. Sarah Lide Fountain to Hannah L. Coker, 10 Feb. 1836, Lide-Coker Family Papers, USC.

34. Serena Lea to Martha Jackson, 19 April, 11 May 1840, Jackson and Prince Family Papers, UNC.

35. Serena Lea to Martha Jackson, 19, 25 July 1840, Henry Lea to Martha Jackson, 19 July 1840, ibid.

36. Serena Lea to Martha Jackson, 5 July 1840, ibid.

37. Ibid., 19, 25 July 1840.

38. Serena Lea to Martha Jackson, 25 April 1842, 5 Jan., 26 March 1846, Emily Rootes Hag to Martha Jackson, 22 April 1846, ibid.

39. Samuel A. Townes to George Franklin Townes, 10 March 1835, Henry Townes to George Franklin Townes, 6 March 1835, Townes Family Papers, USC.

40. Serena Lea to Martha Jackson, 16 Jan. 1829, Jackson and Prince Family Papers, UNC.

41. "For Sale—Real Estate in Mississippi," 482.

42. Robert Gage to James Gage, 25 Dec. 1836 and 1 Jan. 1837 (same letter), James McKibbin Gage Papers, UNC.

43. For the extent and effects of slave emigration, see Tadman, *Speculators and Slaves,* 154–210; Fogel and Engerman, *Time on the Cross,* 44–52. Tadman disputes Fogel and Engerman's estimate that of the 835,000 slaves who moved west between 1790 and 1860, 84 percent did so with their existing owners. According to Tadman this figure seriously underestimates how many slaves were sold west and, by extension, minimizes both the slaves' suffering and the slaveholders' indifference to that suffering. It is important to remember, however, that even when slaves traveled as part of existing households, separation from friends and families on other plantations was common. For a fuller analysis of the slaves' experience of forced emigration, see Baptist, "Creating an Old South."

44. John Wallace to Mary A. Wallace, 11 Aug. 1852, Wallace, Rice, and Duncan Papers, USC.

45. N. B. Powell to Farish Carter, 19 Jan. 1850, Farish Carter Papers, UNC.

46. Ibid., 27 Jan., 7 March 1850.

47. Thomas Harrison to James T. Harrison, 4, 10, 11, 12 Jan. 1836, James T. Harrison Papers, UNC. Isham Harrison named his plantation Greenville, apparently after the area in South Carolina where he was born. Further information about the lives of Thomas, James, and Isham Harrison can be found in Meynard, *The Venturers,* 306–20, 725–29.

48. Thomas Harrison to James T. Harrison, 6, 4 Jan. 1836, Isham Harrison to Thomas Harrison, 10 Feb. 1836, James T. Harrison Papers, UNC.

49. Douglass, *My Bondage and My Freedom,* 177.

50. Charles W. Tait to James A. Tait, 7 Jan. 1851, Tait Family Papers, Auburn. See also Charles W. Tait to James A. Tait, 6 March 1850, Auburn, in which Charles reported to his father that "a great many persons have immigrated to Texas the past winter & consequently land has risen in price a good deal & is still rising."

51. Rebekah Goode to Elizabeth Caroline Tait, 17 Oct. 1837, Sidney Goode to Elizabeth Caroline Tait, 10 Jan. 1837, Tait Papers, ADAH.

52. Rogers, "Migration Patterns," 45–48. By 1850, according to Rogers, 237,000 of the free people born in Alabama still lived there, while over 83,000 had already moved somewhere else. By then, 182,500 free people born in other states had moved to Alabama. Those who left Alabama in the 1850s did so mostly for Mississippi, Texas, Arkansas, and Louisiana. These four states accounted for more than three-fourths of all out-migrants in 1850 and 1860.

53. See Freehling, *Reintegration of American History,* 167, for the statistics. Rogers, "Migration Patterns," estimates that "some 75,000 persons left Georgia for other areas between 1850 and 1860" (48). Tadman, *Speculators and Slaves,* 12, charts the interregional movement of slaves by state for the period 1790–1859. See also Smith, "Migration of Georgians," 307–25.

54. Charles W. Tait to James A. Tait, 25 Dec. 1849, 2 Oct. 1850, Tait Family Papers, Auburn.

55. Maria Lide to Caleb Coker, 16 Sept. 1844, Lide-Coker Family Papers, USC.

56. Eli H. Lide to James Lide, 15 April 1854, ibid.

7. THE PLANTERS' PROGRESS

1. Quoted in Hartwell, "Margaret Lea," 276.

2. *Marion Herald,* quoted in Hartwell, "Margaret Lea," 276.

3. Hartwell, "Margaret Lea," 278; Serena Lea to Martha Jackson, 19 April 1840, Jackson and Prince Family Papers, UNC.

4. Williams, *Sam Houston,* 49; Boles, *South through Time,* 260ff. For information concerning the population of Texas as well as detailed discussions of American emigration to the area, see Chipman, *Spanish Texas,* 205–6, 241.

5. Braider, *Solitary Star,* 159. Sam Houston's account of the battle indicated that it lasted eighteen minutes. See also Pohl, *Battle of San Jacinto;* Lack, *Texas Revolutionary Experience;* Hardin, *Texas Iliad.*

6. Ralph Waldo Emerson, *Journals of Ralph Waldo Emerson, 1820–1872,* ed. Edward Waldo Emerson and Waldo Emerson Forbes (Cambridge, Mass., 1912), 7:206.

7. Marianne Gaillard to John S. Palmer, with note from Thomas Gaillard, 4 June 1844, Marianne Gaillard to John S. Palmer, 29 May 1846, Palmer Family Papers, USC; Thomas R. R. Cobb to Howell Cobb, 12 May 1846, in Phillips, *Correspondence,* 76–77. Marianne Gaillard herself had "lost pounds of flesh" in the midst of "all this commotion," not least because her sons were eager to answer the call of county and country. According to the biographical materials with the Tait papers at the ADAH, Charles W. Tait was born in 1815 and graduated from the University of Alabama in 1834 and from the Medical University of Pennsylvania, also known as Jefferson Medical College, Philadelphia, in 1838. He was an assistant surgeon in the U.S. Navy, 1838–43, as well as a surgeon in the Texas Volunteers during the Mexican War. During the Civil War, Tait was a major in the Texas Volunteers, Confederate States of America. He also served in the General Assembly of Texas before the Civil War. He married Louisa Williams in Lafayette, Texas, on Feb. 14, 1848; the couple had eight children. Tait died in 1878.

8. P. C. Pendleton, "Editor's Table," *Magnolia* 3 (Sept. 1841): 431–32.

9. John C. Calhoun, "Speech on the Importance of Domestic Slavery," in McKitrick, *Slavery Defended,* 18. As James Farmer, *Metaphysical Confederacy,* 16, points out, nations, "even nations built on a foundation of slavery, are not born out of fear alone."

10. George Fitzhugh, "Southern Thought," *De Bow's Review* 23 (1857): 341, quoted in Ashworth, *Slavery, Capitalism, and Politics,* 240.

11. Louisa McCord, "Charity Which Does Not Begin at Home," *Southern Literary Messenger* 19 (April 1853): 194. McCord's article was a response to Harriet Beecher Stowe's *Uncle Tom's Cabin.* See also William Gilmore Simms, "Miss Martineau on Slavery," *Southern Literary Messenger* 3 (Nov. 1837): 567. Simms invokes Ulysses' speech on degree from Shakespeare's *Troilus and Cressida* in defense of universal order and slavery's part in maintaining it. See also Ridgely, *William Gilmore Simms,* 22. For a brilliant discussion of Simms's views of progress and order, see David Moltke-Hansen, "Ordered Progress: The Historical Philosophy of William Gilmore Simms," in O'Brien and Moltke-Hansen, *Intellectual Life,* 126–47.

12. Thomas Roderick Dew, "Abolition of Negro Slavery," *American Quarterly Review* 12 (1832): 189–265, in Faust, *Ideology of Slavery,* 23; William Harper, "Memoir on Slavery," ibid., 78.

13. Thornwell quoted in McCurry, "Two Faces of Republicanism," 1249. Mc-Curry notes the tremendous influence of evangelical ministers on the proslavery defense, writing that "the Biblical defense of slavery was the centerpiece of an organic or familial ideology that encompassed far more than the relation of master and slave." For analysis of the proslavery argument, see, for example, Ford, *Origins of Southern Radicalism*, 350ff.; Fox-Genovese and Genovese, "Divine Sanction of Social Order," 211–34; Fox-Genovese and Genovese, "Religious Ideals," 1–16; Tise, *Proslavery*. For a recent dissection of the various strands of the proslavery argument, see Ashworth, *Slavery, Capitalism, and Politics*, 192–285. The classic compilation of proslavery thought is Elliot, *Cotton Is King, and Pro-Slavery Arguments*.

14. Simpson, "Slavery and Modernism," 80, argues that like their twentieth-century successors, the writers of the slave South addressed "the chief issue in the dialectic between traditionalism and modernism—the nature of man in relation to community. Are we inescapably creatures of community, expressing ourselves properly and truly as men solely through a community of blood, myth, and ritual; or are we truly ourselves as men only when liberated from the bonds of 'organic' community?" In the slave South, Simpson explains, "this issue did not take the form it did under European, or New England, or general American conditions. It took the uniquely intense historical form of the South's efforts to reconcile freedom and community through the development of a modern society founded on chattel slavery." For an extended discussion of this and related matters, see Genovese, *Slaveholders' Dilemma*.

15. Calhoun, "Speech on the Importance of Domestic Slavery," 19.

16. Ibid.

17. Essler, "Agricultural Reform Movement in Alabama, 1850–1860."

18. James Oakes has also addressed the impact of slavery, as well as of "liberal capitalism," on the planters' attitudes toward land and mobility in *Slavery and Freedom* (99–103). Oakes goes so far as to insist that "if it was possible to synthesize slavery and liberal capitalism into a single cultural tradition," then that synthesis would be revealed in correspondence like that of Phillips Fitzpatrick, a young man from a wealthy family who emigrated from Alabama to Texas. Obviously, I agree about the value of such evidence, although I would add the experiences of Phillips Fitzpatrick's sister-in-law, Aurelia Blassingame Fitzpatrick, not to mention her mother, Eliza Townes Blassingame. I also agree with Oakes that slavery generated a general desire for staple-friendly land while encouraging a lack of attachment to particular places. As well, Oakes argues that because "the young man could not expect to inherit his father's estate intact" and the father lacked "the economic power to hold his adult son at home," so it was that "in the liberal South, the bonds of intergenerational dependence were relatively weak" (103). I disagree strongly that emigration reveals how relations between people were becoming as attenuated as those between people and place. Rather, the same relations of slavery that came between planters and place also presented an effective barrier

against their assimilating the assumptions of social atomism and individual autonomy increasingly prevalent elsewhere in the modern world. Thus to the extent that Oakes's prefacing of "capitalist" with "liberal" suggests not just a particular economic context but an internalization of a set of values primarily predicated on the tenets of liberalism or individualism, I do not agree that the evidence supports such a view. As I read the correspondence of people like Fitzpatrick and his kinfolk, it would be difficult to imagine a more interdependent set of human relations.

19. Born in 1823 in Jefferson City, Georgia, Thomas Reed Rootes Cobb was one of his state's most prominent lawyers. The mother of Thomas and his planter-politician brother Howell, was Sarah Rootes Cobb, the older sister of Serena Rootes Lea of Marion (Rootes, "Rootes Family," 210). For a detailed examination of Cobb's life, see McNash, *Thomas R. R. Cobb.*

20. Cobb, *Inquiry into the Law,* ccxv–ccxvi.

21. In *Slavery and Freedom,* 100, James Oakes argues that "slavery required relatively few ties to place and community." In *Ruling Race,* 79, he suggests that given the ubiquity of mobility, "there never was a stable slaveholding society that was not, almost by definition, atypical." I agree that slavery diminished attachment to place but disagree regarding community. Oakes, as did the contemporary critics of emigration, conflates a lack of attachment to place with a weakening of attachment to community or people and, consequently, links demographic mobility to social instability. Yet as Oakes argues in *Slavery and Freedom,* 103, westward expansion was both essential to "the social reproduction of the master class" and a process in which "so many of the elements that went into the socialization of young masters were crystallized" (103). The planters' great success in reproducing both themselves and their society itself reveals an understanding of community that was not grounded in particular places but rather rooted in relations more than strong enough to bridge the distances between East and West.

22. Cobb, *Inquiry into the Law,* ccxiii. Cobb recognized other drawbacks to slavery (most notably the chronic sparseness of population that meant weaker political power at the national level relative to the nonslaveholding regions of the Union). Yet he felt that ultimately what was gained in terms of class, race, and sectional solidarity outweighed what was lost in terms of local attachment and national power. Cobb also turned a northern criticism of slavery, that it repelled immigrants, into a positive feature to be contrasted implicitly with the increasingly heterogeneous North. Cobb believed that white solidarity was strengthened by the fact that "raising their own laborers, there is no inducement for foreign immigration into slaveholding communities. Their citizens imbibe freedom with their mother's milk." Otherwise divergent interpretations of the slave system agree on the presence of white male solidarity, whether viewed as "herrenvolk democracy" or "planter hegemony," at least on the question of slavery. See, for example, Fredrickson, *Black*

Image in the White Mind, chap. 2; Cash, *Mind of the South,* 36ff.; Genovese, "Yeomen Farmers in a Slaveholders' Democracy," in Fox-Genovese and Genovese, *Fruits of Merchant Capital,* 249–64. See Ford, *Origins of Southern Radicalism,* for his interpretation of white male slaveholders and nonslaveholders sharing a commitment to republican ideology in public life. Ashworth, *Slavery, Capitalism, and Politics,* 216–28, analyzes the contradictions and weaknesses of the slaveholders' claims for their society's "racist egalitarianism."

23. James Henley Thornwell, "Slavery and the Religious Instruction of the Coloured Population," *Southern Presbyterian Review* 4 (July 1850), 110–11, quoted in McCurry, "The Two Faces of Republicanism," 1249.

24. S., "Query Addressed to the Hon. Whitemarsh B. Seabrook," *Southern Agriculturist* 7 (May 1834): 239–40. For discussion of the slaveholders' dual role as both lords of the land and lords of labor, see Wright, *Old South, New South,* chap. 2; Ford, *Origins of Southern Radicalism,* 41; Oakes, *Slavery and Freedom,* 99–102. The spiritual and cultural repercussions of the slaves' coming between the slaveholders and their land would trouble agrarians in another time. In Allen Tate's view "the white man got nothing from the Negro, no profound image of himself in terms of the soil" (Tate, "The Profession of Letters in the South," *Essays of Four Decades,* 525). Rubin, *Edge of the Swamp,* 16, discusses Tate's view that "African slavery served to distance rather than unite citizen and land."

25. Douglass, *My Bondage and My Freedom,* 176–77.

26. See Oakes, *Ruling Race,* chaps. 3 and 4, for a discussion that links the slaveholders' evangelicalism to their driving materialism and relates the emigration experience to both. Allen Tate, "Religion and the Old South," *Essays of Four Decades,* 570, argues that Protestantism was the wrong kind of Christianity for the South, being "a non-agrarian and trading religion that had been invented in the sixteenth century by a young finance-capitalist economy: hardly a religion at all but rather a disguised secular ambition."

27. Martha Sarah Howell Means to Claudia Hart Means, 3 May 1847, William Burney Means to Claudia Hart Means, 16 May 1847, Means Family Papers, USC.

28. Mary Ann Hutchinson to Martha Jackson, 4 July, 7 Dec. 1837, Eliza Kennedy to Sarah Jackson, 4 March 1849, Jackson and Prince Family Papers, UNC.

29. Mary Boyd to Jane Gaston, 9 June 1821, Gaston-Crawford Papers, USC.

30. Martha Gaston to Jane Gaston, 17 April 1822, Martha Gamble to Jane Gaston Crawford, 9 March 1860, ibid. Cashin, *Family Venture,* 45, argues that "women commonly compared migration to death, as men almost never did." She cites the example of Mary Maverick's mother's running after her departing daughter and her husband, lamenting that "I will never see you again on earth." It seems to me, however, that it was far more common for women to put the separation and pain caused by emigration in the context of life after death, as Maverick's words

can be read as doing. From this perspective death, for the saved, would bring eternal reunion as well as release from all other earthly troubles.

31. See, for example, James Henley Thornwell to J. D. Witherspoon, 4 Sept. 1856, Witherspoon Family Papers, USC, in which Thornwell sternly warns the younger man of the dangers of self-indulgent grief.

32. Tuan, "Geopiety," 26, discusses how earlier ideas of patriotism grounded in a mystical attachment to place waned with the advent of a Christianity one of whose "express purposes was to loosen man's earthly bonds so that he might more easily enter the kingdom of heaven."

33. Mary Boyd to Jane Gaston, 9 June 1821, Gaston-Crawford Papers, USC.

34. See Fox-Genovese, "Fettered Mind," 629ff. This review essay of Rubin's *Edge of the Swamp* explores, among many of the other issues addressed here, the nature of Simms's understanding of slave society and his work's relation to broader literary explorations of the individual's relation to place and society.

Bibliography

Primary Sources

MANUSCRIPT COLLECTIONS

Alabama Department of Archives and History, Montgomery
    Bolling Hall Papers
    Manly Family Papers
    Alexander B. Meek Papers
    Perry County Collection
    John Seibels Collection
    Tait Family Papers
    Walker Papers
University of Alabama, University
    Gorgas Family Papers
    Basil Manly Papers
    Zachary Meriwether Papers
Auburn University Special Collections, Auburn, Ala.
    Tait Family Papers
William R. Perkins Library, Duke University, Durham, N.C.
    Benson-Thompson Family Papers
    James Douglas Papers
    Hemphill Family Papers
    Alfred Huger Letter Books
    Ebenezer Jackson Letter Book
    George Noble Jones Papers
    Leech Family Papers
    William Sims Papers
    Henry Watson Papers
Special Collections, Robert Woodruff Library, Emory University, Atlanta
    Oliver Family Papers
Hargett Rare Book and Manuscript Library, University of Georgia, Athens
    Champion Family Letters
    John James Gresham Papers
    Hillyer Papers
    Patrick Hues Mell Papers

Oliver H. Prince Papers

Charles Spalding Papers

Southern Historical Collection, University of North Carolina, Chapel Hill

Samuel Agnew Papers

David Wyatt Aiken Papers

George Washington Allen Papers

Anderson and Thornwell Family Papers

John McPherson Berrien Papers

John Peter Broun Papers

Farish Carter Papers

Cobb and Hunter Family Papers

Craft, Fort, and Thorne Family Papers

C. W. Dudley Reminiscences

Elliot-Gonzales Family Papers

Benjamin Fitzpatrick Papers

James McKibbin Gage Family Papers

Gaston-Crawford Family Papers

David Gavin Diary

William P. Graham Papers

Grimball Family Papers

James T. Harrison Papers

Hemphill Family Papers

Heyward and Ferguson Family Papers

Hughes Family Collection

Jackson and Prince Family Papers

Milligan Family Papers

James Milling Papers

Robert Barnwell Rhett Papers

Singleton Family Papers

Springs Family Collection

Elizabeth Furman Talley Papers

Walton Family Papers

Witherspoon and McDowall Family Papers

Presbyterian Church (USA) Department of History, Montreat, N.C.

Fields Bradshaw Papers

Minutes, Hopewell Presbytery, 1834–65

Minutes, Synod of Alabama

"Studies on Slavery and the Presbyterian Church in Alabama, Consisting of Material Taken from Records of the Synod and Presbyteries of Alabama," typescript.

South Carolina Historical Society, Charleston
Thomas Porcher Ravenel Papers
South Caroliniana Library, University of South Carolina, Columbia
Bacot Family Papers
Peter S. Bacot Papers
Berly Family Papers
William Blanding Papers
Mary Davis Brown Papers
Cantey Family Papers
Charles Family Papers
Conway, Black, and Davis Families
Cox Family
Daniel Family Papers
Gaston-Crawford Papers
Gaston, Strait, Wylie, and Baskin Papers
Hemphill Family Papers
David Johnson Papers
Thomas Cassells Law Papers
Lide-Coker Family Papers
Maverick and Van Wyck Papers
John McLees Papers
Mary Hart Means Papers
Noble Family Papers
Odom-Turner Family Papers
Palmer Family Papers
William Moultrie Reid Papers
Singleton Family Papers
James Spann Papers
Townes Family Papers
Wallace, Rice, and Duncan Papers
Waties Family Papers
Witherspoon Family Papers
Eugene C. Barker Texas Historical Center, University of Texas, Austin
Julien Sidney Devereux Papers
Charles William Tait Papers

PERIODICALS

De Bow's Review
Democratic Review

Ladies' Companion
Magnolia
Niles' Weekly Register
Southern Agriculturist
Southern and Western Monthly Magazine and Review
Southern Cultivator
Southern Ladies' Book
Southern Literary Journal
Southern Literary Messenger
Southern Quarterly Review

NEWSPAPERS

Washington, Ga., *Christian Index*
Savannah Daily Republican
Richmond, Va., *Southern Religious Telegraph*

BOOKS

Baldwin, Joseph G. *The Flush Times of Alabama and Mississippi: A Series of Sketches.* 1853. Reprint, Baton Rouge, La., 1987.

Bartram, William. *Travels through North and South Carolina.* Philadelphia, 1791.

Bleser, Carol, ed. *The Hammonds of Redcliffe.* New York, 1981.

———, ed. *Secret and Sacred: The Diaries of James Henry Hammond, a Southern Slaveholder.* New York, 1988.

Burke, Emily. *Pleasure and Pain: Reminiscences of Georgia in the 1840's.* Savannah, 1978.

Carson, James Petigru, ed. *Life, Letters, and Speeches of James Louis Petigru, the Union Man of South Carolina.* Washington, D.C., 1920.

Cobb, Thomas R. R. *An Inquiry into the Law of Negro Slavery in the United States of America. To Which Is Prefixed, an Historical Sketch of Slavery.* Philadelphia, 1858.

Darby, William. *The Emigrant's Guide to the Western and Southwestern Territories.* New York, 1818.

De Bow, J. D. B., comp. *Statistical View of the United States . . . Being a Compendium of the Seventh Census.* Washington, D.C., 1854.

Douglass, Frederick. *My Bondage and My Freedom.* 1855. Reprint, New York, 1969.

Elliot, E. N., ed. *Cotton Is King, and Pro-Slavery Arguments.* 1860. Reprint, New York, 1968.

Exley, Jo Ella, ed. *Texas Tears and Texas Sunshine: Voices of Frontier Women.* College Station, Tex., 1985.

Faust, Drew Gilpin, ed. *The Ideology of Slavery: Proslavery Thought in the Antebellum South, 1830–1860.* Baton Rouge, La., 1981.

Featherstonehaugh, George William. *Excursion through the Slave States, from Washington on the Potomac to the Frontier of Mexico; with Sketches of Popular Manners and Geological Notices.* New York, 1844.

Freehling, William W., ed. *The Nullification Era: A Documentary Record.* New York, 1967.

Fulkerson, H. S. *Random Recollections of Early Days in Mississippi.* Vicksburg, Miss., 1885.

Green, Fletcher M., ed. *The Lides Go South . . . and West: The Record of a Planter Migration in 1835.* Columbia, S.C., 1952.

Hodgson, Adam. *Letters from North America, Written during a Tour in the United States and Canada.* 2 vols. London, 1824.

Holley, Mary Austin. *Texas: Original Narratives of Texas History and Adventure.* 1836. Reprint, Austin, Tex., 1935.

Hooper, Johnson J. *Adventures of Simons Suggs.* Philadelphia, 1845.

Kirkland, Caroline. *Western Clearings.* New York, 1845.

Legaré, Mary Swinton, ed. *Writings of Hugh Swinton Legaré.* 2 vols. 1846. Reprint, New York, 1970.

Lewis, Henry Clay. *Odd Leaves from the Life of a Louisiana Swamp Doctor.* Philadelphia, 1850.

Longstreet, Augustus Baldwin. *Georgia Scenes, Characters, Incidents, &c., in the First Half Century of the Republic.* Augusta, Ga., 1835.

Lyell, Sir Charles. *A Second Visit to the United States of North America.* 2 vols. New York, 1849.

Martineau, Harriet. *Retrospect of Western Travel.* London, 1838.

McKitrick, Eric L., ed. *Slavery Defended: The Views of the Old South.* Englewood Cliffs, N.J., 1963.

Meek, Alexander Beaufort. *Romantic Passages in Southwestern History; Including Orations, Sketches, and Essays.* Mobile, Ala., 1857.

Meriwether, Robert L., et al., eds. *The Papers of John C. Calhoun.* 22 vols. to date. Columbia, S.C., 1959–.

Myers, Robert Manson, ed. *The Children of Pride: A True Story of Georgia and the Civil War.* New Haven, 1972.

Oliphant, Mary C. Simms, Alfred Taylor Odell, and T. C. Duncan Eaves, eds. *The Letters of William Gilmore Simms.* 5 vols. Columbia, S.C., 1952.

Phillips, Ulrich B., ed. *The Correspondence of Robert Toombs, Alexander H. Stephens, and Howell Cobb.* 1911. Reprint, New York, 1970.

Power, Tyrone. *Impressions of America, during the Years 1833, 1834, and 1835.* 2 vols. London, 1836.

Ramsay, David. *Ramsay's History of South Carolina, from Its First Settlement in 1670 to the Year 1809.* 1809. Reprint, Newberry, S.C., 1858.

Rogers, Carlton. *Incidents of Travel in the Southern States and Cuba. With a Description of the Mammoth Cave by C. H. R.* New York, 1863.

Simms, William Gilmore. *Poems Descriptive, Dramatic, Legendary, and Contemplative.* 2 vols. New York, 1853.

——. *Richard Hurdis: A Tale of Alabama.* 1838. Reprint, New York, n.d.

——. *The Social Principle: The True Source of National Permanence. An Oration Delivered before the Erosophic Society of the University of Alabama, at Its Twelfth Anniversary, December 13, 1842.* Tuscaloosa, Ala., 1843.

——. *Views and Reviews in American Literature, History, and Fiction.* Ed. C. Hugh Holman. Cambridge, Mass., 1962.

Spalding, Thomas. *Address of Hon. Thomas Spalding before the Union Agricultural Society, Darien, Georgia. 13 May 1824.* Griffin, Ga., n.d.

Taylor, John. *Arator: Being a Series of Agricultural Essays, Practical and Political: in Sixty-Four Numbers.* Ed. M. E. Bradford. Indianapolis, 1977.

Tocqueville, Alexis de. *Democracy in America.* Ed. J. P. Mayer. Trans. George Lawrence. 2 vols. in 1. Garden City, N.J., 1969.

Townes, Samuel A. *The History of Marion, Alabama.* 1844. Reprint, ed. Tom Skinner and Lee Ketcham, Birmingham, Ala., 1985.

Trollope, Anthony. *North America.* 1862. Reprint, ed. Robert Mason, Harmondsworth, U.K., 1968.

ARTICLE

Townes, S. A. "The History of Marion: Sketches of Life in Perry County, Alabama." *Alabama Historical Quarterly* 14 (1952): 171–229.

Secondary Sources

BOOKS

Abernethy, Thomas Perkins. *The Formative Period in Alabama, 1815–1828.* University, Ala., 1965.

Ashworth, John. *Slavery, Capitalism, and Politics in the Antebellum Republic,* vol. 1, *Commerce and Compromise, 1820–1850.* Cambridge, 1995.

Atack, Jeremy, and Fred Bateman. *To Their Own Soil: Agriculture in the Antebellum North.* Ames, Iowa, 1987.

Bailey, Hugh C. *John Williams Walker: A Study in the Political, Social, and Cultural Life of the Old Southwest.* University, Ala., 1964.

Bancroft, Frederic. *Calhoun and the South Carolina Nullification Movement.* Baltimore, 1928.

———. *Slave-Trading in the Old South.* Baltimore, 1931.

Barker, Eugene C. *The Life of Stephen F. Austin, Founder of Texas, 1793–1836: A Chapter in the Westward Movement of the Anglo-American People.* Austin, Tex., 1949

Barney, William L. *The Secessionist Impulse: Alabama and Mississippi in 1860.* Princeton, N.J., 1974.

Barnwell, John. *Love of Order: South Carolina's First Secession Crisis.* Chapel Hill, N.C., 1982.

Barron, Hal S. *Those Who Stayed Behind: Rural Society in Nineteenth-Century New England.* New York, 1984.

Bartlett, C. J., ed. *Britain Pre-eminent: Studies of British World Influence in the Nineteenth Century.* London, 1969.

Bartlett, Irving H. *John C. Calhoun: A Biography.* New York, 1993.

Bell, Malcolm. *Major Butler's Legacy: Five Generations of a Slaveholding Family.* Athens, Ga., 1987.

Bender, Thomas. *Community and Social Change in America.* Baltimore, 1982.

Berman, Marshall. *All That Is Solid Melts into Air: The Experience of Modernity.* New York, 1982.

Billington, Ray Allen. *Westward Expansion: A History of the American Frontier.* New York, 1967.

Bleser, Carol, ed. *In Joy and in Sorrow: Women, Family, and Marriage in the Victorian South, 1830–1900.* New York, 1991.

Boles, John. *The South through Time: A History of an American Region.* Englewood Cliffs, N.J., 1995.

Boles, John, and E. T. Nolen, eds. *Interpreting Southern History: Historiographical Essays in Honor of Sanford W. Higginbotham.* Baton Rouge, La., 1987.

Bolton, Charles. *Poor Whites of the Antebellum South: Tenants and Laborers in Central North Carolina and Northeast Mississippi.* Durham, N.C., 1994.

Bondurant, John P. *The First United Methodist Church, Athens, Georgia: Some History and Recollections, and Its Trustees.* Athens, Ga., 1988.

Bonner, James C., and Lucien E. Roberts, eds. *Studies in Georgia History and Government.* Athens, Ga., 1940.

Bowman, Shearer Davis. *Masters and Lords: Mid-19th Century U.S. Planters and Prussian Junkers.* New York, 1993.

Boydston, Jeanne. *Home and Work: Housework, Wages, and the Ideology of Labor in the Early Republic.* New York, 1990.

Braden, Waldo W., ed. *Oratory in the Old South, 1820–1860.* Baton Rouge, La., 1970.

Braider, Donald. *Solitary Star: A Biography of Sam Houston.* New York, 1974.

Brown, Roger H. *The Republic in Peril: 1812.* New York, 1964.

Burton, Orville V. *In My Father's House Are Many Mansions: Family and Community in Edgefield, South Carolina.* Chapel Hill, N.C., 1985.

Candler, Allen Daniel, and Clement A. Evans, eds. *Georgia; Comprising Sketches of Counties, Towns, Events, Institutions, and Persons.* 4 vols. Atlanta, 1904.

Cash, W. J. *The Mind of the South.* 1941. Reprint, New York, 1969.

Cashin, Joan E. *A Family Venture: Men and Women on the Southern Frontier.* 1991. Reprint, Baltimore, 1994.

Censer, Jane Turner. *North Carolina Planters and Their Children, 1800–1860.* Baton Rouge, La., 1984.

Chaplin, Joyce E. *An Anxious Pursuit: Agricultural Innovation and Modernity in the Lower South, 1730–1815.* Chapel Hill, N.C., 1993.

Chipman, Donald. E. *Spanish Texas, 1519–1821.* Austin, Tex., 1992.

Clark, Christopher. *The Roots of Rural Capitalism: Western Massachusetts, 1780– 1860.* Ithaca, N.Y., 1990.

Clark, Thomas D., and John D. W. Guice. *Frontiers in Conflict: The Old Southwest, 1795–1830.* Albuquerque, N.Mex., 1989.

Clinton, Catherine, and Nina Silber, eds. *Divided Houses: Gender and the Civil War.* New York, 1992.

Collins, Bruce. *White Society in the Antebellum South.* New York, 1985.

Conzen, Michael P., ed. *The Making of the American Landscape.* Boston, 1990.

Cott, Nancy F. *The Bonds of Womanhood: "Woman's Sphere" in New England, 1780–1835.* New Haven, 1977.

Coulter, E. Merton. *Georgia: A Short History.* 2d ed. rev. and enl. Chapel Hill, N.C., 1960.

Cowdrey, Albert E. *This Land, This South: An Environmental History.* Lexington, Ky., 1983.

Curtin, Philip D. *The Atlantic Slave Trade: A Census.* Madison, Wis., 1969.

Dangerfield, George. *The Awakening of American Nationalism, 1815–1828.* New York, 1965.

Davis, Charles S. *The Cotton Kingdom in Alabama.* Montgomery, Ala., 1939.

Demaree, Albert Lowther. *The American Agricultural Press, 1819–1860.* New York, 1941.

Dick, Everett. *The Dixie Frontier: A Social History of the Southern Frontier from the First Transmontane Beginnings to the Civil War.* New York, 1948.

———. *The Lure of the Land: A Social History of the Public Lands from the Articles of Confederation to the New Deal.* Lincoln, Nebr., 1970.

Dillingham, William B., and Hennig Cohen, eds. *Humor of the Old Southwest.* 3d ed. Athens, Ga., 1994.

Dodd, Donald B., comp. *Historical Statistics of the States of the United States: Two Centuries of the Census, 1790–1990.* Westport, Conn., 1993.

Drinnon, Richard. *Facing West: The Metaphysics of Indian-Hating and Empire Building.* Minneapolis, 1980.

Eadie, John W., ed. *Classical Traditions in Early America.* Ann Arbor, Mich., 1976.

Earle, Carville. *Geographical Inquiry and American Historical Problems.* Stanford, Calif., 1992.

Farmer, James Oscar, Jr. *The Metaphysical Confederacy: James Henley Thornwell and the Synthesis of Southern Values.* Macon, Ga., 1986.

Farragher, John Mack. *Women and Men on the Overland Trail.* New Haven, 1979.

Faust, Drew Gilpin. *James Henry Hammond and the Old South: A Design for Mastery.* Baton Rouge, La., 1982.

———. *A Sacred Circle: The Dilemma of the Intellectual in the Old South, 1840–1860.* Baltimore, 1977.

Fender, Stephen. *Sea Changes: British Emigration and American Literature.* Cambridge, 1992.

Fischer, David Hackett, and James C. Kelly. *Away, I'm Bound Away: Virginia and the Westward Movement.* Richmond, 1993.

Flanders, Ralph. *Plantation Slavery in Georgia.* Chapel Hill, N.C., 1933.

Fogel, Robert William, and Stanley L. Engerman. *Time on the Cross: The Economics of American Negro Slavery.* Boston, 1974.

Ford, Lacy. *Origins of Southern Radicalism: The South Carolina Upcountry, 1800–1860.* New York, 1988.

Foust, James D. *The Yeoman Farmer and Westward Expansion of U.S. Cotton Production.* New York, 1975.

Fox-Genovese, Elizabeth. *Within the Plantation Household: Black and White Women of the Old South.* Chapel Hill, N.C., 1988.

Fox-Genovese, Elizabeth, and Eugene D. Genovese. *Fruits of Merchant Capital: Slavery and Bourgeois Property in the Rise and Expansion of Capitalism.* New York, 1983.

Fredrickson, George M. *The Black Image in the White Mind: The Debate on Afro-American Character and Destiny, 1817–1915.* New York, 1972.

Freehling, William W. *Prelude to Civil War: The Nullification Controversy in South Carolina, 1816–1836.* New York, 1968.

———. *The Reintegration of American History: Slavery and the Civil War.* New York, 1994.

——. *The Road to Disunion: Secessionists at Bay, 1776–1854.* New York, 1990.

Gates, Paul W. *The Farmer's Age: Agriculture, 1815–1860.* New York, 1960.

Genovese, Eugene D. *From Rebellion to Revolution: Afro-American Slave Revolts in the Making of the New World.* New York, 1981.

——. *The Political Economy of Slavery: Studies in the Economy and Society of the Slave South.* New York, 1967.

——. *Roll, Jordan, Roll: The World the Slaveholders Made.* New York, 1974.

——. *The Slaveholders' Dilemma: Freedom and Progress in Southern Conservative Thought, 1820–1860.* Columbia, S.C., 1992.

——. *The World the Slaveholders Made: Two Essays in Interpretation.* New York, 1971.

Gerster, Patrick, and Nicholas Cords, eds. *Myth and Southern History,* vol 1, *The Old South.* 2d ed. Urbana, Ill., 1989.

Gibson, James R., ed. *European Settlement and Development in North America: Essays on Geographical Change in Honour and Memory of Andrew Hill Clark.* Toronto, 1978.

Going, William T. *Essays on Alabama Literature.* University, Ala., 1975.

Gonzales, John Edmond, ed. *A Mississippi Reader: Selected Articles from the Journal of Mississippi History.* Jackson, Miss., 1980.

Grammer, John M. *Pastoral and Politics in the Old South.* Baton Rouge, La., 1996.

Gray, Lewis. *History of Agriculture in the Southern United States to 1860.* 2 vols. Washington, D.C., 1933.

Guilds, John Caldwell. *Simms: A Literary Life.* Fayetteville, Ark., 1992.

Hall, Catherine. *White, Male, and Middle-Class: Explorations in Feminism and History.* New York, 1992.

Hardin, Stephen L. *Texian Iliad: A Military History of the Texas Revolution, 1835–1836.* Austin, Tex., 1994.

Horsman, Reginald. *The Frontier in the Formative Years, 1783–1815.* New York, 1970.

——. *Josiah Nott of Mobile: Southerner, Physician, and Racial Theorist.* Baton Rouge, La., 1987.

——. *The War of 1812.* New York, 1969.

Hudson, Charles. *The Southeastern Indians.* Knoxville, Tenn., 1976.

Hyam, Ronald. *Britain's Imperial Century, 1815–1914: A Study of Empire and Expansion.* London, 1976.

Inge, M. Thomas, ed. *The Frontier Humorists: Critical Views.* Hamden, Conn., 1975.

Johnson, Paul. *The Birth of the Modern: World Society, 1815–1830.* New York, 1991.

Klein, Rachel N. *Unification of a Slave State: The Rise of the Planter Class in the South Carolina Backcountry, 1760–1808.* Chapel Hill, N.C., 1990.

Kolchin, Peter. *American Slavery, 1619–1877.* New York, 1993.

———. *Unfree Labor: American Slavery and Russian Serfdom.* Cambridge, Mass., 1987.

Kolodny, Annette. *The Land before Her: Fantasy and Experience of the American Frontiers, 1630–1860.* Chapel Hill, N.C., 1984.

Kousser, J. Morgan, and James M. McPherson, eds. *Region, Race, and Reconstruction: Essays in Honor of C. Vann Woodward.* New York, 1982.

Kovacik, Charles F., and John J. Winberry. *South Carolina: A Geography.* Boulder, Colo., 1987.

Kulikoff, Allan. *The Agrarian Origins of American Capitalism.* Charlottesville, Va., 1992.

Lack, Paul D. *The Texas Revolutionary Experience: A Political and Social History, 1835–1836.* College Station, Tex., 1992.

Lathrop, Barnes F. *Migration into East Texas, 1835–1860: A Study from the United States Census.* Austin, Tex., 1949.

Lears, T. J. Jackson. *Fables of Abundance: A Cultural History of Advertising in America.* New York, 1994.

———. *No Place of Grace: Antimodernism and the Transformation of American Culture, 1880–1920.* New York, 1981.

Lerner, Max. *America as a Civilization: Life and Thought in the United States Today.* New York, 1957.

Loveland, Anne C. *Southern Evangelicals and the Social Order, 1800–1860.* Baton Rouge, La., 1980.

Lowe, Richard G., and Randolph B. Campbell. *Planters and Plain Folk: Agriculture in Antebellum Texas.* Dallas, 1987.

Lowenthal, David. *George Perkins Marsh: Versatile Vermonter.* New York, 1958.

Lowenthal, David, and Martyn J. Bowden, eds. *Geographies of the Mind: Essays in Historical Geography.* New York, 1976.

Lumpkin, Katherine Du Pre. *The Making of a Southerner.* Reprint, Athens, Ga., 1991.

Lynn, Kenneth S. *Mark Twain and Southwestern Humor.* Westport, Conn., 1959.

Lytch, William E. *The Cradle of Texas Presbyterianism: A History of the Memorial Presbyterian Church, San Augustine, Texas.* Franklin, Tenn., 1993.

Marks, Paula Mitchell. *Turn Your Eyes towards Texas: Pioneers Sam and Mary Maverick.* College Station, Tex., 1989.

Marsden, George. *Fundamentalism and American Culture: The Shaping of Twentieth-Century Evangelism, 1870–1925.* New York, 1980.

Mathew, William M. *Introduction to Agriculture, Geology, and Society in Antebellum South Carolina: The Private Diary of Edmund Ruffin, 1843.* Athens, Ga., 1992.

Mathis, Gerald Ray. *John Horry Dent: South Carolina Aristocrat on the Alabama Frontier.* University, Ala., 1979.

McClelland, Peter D., and Richard J. Zeckhauser. *Demographic Dimensions of the New Republic: American Interregional Migration, Vital Statistics, and Manumissions, 1800–1860.* New York, 1982.

McCoy, Drew R. *The Elusive Republic: Political Economy in Jeffersonian America.* New York, 1980.

McLoughlin, William G. *After the Trail of Tears: The Cherokees Struggle for Sovereignty, 1839–1880.* Chapel Hill, N.C., 1993.

———. *Cherokees and Missionaries, 1789–1839.* New Haven, 1984.

McMaster, Fitz Hugh. *History of Fairfield County, South Carolina.* Columbia, S.C., 1946.

McNash, William. *Thomas R. R. Cobb (1823–1862): The Making of a Southern Nationalist.* Macon, Ga., 1983.

McNeill, William H. *The Great Frontier: Freedom and Hierarchy in Modern Times.* Princeton, N.J., 1983.

McNeill, William H., and Ruth S. Adams, eds. *Human Migration: Patterns and Policies.* Bloomington, Ind., 1978.

Meinig, D. W. *The Shaping of America: A Geographical Perspective on 500 Years of History,* vol. 2, *Continental America, 1800–1867.* New Haven, 1993.

———, ed. *The Interpretations of Ordinary Landscapes: Geographical Essays.* New York, 1979.

Meyers, Marvin. *The Jacksonian Persuasion: Politics and Belief.* New York, 1957.

Meynard, Virginia G. *The Venturers: The Hampton, Harrison, and Earle Families of Virginia, South Carolina, and Texas.* Easley, S.C., 1981.

Miller, Perry. *The New England Mind: From Colony to Province.* Cambridge, Mass., 1953.

Miller, Randall M., and John David Smith, eds. *The Dictionary of Afro-American Slavery.* New York, 1988.

Moffatt, Charles Hill. *Charles Tait, Planter, Politician, and Scientist of the Old South.* Nashville, 1948.

Moore, John Hebron. *The Emergence of the Cotton Kingdom in the Old Southwest: Mississippi, 1770–1860.* Baton Rouge, La., 1988.

Nagel, Paul C. *One Nation Indivisible: The Union in American Thought, 1776–1861.* New York, 1964.

Namier, Lewis. *England in the Age of the American Revolution.* 2d ed. London, 1966.

Nirenstein, Virginia King. *With Kindly Voices: A Nineteenth-Century Georgia Family.* Macon, Ga., 1984.

Noble, Andrew, ed. *Edwin Muir: Uncollected Scottish Criticism.* London, 1982.

Oakes, James. *The Ruling Race: A History of American Slaveholders.* New York, 1982.

———. *Slavery and Freedom: An Interpretation of the Old South.* New York, 1990.

O'Brien, Michael. *Rethinking the South: Essays in Intellectual History.* Baltimore, 1988.

O'Brien, Michael, and David Moltke-Hansen, eds. *Intellectual Life in Antebellum Charleston.* Knoxville, Tenn., 1986.

Otto, John Solomon. *The Southern Frontiers, 1607–1860: The Agricultural Evolution of the Colonial and Antebellum South.* Westport, Conn., 1989.

Owsley, Frank Lawrence, Jr. *Plain Folk of the Old South.* Chicago, 1965.

———. *Struggle for the Gulf Borderlands: The Creek War and the Battle of New Orleans, 1812–1815.* Gainesville, Fla., 1981.

Pease, William H., and Jane H. Pease. *The Web of Progress: Private Values and Public Styles in Boston and Charleston, 1828–1843.* Athens, Ga., 1991.

Perry, Lewis. *Boats against the Current: American Culture between Revolution and Modernity, 1820–1860.* New York, 1993.

Phillips, Ulrich Bonnell. *American Negro Slavery: A Survey of the Supply, Employment, and Control of Negro Labor as Determined by the Plantation Regime.* New York, 1918.

———. *Georgia and States' Rights: A Study of the Political History of Georgia from the Revolution to the Civil War.* Washington, D.C., 1902.

———. *The Slave Economy of the Old South: Selected Essays in Economic and Social History.* Baton Rouge, La., 1968.

Pohl, James W. *The Battle of San Jacinto.* Austin, Tex., 1989.

Prucha, Francis Paul. *The Great Father: The United States Government and the American Indians.* Lincoln, Nebr., 1984.

Ransom, Roger L. *Conflict and Compromise: The Political Economy of Slavery, Emancipation, and the American Civil War.* New York, 1989.

Rasmussen, Wayne D., ed. *Agriculture in the United States: A Documentary History.* New York, 1975.

Reichstein, Andreas V. *Rise of the Lone Star: The Making of Texas.* Trans. Jeanne R. Wilson. College Station, Tex., 1989

Ridgely, J. V. *William Gilmore Simms.* New York, 1962.

Roark, James L. *Masters without Slaves: Southern Planters in the Civil War and Reconstruction.* New York, 1977.

Rogin, Michael P. *Fathers and Children: Andrew Jackson and the Subjugation of the American Indian.* New York, 1975.

Rohrbough, Malcolm. *The Land Office Business: The Settlement and Administration of American Public Lands, 1789–1837.* New York, 1968.

———. *The Trans-Appalachian Frontier.* New York, 1978.

Rubin, Louis D. *The Edge of the Swamp: A Study in the Literature and Society of the Old South.* Baton Rouge, La., 1989.

———, ed. *The Comic Imagination in American Literature.* New Brunswick, N.J., 1973.

———, ed. *I'll Take My Stand: The South and the Agrarian Tradition.* Baton Rouge, La., 1983.

Scott, Anne Firor. *The Southern Lady: From Pedestal to Politics, 1830–1930.* Chicago, 1970.

Scott, Joan Wallach. *Gender and the Politics of History.* New York, 1988.

Seale, William. *Sam Houston's Wife: A Biography of Margaret Lea Houston.* 1970. Reprint, Norman, Okla., 1992.

Sellers, Charles. *The Market Revolution: Jacksonian America, 1815–1846.* New York, 1991.

SenGupta, Gunja. *For God and Mammon: Evangelicals and Entrepreneurs, Masters and Slaves in Territorial Kansas, 1854–1860.* Athens, Ga., 1996.

Simpson, Lewis. *The Brazen Face of History: Studies in the Literary Consciousness in America.* Baton Rouge, La., 1980.

Smith, Alfred Glaze, Jr. *Economic Readjustment of an Old Cotton State: South Carolina, 1820–1860.* Columbia, S.C., 1958.

Stuck, Goodloe. *End of the Land: A South Carolina Family on the Louisiana Frontier.* Ruston, La., 1992.

Tadman, Michael. *Speculators and Slaves: Masters, Traders, and Slaves in the Old South.* Madison, Wis., 1989.

Tate, Allen. *Essays of Four Decades.* Chicago, 1968.

Tawney, R. H. *Religion and the Rise of Capitalism: A Historical Study.* Gloucester, Mass., 1962.

Thornton, J. Mills, III. *Politics and Power in a Slave Society: Alabama, 1800–1860.* Baton Rouge, La., 1977.

Tise, Larry. *Proslavery: A History of the Defense of Slavery in America, 1701–1840.* Athens, Ga., 1987.

Tompkins, Alma Cole. *Charles Tait.* Alabama Polytechnic Institute Historical Papers. 4th ser., no. 2. Auburn, Ala., 1910.

Turner, Frederick Jackson. *Rise of the New West, 1819–1829.* The American Nation: A History, vol. 14. New York, 1906.

Viereck, Peter. *The Unadjusted Man—A New Hero for Americans: Reflections on the Distinction between Conforming and Conserving.* Boston, 1956.

Wallace, Anthony F. C. *The Long, Bitter Trail: Andrew Jackson and the Indians.* New York, 1993.

Watson, Charles S. *From Nationalism to Secessionism: The Changing Fiction of William Gilmore Simms.* Westport, Conn., 1993.

Weber, Max. *The Protestant Ethic and the Spirit of Capitalism.* 2d ed. London, 1976.

Williams, John Hoyt. *Sam Houston: The Life and Times of the Liberator of Texas, an Authentic American Hero.* New York, 1993.

Wilson, Charles R., ed. *The Encyclopedia of Southern Culture.* Chapel Hill, N.C., 1989.

Wright, Gavin. *Old South, New South: Revolutions in the Southern Economy since the Civil War.* New York, 1986.

———. *The Political Economy of the Cotton South: Households, Markets, and Wealth in the Nineteenth Century.* New York, 1978.

Wyatt-Brown, Bertram. *Southern Honor: Ethics and Behavior in the Old South.* New York, 1982.

———. *Yankee Saints and Southern Sinners.* Baton Rouge, La., 1985.

ARTICLES

Allen, Lee N. "Biographical Sketch of Samuel A. Townes." In *The History of Marion, Alabama* (1844), ed. Tom Skinner and Lee Ketcham, xv–xxv. Reprint, Birmingham, 1985.

Bailey, Hugh C. "John Williams Walker and the 'Georgia Machine' in Early Alabama Politics." *Alabama Review* 8 (July 1955): 179–95.

Barrett, Kayla. "The Whitfields Move to Alabama: A Case Study in Westward Migration, 1825–1835." *Alabama Review* 48 (April 1995): 96–113.

Cashin, Joan E. "Landscape and Memory in Antebellum Virginia." *Virginia Magazine of History and Biography* 102 (Oct. 1994): 477–500.

Censer, Jane Turner. "Southwestern Migration among North Carolina Planter Families: 'The Disposition to Emigrate.'" *Journal of Southern History* 57 (Aug. 1991): 407–26.

Chappell, Gordon T. "John Coffee: Land Speculator and Planter." *Alabama Review* 22 (Jan. 1969): 24–43.

———. "Some Patterns of Land Speculation in the Old Southwest." *Journal of Southern History* 15 (Nov. 1949): 461–68.

Coulter, E. Merton. "The Nullification Movement in Georgia." *Georgia Historical Quarterly* 5 (March 1921): 3–39.

Craven, Avery. "Georgia and the South." *Georgia Historical Quarterly* 23 (Sept. 1939): 219–35.

Doster, James F. "Land Titles and Public Land Sales in Early Alabama." *Alabama Review* 16 (April 1963): 108–24.

Earle, Carville. "The Myth of the Southern Soil Miner: Macrohistory, Agricultural Innovation, and Environmental Change." In *The Ends of the Earth: Perspectives on Modern Environmental History,* ed. Donald Worster, 175–210. New York, 1988.

Essler, Elizabeth McTyeire. "The Agricultural Reform Movement in Alabama, 1850–1860." *Alabama Review* 1 (Oct. 1948): 243–60.

Faust, Drew Gilpin. "The Rhetoric and Ritual of Agriculture in Antebellum South Carolina." In *Southern Stories: Slaveholders in Peace and War,* 29–53. Columbia, Mo., 1992.

Fox-Genovese, Elizabeth. "Antebellum Southern Households: A New Perspective on a Familiar Question." *Review* 7 (1983): 215–53.

——. "The Fettered Mind: Time, Place, and the Literary Imagination of the Old South." *Georgia Historical Quarterly* 74 (Winter 1990): 622–50.

——. "Social Order and the Female Self: The Conservatism of Southern Women in Comparative Perspective." In *What Made the South Different?* ed. Kees Gispen. Jackson, Miss., 1990.

——. "Stewards of Their Culture: Southern Women Novelists as Social Critics." In *Stepping Out of the Shadows: Alabama Women, 1819–1990,* ed. Mary Martha Thomas, 11–27. Tuscaloosa, Ala., 1995.

Fox-Genovese, Elizabeth, and Eugene D. Genovese. "The Divine Sanction of Social Order: Religious Foundations of the Southern Slaveholders' World View." *Journal of the American Academy of Religion* 55 (Summer 1987): 211–34.

——. "The Religious Ideals of Southern Slave Society." *Georgia Historical Quarterly* 70 (Spring 1986): 1–16.

Gray, Daniel Savage. "Frontier Journalism: Newspapers in Antebellum Alabama." *Alabama Historical Quarterly* 37 (Fall 1975): 183–91.

Hartwell, Joan M. "Margaret Lea of Alabama, Mrs. Sam Houston." *Alabama Review* 17 (Oct. 1964): 271–79.

Hoole, Wm. Stanley. "Alabama and W. Gilmore Simms, Part II." *Alabama Review* 16 (July 1963): 185–99.

Jackson, Harvey, Jr., and Harvey H. Jackson III. "Moving to Alabama: The Joel Spigener–William K. Oliver Letters, 1833–1834." *Alabama Review* 48 (Jan. 1995): 16–42.

Johnson, Michael P. "Planters and Patriarchy: Charleston, 1800–1860." *Journal of Southern History* 46 (Feb. 1980): 45–72.

Kerber, Linda K. "Separate Spheres, Female Worlds, Woman's Place: The Rhetoric of Women's History." *Journal of American History* 75 (June 1988): 9–39.

Lynch, William O. "The Westward Flow of Southern Colonists before 1861." *Journal of Southern History* 9 (Aug. 1943): 303–27.

McCurry, Stephanie. "The Two Faces of Republicanism: Gender and Proslavery Politics in Antebellum South Carolina." *Journal of American History* 78 (March 1992): 1245–64.

McKenzie, Robert H. "Newspapers and Newspaper Men during Tuscaloosa's Capital Period, 1826–1846." *Alabama Historical Quarterly* 44 (1982): 187–201.

McNair, Donald. "Backwoods Humor in the Pendleton, South Carolina, *Messenger,* 1810–1851." In *South Carolina Journals and Journalists,* ed. James B. Meriwether, 225–32. Spartanburg, S.C., 1975.

O'Brien, Michael. "The Lineaments of Antebellum Southern Romanticism." *Journal of American Studies* 20 (1986): 165–88.

——. "The Nineteenth-Century American South." *Historical Journal* 24 (Sept. 1981): 751–63.

Owsley, Frank Lawrence. "John Williams Walker." *Alabama Review* 9 (April 1956): 100–19.

———. "The Pattern of Migration and Settlement on the Southern Frontier." *Journal of Southern History* 11 (May 1945): 147–76.

Pennington, Edgar Legaré. "The Episcopal Church in the Alabama Black Belt, 1822–1836." *Alabama Review* 4 (April 1951): 117–26.

Roberts, Frances. "Politics and Public Land Disposal in Alabama's Formative Period." *Alabama Review* 22 (July 1969): 163–74.

Roff, Sandra. "Visions of a New Frontier: Nineteenth-Century Texas Guidebooks in the New York Public Library and New-York Historical Society Collections." *East Texas Historical Journal* 29 (Fall 1991): 15–25.

Rogers, Tommy. "The Great Population Exodus from South Carolina 1850–1860." *South Carolina Historical Magazine* 68 (Jan. 1967): 14–21.

———. "Migration Patterns of Alabama's Population, 1850 and 1860." *Alabama Historical Quarterly* 28 (1966): 45–48.

Rogers, William Warren, Jr. "'The Husbandman That Laboureth Must Be First Partaker of the Fruits' (2 Timothy 2:6): Agricultural Reform in Ante Bellum Alabama." *Alabama Historical Quarterly* 40 (1970): 37–50.

Rootes, T. R. "The Rootes Family." *Virginia Historical Magazine* 4 (1896): 206–13.

Schaefer, Donald F. "A Statistical Profile of Frontier and New South Migration, 1850–1860." *Agricultural History* 59 (Oct. 1985): 563–78.

Sederberg, Nancy B. "Antebellum Southern Humor in the Camden Journal, 1826–1840." *Mississippi Quarterly* 27 (1973–74): 41–74.

"Settlement and Early History of Perote." *Alabama Historical Quarterly* 20 (1958): 481–86.

Shields, Johanna Nicol. "A Social History of Antebellum Alabama Writers." *Alabama Review* 42 (July 1989): 163–91.

Smith, R. Marsh. "Migration of Georgians to Texas." *Georgia Historical Quarterly* 20 (1936): 307–25.

Smith, Warren I. "The Farm Journal of John Horry Dent, 1882–1884." *Georgia Historical Quarterly* 42 (March 1958): 44–53.

Turner, Arlin. "Realism and Fantasy in Southern Humor." *Georgia Review* 12 (1958): 451–57.

Turner, Frederick Jackson. "The Colonization of the West." *American Historical Review* 11 (1906): 303–27.

Welter, Barbara. "The Cult of True Womanhood, 1820–1860." *American Quarterly* 18 (1966): 151–74.

West, James L. W., III. "Early Backwoods Humor in the Greenville Mountaineer." *Mississippi Quarterly* 25 (1971): 69–82.

DISSERTATIONS

Baptist, Edward E. "Creating an Old South: The Plantation Frontier in Jackson and Leon Counties, Florida, 1821–1860." Ph.D. diss., University of Pennsylvania, 1997.

Deschamps, Margaret Burr. "The Presbyterian Church in the South Atlantic States, 1801–1861." Ph.D. diss., Emory University, 1952.

Dye, Renee. "Sociology for the South: Representations of Caste, Class, and Social Order in the Fiction of William Gilmore Simms." Ph.D. diss., Emory University, 1994 (Ann Arbor: UMI: 9524619).

Johnston-Miller, Mary Margaret. "'Heirs to Paternalism': Elite White Women and Their Servants in Alabama and Georgia, 1861–1874." Ph.D. diss., Emory University, 1994.

Index

The American South Series